# T · R · A · P · P · E · D

# T·R·A·P·P·E·D

## Michael Jackson and the Crossover Dream

## Dave Marsh

**BANTAM BOOKS**
TORONTO · NEW YORK · LONDON · SYDNEY · AUCKLAND

TRAPPED: MICHAEL JACKSON AND THE CROSSOVER DREAM
A Bantam Book / December 1985

Book Design by Nicola Mazzella.

**Library of Congress Cataloging-in-Publication Data**

Marsh, Dave.
  Trapped: Michael Jackson and the crossover dream.

  1. Jackson, Michael, 1958–    .  2. Rock musicians—
United States—Biography.  I. Title.
ML420.J175M35  1985   784.5'4'00924  [B]     85-47804
ISBN 0-553-34241-X (pbk.)

Published simultaneously in the United States and Canada

Bantam Books are published by Bantam Books, Inc. Its trademark,
consisting of the words "Bantam Books" and the portrayal of a
rooster, is Registered in U.S. Patent and Trademark Office and in
other countries. Marca Registrada. Bantam Books, Inc., 666 Fifth
Avenue, New York, New York 10103.

PRINTED IN THE UNITED STATES OF AMERICA

S    0  9  8  7  6  5  4  3  2  1

*For George Travis,*
*who does it right*

# Acknowledgments

I'd like to thank the following for offering insights and leads, general ideas and sometimes just plain late-night conversation: Gerri Hirshey, John Hughes, Larry Reagan, Gladys Johnson, Milo Miles, Denise Worrell, Jay Cocks, Ken Barnes, Lee Ballinger, Greil Marcus, Steve Popovich, Ron Alexenburg, Barbara Hall and Lenore Travis for putting up with the L.A. shows, Mikal Gilmore for hearing me out and a host of music industry figures who will, for once, be thrilled to maintain their anonymity. Especial thanks are due Gerri Hirshey for lending invaluable insights and materials.

For once, an author thanks his wife more than perfunctorily: Barbara Carr *asked* me to write an open letter to Michael, thinking it would shut me up about the whole situation. Sorry it worked out that way. My friend and agent, Sandra Choron, was the person with the perceptivity to see a book in the idea, for which I think I thank her. Lou Aronica, my editor at Bantam, deserves special thanks for his patience and sympathetic understanding and pushing me to do it right.

*He had ecstasies innumerable that other children can never know; but he was looking through the window at the one joy from which he must be for ever barred.*

*Peter Pan*

# O · N · E

This story begins simply enough. In November 1982, Epic Records released *Thriller,* Michael Jackson's second solo album for the label. To no one's surprise, *Thriller* was an instantaneous smash, a hit "out of the box," in record industry parlance. CBS had been counting on it. Sales of recorded music were slumping, but Michael's previous solo album, *Off the Wall,* had sold eight million copies, so CBS was prepared to do tonnage (to again lapse into industrial vernacular) on the follow-up.

Nevertheless, *Thriller* got out of hand, selling more and faster than anyone could have predicted. In the face of a record business mired in its worst slump of the past twenty-five years, Michael Jackson had made the most commercially successful music in history. *Thriller* topped *Billboard*'s album chart for thirty-seven weeks (a record), and it sold more than twenty million copies in the United States (a record), with a worldwide total of more than thirty million (a record). It also spawned seven hit singles (a record), which sold who knows how many additional copies (probably a record), and three music videos that revolutionized that infant medium. One of them, the fourteen-minute (a record), one-million-dollar (a record) John Landis production of "Thriller," was made into a commercial videotape, *The Making of Michael Jackson's "Thriller,"* which topped sales charts in that field. By the beginning of 1984, more than a year after *Thriller*'s release (by which time, most popular albums have either dropped off the charts or slumped dramatically), *Thriller* was still Top 10 and Michael Jackson was the most famous star pop music had produced since the Beatles, or maybe Elvis Presley.

His appeal crossed lines and smashed barriers. A generation of American kids had grown up listening to radio broadcasts that were almost as strictly segregated as they were before Elvis Presley, Alan Freed, Little Richard, Chuck Berry, Fats Domino, and the other pioneers of rock & roll. Michael Jackson's music brought black sounds and faces back to the center of all pop; he created, in fact, the first *pervasively* popular music, with appeal in almost every segment of the audience, since the demise of the Beatles. "Billie Jean" and "Beat It," the best of his hits, fused dance beat and funk groove with rock lyricism and drive, even incorporating heavy-metal guitar. His triumph over apartheid broadcasting was personal and transitory, but it left a lasting residual effect. In early 1984, then, Michael Jackson was more than a star—he looked like a certified pop culture hero.

He had already conquered network television, with a devastating appearance on NBC's May 1983 special *Motown 25,* a silver anniversary tribute to the label that had nurtured and exploited him for the first seven years of his recording career. Performing a medley of Jackson 5 hits with his brothers, then ripping into "Billie Jean" with a knock-'em-dead dance routine, Michael stole the show from such seasoned and exciting performers as Marvin Gaye, Diana Ross, Stevie Wonder, Lionel Richie, and Smokey Robinson. His bopping and strutting, already fabled from the showing of his videos on cable's MTV, swept the nation. His high-water black trousers, white socks with black loafers, and single, sequined black glove became a teenybopper uniform. Half the kids in America stayed up late trying to learn his forward-gliding-backward step, the "moonwalk." Nielsen said that *Motown 25* drew an audience of forty-seven million. A good guess is that as many as half tuned in especially to see Michael. No one could have watched unimpressed.

Nine months later, in February 1984, Michael Jackson once again stole a prime-time TV special from his peers. This time it was those peers who put him up to it, by awarding him eight Grammys, the record industry equivalent of Oscars, for everything from Record of the Year to Best Children's Album (for a narrative reading of the *E.T. Storybook*). Michael went through the ceremony tight-lipped, thanking his parents, paying brief tribute to Jackie Wilson, acknowledging "my friend" Katharine Hepburn by briefly lifting his sunglasses.

On a bitterly cold night in March, Michael Jackson was feted at a black-tie ceremony held in the central hall of the American Museum of Natural History in New York City. CBS Records put on the spread and invited a host of celebrities to honor Jackson for selling twenty-five million copies of *Thriller* and for the album's inclusion in the *Guinness Book of World Records* as the largest-selling LP of all time. But the event ended on a sad note when Michael commented that being listed in the *Book of World Records* made him feel for the first time that he'd accomplished something.

Maybe it was an omen, for immediately afterward, the consensus surrounding Jackson and his works began to fall apart. His Jehovah's Witness brethren criticized his videos, especially "Thriller," which toyed with occult imagery. Editorialists in almost all the national news media attacked him as a decadent, subliterate wimp upon whom the nation's youth were wasting time and dollars. Muslim rabble-rouser Louis Farrakhan snarled that Michael was "sissified," a poor—indeed, dangerous—example to young American manhood. Jerry Falwell more or less agreed. Educators also got into the act: Most notoriously, the administration at a high school in Bound Brook, New Jersey, expelled several students for dressing like Michael.

It is a function of rock & roll stars, of which Michael Jackson is marginally one, to outrage editorialists, preachers, and teachers, of course. Significantly, no one even tried to lay a glove on *Thriller*'s music; it continued to be beyond any blemish or reproach. But the consensus about Michael Jackson had been shattered once and for all. In its place stood controversy—teapot tempests, no doubt, but suggestive of the forces that consistently oppose not only popular music and popular culture in general, but the kind of cultural breakthroughs epitomized by the ascendance of Michael Jackson and *Thriller*.

Then the Jacksons (the name of the family group once it left Motown) announced that they would do a summer concert tour.

Rumors had been flying since midwinter that they would attempt something of the sort. Behind the scenes, the reasons given were unusual. By his own admission, Michael Jackson hated touring. He had no need to make more money (his records and videos had earned royalties of well over fifty million dollars since the release of *Thriller*). But his family was used to his support. His brothers and his father (their on-and-off manager) counted on Michael's presence in the Jacksons to attract paying customers, selling many more tickets and records than the other brothers could ever have done on their own.

Now, it was said, Michael wanted to cut loose from his large and bickering family. They were pressuring him (as only a large, contentious family can) to do another tour, a set of shows that would make enough money to set them up for a long while, even without his presence. And Michael, it was said, agreed to do such a tour, just to keep the family on an even keel . . . or just to be shut of them.

The behind-the-scenes rumors about their touring plans were not good. The rifts in the Jackson clan were obvious and increasing. The tour was announced with Don King, the boxing promoter and former felon, as copromoter with their parents (still partners despite the fact that Mrs. Jackson had filed for divorce). And it was said that the Jacksons were already squabbling over who got what cut, who spent how much time in the spotlight, how to choose their repertoire, what shape the stage would be, each and every one of the thousands of decisions involved in producing a large-scale stadium tour.

About this time—even before the tour signed on that noted bumbler Chuck Sullivan or was accused of being a safety hazard or was roasted for being both spendthrift and tightfisted or was ripped for presenting a jive and lackluster spectacle or was flogged for its exorbitant, thirty-dollar ticket price and exclusionary ticket-selling format—long before any of that came to the fore, it became clear that this was a story that needed telling. And not just telling—the tale required interpretation and analysis. Flatly recited, the facts were mystifying. Someone had to sit down and try to divine just how things had reached the point where the most beloved culture hero of one year was being reviled, not just discarded but mocked and attacked. And mocked and attacked not only by those whose social role dictated disapproval of all pop stars, but by a significant number of those who'd formed the near-unanimous consensus around him less than a year before.

One wished deeply that Michael Jackson would try to make sense of his own story. But this was unlikely, if not impossible. He was virtually mute in public; he did no interviews after *Thriller*'s release. He had never been eloquent nor very interested in questions about the implications of his work or his fame. He never displayed any eagerness to confront the several anomalies presented by his stature and persona.

As he became more famous, Michael just became that much more obtuse. His rare public appearances, at press conferences and the like, were given in Coolidge-like silence, his face perpetually hidden behind mirrored shades, his body usually draped in a bellman's uniform. He'd often described his goals in terms of "escapism." Now he seemed really to have fled.

In any event, a Michael Jackson statement expressing his impressions of what his life had been like would do only part of the job. Also needed was some sense of dialogue between Michael and his huge audience, with the part that remained loyal and the part that had defected. Michael, however, was terrified of audience/artist interactions, as immobilized by fear of mobs as Elvis or John Lennon.

There was no way to compel such a dialogue. But there was a way to initiate an exchange, to convey enough of the untold parts of the story to clear the space necessary for telling the story of Michael Jackson more clearly. You could write him a letter. But rather than sealing it and dropping it in the mail, you'd have to publish it openly.

# T · W · O

Dear Michael,

What happened?

There you were at the top of the charts and then, it seemed quite suddenly, somebody stuck a pin in your balloon, and as the air leaked away, it became harder and harder to see your triumphs. By now, those victories have had so much mud slung at them (and by pros in the "media" and in the music business), they're so daubed with hostility and confusion, resentment and distraction that it's just about all anybody can do to remember how completely you consolidated the public's affection in those few brief months from the beginning of 1983 through the middle of 1984.

In those days, you soared higher than any other pop star has ever climbed. Nobody else—certainly not any entertainer or athlete, definitely not a black one—has ever experienced such unanimous adulation. And while I guess there are those who'd say that you did it all with fluff and half-baked magic, dance beats, smooth moves, and mirrors, I'd say that you revealed how much magic can still be made by drawing us together with devices that aren't so simple as they might seem.

Nevertheless, the setbacks are undeniable and so pervasive that by now the time of your triumph recedes from our memory. So I wonder if we don't need reminding that, however

much your consensus may have shrunk, you're still one of the
most widely beloved, most influential figures of all time, not
just of our era but ever.

In those months of your rise, the very name Michael Jackson
became a totem. The bond between you and your fans seemed
so powerful that it would overwhelm all barriers, cross over all
boundaries. That bond was a version of a dream, its expression
essentially American but truly worldwide, in which all opposites are reconciled, sexual and racial and political contradictions
extinguished or, rather, fused one unto the other, through sheer
goodwill. For the shimmering moment in which you peaked,
the message was transmitted through your relentless beat and
shy, smiling face, encompassing all innocence yet knowing for
certain where the secret heart of the matter—the key to taking
joy in life itself—was hidden.

Of course it couldn't last. The dream of which I speak is too
utopian to be realized, whether right here and now or in an
afterlife. It's only something to which we aspire, not something
we're really ever going to possess. But that makes it no less
valuable as a dream, not as long as so many people cherish it.
It's the one thing that might yet keep humanity from destroy-
ing itself, I think, and maybe that's why, when the bond that
wed us to you and your sense of joy was fractured—given even
so much as a hairline wound—it felt as though the whole
structure had collapsed and dragged us down with it.

People got nasty. Before the breach, the parodies were affec-
tionate, on the childishly witty level of Weird Al Yankovic's
"Eat It," the junk food version of "Beat It." (Made doubly
resonant by the fact that Yankovic's recast lyric was a shopping
list of things you'd never allow to cross your lips.) After the
breakdown, you were fair game, and sport was made of your
nose job and your skinniness. You were accused of being a
hermaphrodite, an illiterate, several kinds of clown, and the
only kind of damn fool that there is. Some said you were crazy,
others only callous.

And all of this just because you went out to do a concert tour
with your brothers that began, let's face it, in a blitzkrieg of
hype and was staged by bumblers who couldn't keep a secret if
their lives and those of their children depended upon it. Consequently, every risqué remark, personal foible, and familial squab-

ble on the tour was exposed to a level of scrutiny that the Holy
Family's life couldn't endure.

At least partly because no one stepped in to heal it, the crack
in the consensus around you widened. Suddenly, to a surprisingly large number of people, your thirty-dollar concert tickets
made you a gouger and your taste for Og Mandino's banal
self-help literature (not to mention your Jehovah's Witness ties)
made you a boob. You went from Mr. Do-No-Wrong to a
*villain*.

Some of this disillusionment was justified. You'd already
reaped millions from record and video sales and didn't need
ticket prices that were somewhere around double what anybody
else was getting for similar shows—and don't tell me about
supporting your brothers, because even if the billing says the
Jacksons, it was Michael we were paying to see, and therefore
you've got to take that much more responsibility and control.
Let's face it, even an old Michael Jackson fan like myself had to
have some nasty questions and negative attitudes snarling up his
mind.

On the other hand, a lot of the criticism directed at you was
simply founded in malice, the ugly flip side of that dream of
brotherhood. In this nightmare, all success is resented, and
none more so than that that comes to a skinny black kid
without family connections or any kind of cultural credentials.

However prepared you were for megastardom, Michael (and
everyone I've ever met who knows you says that you were after
it from the moment you began to make *Thriller*), I know that
you could never have been prepared for the backlash against not
it, but *you*. There's no way to ready yourself to confront the
meanness of spirit inherent in the nightmare side of the dream.
But it's also pretty obvious that with a little foresight you
could have escaped a lot of the attacks and feelings of betrayal
from people who were arguably "on your side"; one of the most
bitter lessons of your fall from grace (though exactly who will
learn it, I don't know—maybe the next guy to fit himself for
such a large pair of shoes) is that it is simpler and more pleasant
to take your time, do things right, operate on a smaller scale, or
often not do anything at all in order to escape the bitterest
consequences of a single dumb move when you've become the
"biggest in the world."

Elvis Presley faded into obscurity on the heels of forty lousy movies, but he never faced a year in which he pissed off so many people as you did in 1984. For all the contempt for himself as a redneck hillbilly rube that Elvis had to swallow, there was never a time when the snubs reached such a fever pitch as they did in your case. Across the board, publications both liberal and reactionary—*Time, The Nation, The New Republic, The Wall Street Journal, The Washington Post, The National Review*—found a way to sneer or jeer, to pick you apart or simply to use you as a whipping boy for the idea that most Americans cannot and do not and never will possess any sense of culture, much less have the ability to create some.

Not even Elvis had to deal with quite this level of denigration. Anyhow, when Elvis was belittled and attacked, he kind of naturally stepped back into line, which you can't, since black and rich and famous is already too far out of line for some. Not that you've really ever done anything deliberately outrageous— you sure never claimed to be bigger than Jesus—but the idea of a black man performing such a massively successful and enticing act of unification had to be nipped in the bud. Somebody must have feared that otherwise people might get the idea that the things that hold them separate are either bullshit or . . . visited upon them for reasons other than the obvious. There are a lot of suburban kids out there who are going to have a hard time believing that their white skin is an automatic sign of superiority after having spent the happiest years of their childhood trying to be just like you. Not that they won't be given lots of opportunity and encouragement to deny it.

Still, in the end, you'd have to say that you cooperated in your own demise almost as much as Elvis Presley did. You didn't make a string of putrid movies or sing moronic songs or in any other way debase your art. But the perfect parallel to Elvis's adventures in gluttony is your obsession with weekly fasting and frequent purgative enemas—a habit symptomatic of the fact that in the end you're just as isolated, as completely cut off from the world that the rest of us inhabit, as Elvis ever was. More than Demerol or Pepsi-Cola, that's what really killed Elvis. You'll survive far longer, I think, if only because you've learned from such hard lessons, but I wonder if spending your life stretched taut to hold back the world at every passing second will be measurably more pleasant.

Well, those are the words of someone who would surely like to talk this over face to face and knows he won't be able to. And to tell the truth, I don't see much reason why you'd want to expose yourself to a writer you don't know, especially not to talk about things that make you uncomfortable. And especially not when it would compete with your own, authorized, Jacqueline Onassis-edited volume.

But there's more to your avoidance of the press than that. "He's been doing interviews all his life," one ex-Motown employee said of you. "There's nothing in it for him. To him, it's a game of cat-and-mouse. He gets no pleasure out of it—why should he do it? There's no reason why Michael Jackson should ever do an interview again. He's got what he wanted. He's got his freedom, his respect as an adult artist. . . ."

What I wonder is: Do you still think that you have all that? The curse of your search for a place in the world is the notion of respectability; it's the very thing that allowed your triumph to be chipped away. Are you "free"? I doubt you feel that way when, walking past a newsstand, wearing a disguise, you spot another headline linking you as a lover with someone you've met twice (or not at all). Or when you have to explain to someone the innumerable everyday things it isn't wise for you to do, because if you go to a certain place at the wrong time, some ugly or simply silly but at least unpleasant stuff is going to happen (or maybe not, but why take the chance?).

And I'll go on wondering because that Motown vet is right. What's in it for you? Just like that damnable tour, it's a no-win proposition from the start. You have nothing to gain from gabbing because people couldn't like you any more than they already have; there isn't any greater degree of affection, much less notoriety, to be gained. There's no hope we'd gain a greater compassion for your situation, either, because your other interviews indicate that you have no idea of how to explain your plight to anybody in comprehensible terms.

I'd like to have a chance to ask you about the very premises of your success, the basic goals behind what you have done. What's the nature of your fame—is it an end in itself? Were there other options? If I were you, I'd likely prefer to not even think about a situation from which there's no escape in any case.

But open letters aren't written just for the two of us, Michael. They're written for the people peering over our shoulders, so they can place themselves in a broader public discussion, however they're able to do it. So it makes sense to carry on and lay out the facts even if you don't especially want to be bothered with them.

There's a final element of what you might have to say on the subject of yourself and your public imprisonment as a pop star that interests me. I wonder whether if by chance you summoned up the courage and interest to face the questions I have in mind, you'd even be able to answer them. If the questioning headed in that direction, I have a hunch I'd be talking to myself anyhow.

Which doesn't mean anybody here thinks you're dumb. To the contrary. When John Branca, your lawyer, says that you're "very informed and aware of what is going on in [your] life," that you're your "own Rasputin," I take the words literally. Remember, Rasputin's job was to mystify the obvious, to deflect attention from what was really going on, which was that the situation had kiltered so far out of control that the czar and his entourage were in mortal jeopardy.

So what I'm trying to say has nothing to do with whether you're "ready" to have such a discussion, either. That would imply that you were preparing to eventually tackle such difficult and abstract and even ugly matters. There is no evidence that this could be true. After all, you're the man who identifies with stiff and unyielding mannequins, perfectly posed but changeless and dead. The obsession isn't new. It's as old as your career, which is to say, you've had it all your life. In a 1974 Chicago *Tribune* story, your brothers recounted an incident from the early days of the Jackson 5's celebrity. During this teen idol phase, you and the group were surrounded by raving fans in a San Francisco department store. We all panicked, they said, but not Michael. You froze in place and tried to convince the fans that you were a mannequin.

It didn't work. A decade later, though, you told Gerri Hirshey, when she was writing her *Rolling Stone* profile and doing your final formal interview, all about your mannequin collection. All of them had personalities that you could identify with, you said. And in almost the same breath, you described how much more comfortable you were onstage than off. "I feel like there are angels on all corners, protecting me. I could sleep onstage," you claimed. About real life, inhabited by humans rather than angels or mannequins, you seemed a great deal less certain.

So do many of your friends. "On some level, I don't know whether it's conscious or not, Michael knows that he has to stand off the demands of reality and protect himself," said Jane Fonda. "His intelligence is instinctual and emotional, like a child's. If any artist loses that childlikeness, you lose a lot of creative juice. So Michael creates around himself a world that protects his creativity."

Well, sure. Maybe. Keeping those juices flowing isn't of much use if they aren't channeled. When all that extra energy bubbles over into one of the explosive leaps in your dance routines, it's hard to conceive of any better way to spend your time, but take protecting those instincts another step or two further and the result isn't insulation, it's a cocoon. Then the energy begins to build without an outlet and feeds back into the system, just like a guitar does through an amplifier. And just as in music, the feedback distorts the signal and your perception goes fuzztone. Which is okay, too, that's a great sound. Except where it happens when you ought to be at your most lucid.

And I'll tell you the truth, Michael, I'm not so sure that hiding out this way won't inevitably lead you to a situation that's frighteningly close to that of Elvis Presley: a demise too young and too hideous to contemplate. Living at twenty-six in the house you grew up in is one thing, especially for somebody who apparently feels pretty rootless. But it's another matter to say to Hirshey: "If I moved out now, I'd die of loneliness." And it's yet another to say, "Most people who move out go to discos every night. They party every night. They invite friends over and I don't do any of those things."

What a bizarre vision of how other people live! "Most people" don't do anything of the kind "every night"—to start with, they can't afford it. Even most stars aren't out and about "every night." Even if the friends you've made do act like that—whatever Liza Minnelli and Andy Warhol may get up to—how frightened of your own passions, how dubious of your own self-control can you be? I mean, do you really need to live with your mom as an excuse for staying home at night?

What's revealed in those statements is more than a fear of your own capacities and desires. It's a lack of self-knowledge. As a result, it's believable when you say that what you hate about interviews is that "an interviewer can interpret something totally different from what the person [meant]. . . . I think it's wrong, it's cruel, it's ridiculous . . . I just don't want to deal with what people say and how they say it and make up things."

Those are just the kind of things that do need to be dealt with by any writer who approaches your story, Michael. Otherwise, no one will ever tell it right. For at this stage, there are undeniably two Michael Jacksons: the guy who lives your daily life and the one that the rest of us (with much cooperation from the original) have invented. You may resent this—you may especially resent the fact that the Other Michael, the one you made up in a manner quite similar to the way that your friend Steven Spielberg dreamed up E.T., is so easily and constantly confused with the original you. You may hate it when you are expected to act like your Other *all the time.* But you've been so mute publicly, so unrevealing of yourself, and so much has been invested in that Other by everybody else (myself included) that to talk about just one version of Michael Jackson is impossible.

While I don't know whether my letters will reach the Original Michael, I know that the Other will listen attentively, for a portion of him resides somewhere within everyone his music has reached. So, in finding some things about you that we might hope are true, in thinking about them in different ways than they're usually allowed to be thought about, maybe we can also learn something about ourselves. That way, no matter how gruesome you may find the prospect personally, we all might learn a little bit more about each other.

But where to start? At the beginning, of course.

# T ◆ H ◆ R ◆ E ◆ E

Michael Jackson lives today in a house high in the hills of Encino, just a few minutes' drive from Hollywood and Beverly Hills. It is one of America's wealthiest residential neighborhoods. The house in which he spends most of his time is huge, built in English Tudor style. It's reached only after one passes through iron gates watched at all hours by professional security guards and closed-circuit cameras. The grounds are lavishly landscaped with shrubs and trees, some strung with tiny white lights in the fashion of Copenhagen's Tivoli Gardens. Like every other house in these precincts, the Jacksons' has a swimming pool, but this pool is elaborate even for Encino, with four bearded Neptune fountainheads and a large mosaic of a parrot. A Jacuzzi whirlpool bath is nearby. There is also a pond on the property, where two pairs of swans—one white, one black—reside.

Also on the grounds is a full-scale zoo with deer, a llama, a ram, live parrots, and Michael's pet boa constrictor, Muscles. There used to be a pair of peacocks, too, until their mating grew too boisterous. There is a four-car, two-story garage, the upper chamber given over to a picture gallery containing several hundred pictures of the Jackson clan and several dozen boxes of cards and gifts sent by fans.

Inside the house are a vast game room with the most up-to-date video units as well as classic arcade machines; a large kitchen with white tile floors and chrome-and-black ovens; spacious living and dining areas with furniture speckled with gold ornamentation; a den with a bar area that's really a soda fountain; and a screening room with three dozen seats. A circular staircase leads upstairs to six bedrooms and several bathrooms.

Not all of the bedrooms are occupied today because four of Michael's brothers and two of his sisters have married and moved out. But when the Jacksons first moved to Encino, journalists were amused that the family, with eight of its nine children living at home, had bought a place where the teen idol Michael had to share a bedroom with Marlon and Randy, the two brothers closest to him in age.

Yet to Michael, Marlon, Randy, and the rest of the Jacksons, their Encino home must have seemed unaccountably spacious. Before moving to California, they had not slept three to a room. Back in Gary, Indiana, in their house at 2300 Jackson Street, there were only two bedrooms, which meant that all nine kids slept in the same room. (Maureen, the eldest, got married and moved out just a year or so before the move west.)

The house at 2300 Jackson Street sits on a corner lot (since Gary is laid out on a grid, the cross street is 23rd) in the midst of a tidy but impoverished neighborhood. The lot is at most a hundred feet deep and about half as wide. There is no garage. Except for the patch of lawn, there is no landscaping, though a few plants cling humbly to the building's foundation. The house has brick and aluminum siding, and it's painted bright white, unusual in a neighborhood where colors are more often muted, and the kind of ambitious "home improvements" suggested by the siding appear to be otherwise unknown.

The brightest area in the Jacksons' old neighborhood, in fact, lies just across the alleyway that runs along the back of the house. It's the Roosevelt High School football field, with brilliant green turf and freshly painted stands for perhaps two or three thousand fans. The field stands next to an asphalt playground with basketball hoops. Just beyond the playground is the high school itself, a massive building of institutional brick with a spacious front lawn on 24th Street that gives it the appearance of a campus. Together, the play areas and the school suggest that Jackson Street should have been a livable place to bring up kids.

Gladys Johnson says that it was. She knows because she has lived in the neighborhood for nearly thirty years and in Gary all of her life. From 1956 to 1969, Mrs. Johnson was the principal of Garnett Elementary School, which stands three blocks away. During those years, all of the Jackson children, except Janet, who was born in 1967, attended Garnett. Mrs. Johnson remembers them and their time well.

"We were the first or second black family to live in this neighborhood. The stores and so on were all owned by whites, but they sent their kids to schools in other neighborhoods. It wasn't within the rules, but the administration cooperated with them." Mrs. Johnson knows about fighting school board administrators. She became a principal in 1953 "when it was unheard of for one of us [blacks] to be a principal," and she fought many battles to integrate the city's schools.

"When I taught at the Pulaski School, we had one building that was all black and one that was all white. I was in the first group to integrate and I remember that the floor plans of the two schools were identical, but the finish was completely different. They had *polished* wooden floors and so on. At the end of the second year, the supervisor told the white teachers that they might want to apply for a transfer. So I made sure that I was also able to transfer." Thus did separate-but-equal rule not only the South but also up North.

"In the sixties, things were changing," she remembered. "All the families who lived on Jackson Street then were black— Negro families, as I prefer to say. So the Jacksons lived in a totally black community. There are a few older houses across the street, but their houses were built twenty or twenty-five years ago; there's nothing pretentious about them, but they had four or five rooms. No basement, of course."

The neighborhood is anything but a slum. This can especially be seen in light of the neighborhood around 825 Jackson Street, another address often given for the Jackson family. Maybe they never actually lived there, but the comparison is instructive. On this part of Jackson Street, much nearer downtown and the steel mills, many houses are boarded up, and the more spacious lots look weedy and dangerous. Owners post signs warning of guard dogs and worse. Nearby are the landmarks of desperate poverty: a housing project, a blood bank, groceries advertising the cheapest cuts of organ meat. To be specific, 825 Jackson Street stands in the midst of a slum—not an especially horrific one by the standards of New York or Chicago, but among the worst that Gary has to offer.

It is also in the oldest part of the city, less than ten blocks from the huge Gary Works, the U.S. Steel complex that stretches for ten miles along what should be the city's lakefront. There is no access to Lake Michigan here, however, none of the towering high-rise construction that characterizes Chicago's Gold Coast. It is impossible to see any vestige of the sand dunes and swamps that once marked the southern terminus of the lake. Gary was not built for pleasure and comfort.

It was created by men many of whom never set foot in it, the board of directors of the U.S. Steel Corporation. U.S. Steel, founded in 1901 as a trust that controlled the largest deposits of iron ore in North America, the most massive steel mills, and the rail and shipping lines on which raw materials and finished products traveled, had by 1905 outgrown the capacity of its South Works mill in Chicago.

The company, spearheaded by board chairman Elbert Gary and board member Marshall Field, of the Chicago department store family, decided to build the largest steel mill in the world and scooped up ten miles of the southernmost lakefront. Its rail tracks ran straight through the site, which was located on a convenient water route from the Mesabi Range, controlled by U.S. Steel, on the shores of Lake Superior. It had huge supplies of fresh water. And when the Gary Works opened, in 1906, it immediately produced one-twelfth of all the steel produced in America, 1.75 million tons, a production capacity that was to almost triple by the end of World War I.

The city was thrown up as an afterthought. U.S. Steel needed to have its workers close to its production center, but it wanted to avoid the more onerous (to the company) aspects of a true company town. So the workers were paid in cash, not script; they bought their groceries and furniture from independent merchants; their housing wasn't subsidized by the company.

But U.S. Steel still controlled Gary, in its geography (the company shifted the course of the Grand Calumet River a quarter mile south, and all the residential and business areas were located below the new river banks), in its real estate (a third of the city's land was occupied by either industrial or railroad property, triple the U.S. average, and the largest single real estate company in town was the corporation-controlled Gary Land Co.), and in its politics (symbolized by U.S. Steel's donation of the land for the City Hall, the federal building, the armory, the public library, two hospitals, and the public auditorium). By the Depression, Judge Gary had donated five million dollars to the city, including paying for the YMCA building, which was built on land donated by the Gary Land Co. And the steelworkers worked eighty-four-hour weeks . . . when there was work.

The result was a city gray, bleak, and dreary, full of bars (two-hundred thirty-eight in 1911, when the population was just over 12,000), riddled with gambling and whores and vice of all kinds, a wide-open town. You could learn to love it, but it was just as reasonable to scheme with all your might to leave it, to dream up plans for busting out. So Joe Jackson and his sons dreamed.

There were blacks in the work crews that built the Gary Works—two-hundred fifty out of six thousand on the construction gang. In 1910, two percent of the city was black, a not untypical percentage for a Northern industrial town. By 1920, that figure had reached 10 percent, and by 1930, 18 percent. The proportion of those employed by U.S. Steel was similar.

Most of the new black population came from the South; the movement off the land began with World War I, when the flood of European immigration was stilled (and even reversed, as some European-Americans returned to their native lands to fight). For the first time, many jobs in Northern industries were open to blacks, who were only too glad to escape the destitution and degradation of their Southern peonage, especially since the cotton-based economy had been ravaged by boll weevils and floods.

But Gary was not the promised land. In the twenties, the

city's integrated central district was broken up, and segregated housing was built as early as World War I (a project spurred along, needless to say, by the Gary Land Co.). By the early thirties, only 20 percent of the blacks owned their own homes, although 40 percent of the whites did, and black renters were paying rates 20 percent higher than white tenants. Ten years later, Gary was one of the most rigidly segregated cities in the United States.

The situation was no better at the Gary Works. A 15 percent quota on the number of black employees in skilled trades was established in 1924, but almost half the unskilled labor was provided by blacks and Mexicans. Black workers thus worked in the most dangerous, filthy jobs in the mill, the coke ovens and blast furnaces. As a result, black steelworkers had lung cancer rates ten times higher than white ones. Blacks were also paid less, even after unionization. By the end of World War II, about a quarter of U.S. Steel's Gary workforce was black, but even as late as 1966, only two percent of black workers were in white-collar or foreman jobs.

Joe Jackson and Katherine Scruse grew up in this environment as typical members of the black community. (Katherine was born in Alabama. She actually lived in nearby East Chicago, Indiana, in her youth, but the situation there was no improvement on Gary.) Their parents came from the South—Tennessee and Alabama—bringing their culture with them. "I grew up on country and western because of my father," Katherine told Gerri Hirshey. "Every day we would have the radio on. *Suppertime Frolic* it was called and every evening around suppertime we'd listen until it went off. That's all my sisters and I knew was country and western."

Joe Jackson, the eldest of six children born to Samuel and Chrystal Jackson, grew up in Gary on Buchanan Street, only a few blocks from where he raised his own brood. His mother was also musical. "I can play anything I pick up," she said. "But my parents were common people—Mama and Daddy were farmers—and didn't have money to give me lessons." Joe and his brothers developed a taste for blues, the kind being developed in nearby Chicago, where the rhythms and poetic traditions of the Mississippi Delta were being transformed into wilder, electrified, industrialized sounds.

Like their parents, Joseph and Katherine got married young, in 1949. They had their first child, Maureen, in 1950, the second, Sigmund Esco (called Jackie), in '51. Then came Toriano Adaryl (Tito) in 1953, Jermaine in '54, LaToya in '55, Marlon in '57, Michael in '58, and Randy in '61. The final child, Janet, did not arrive until 1967. Joe went to work in the mill to support them all, becoming a crane operator. Like most of the other men, he tried to—had to—keep something going on the side. In the early 1950s, that meant a rhythm and blues band, the Falcons, formed with his brothers. He said they "mostly worked colleges and bars."

"We tried to be professional," he remembered. "But we couldn't get the right type of management, guidance or contacts, so we never did anything serious with it." Within a few years, the group split up for lack of prospects.

But while they lasted, the Falcons kept the Jackson brothers fascinated. "The boys would listen to the things we were trying to do at rehearsals," Joe remembered. "There were always instruments lying around. If you're around something enough, you're gonna take part in it."

When the Falcons folded, Joe put the guitar in his bedroom closet, from which it emerged only when Katherine decided to lead the kids in singing songs she remembered from her youth—country songs like "You Are My Sunshine" and Roy Acuff's "Wabash Cannonball" and "The Great Speckled Bird," folk songs like "Cottonfields." (She'd dreamed of a singing career herself, but "who ever heard of a black person getting anywhere by singing country and western back in the forties?") Joe told the kids that the guitar was not to be messed with, promising pain if they should violate his command.

And Joe Jackson was that kind of father. Standing just under six feet, with green eyes, a pencil mustache, and a large black mole on his right cheek, he was one formidable figure. Though he spoke softly, there was an aspect to his gaze that told not just his children but the world that he was not to be trifled with, that he could more than take care of himself in a pinch. "He was the man of the house and when I say a man, I don't mean he wears a moustache," his cousin Tim Brown once said. "He had dignity and pride and he held his family together."

He came by those traits honestly. "My father was very

strict," Joe said. "He was a schoolteacher and he treated me just like the rest of the kids in school. I'm glad that happened." His mother and his wife both agree, indeed seem proud that at a time and in a place where many parents were lax, Joe did not spare the rod. "The father did not allow them to group with the other boys," says Chrystal Jackson, by way of explaining her grandsons' successes. "The Bible says that bad associations spoil youthful habits. Their place was always in the home. And that's the way I raised my family, too."

The pressure was especially felt by the older children—"After you instill in the two oldest what they can and can't do," Katherine said, "the others automatically follow"—but it was felt as a constant force by the younger ones as well. "We were always sheltered, Mommy and Daddy's babes," said Jermaine. "We used to have to be in before the street lights were lit. . . . We loved going to school because it was the only time when we could play and let off steam doing things like physical education."

Even at school, Gladys Johnson recalls, the Jackson children "were somewhat isolated. When school was over, they went right home. They weren't in anything at school—I think that some of them played in Little League, but that was all. My working day was over at 5 P.M., and when I would leave the building, as I walked by their house, I could hear them practicing. They had a strict sense of what they should do."

The discipline Joe Jackson enforced was perhaps not quite as rare as it might have been composed of in other Gary neighborhoods lived families equally poor but less well assimilated into urban life. Mrs. Johnson can remember having to teach children who had spent their first few years living on Southern farms what a toilet was. "Some of them wanted to use the floor drains, or stand on the bowl."

In contrast, the families of the children who attended Garnett Elementary had grown up in the city and shared its values. "The children's families were supported by the steel mill," Mrs. Johnson said, "but their base was also in the high school diplomas that the parents had. I opened up two new schools and that was definitely the difference. [At Garnett], the parents at least had a high school education—whether they lived in the projects or not."

In addition to their father's stern attitude, there was another factor in the Jackson children's circumspect behavior. Katherine Jackson is a Jehovah's Witness (as is Joe's mother, Chrystal). Witnesses do not recognize secular holidays, such as birthdays, and regard religious ones such as Christmas and Easter as "pagan celebrations." They also reject the power of the state, thus refusing to pledge allegiance to the flag, for instance. From an early age, children raised within the Witness church are expected to participate in the famous door-to-door literature distribution and to exhibit "discipline and mental-regulating." (Witness literature even boasts that children are described in the Bible as comparable to slaves.) All of this further isolated the Jackson children.

"They didn't force their religion on anyone," Mrs. Johnson said. "At Christmas, Easter or a party of some kind, they didn't make a big point of it, they simply absented themselves from school. Of course, they never stood for the pledge of allegiance to the flag, but they were so quiet about it, they were almost unnoticed. Their parents were always cooperative."

Finally, there was the factor of poverty. Joe Jackson's job paid him a comparatively good wage, but the family was so large that they simply couldn't do some of the things that other families, even other steadily employed working-class families, might. For instance, Mrs. Johnson says that one reason there are few pictures from the Jacksons' school years is that they never had school pictures taken. "They never bought the pictures. And I soon learned that many of the families wouldn't buy the pictures, so I insisted that a deposit be taken before the pictures were done." Mrs. Jackson remembered that Jackie and Rebbie, the two oldest kids, were given dance and piano lessons until "more children came [and] we couldn't afford it."

Reined in as they were, the Jackson brothers had to have some form of release. Their mother did her best to keep them occupied with games—Scrabble, Monopoly, a card game called "Tonk"—and with music. Their parents taught the kids harmony. "We started singing country and western music," Jackie recalled. "My mother just loved that kind of music and it was all we heard around the house. We would harmonize with my mother. When I was a little bitty baby, my mama would rock me . . .'—we'd be singin'. Television was broke, you just went to singin' in harmony."

And the singing became more important as Gary's neighborhoods filled with singing groups. It was the doo-wop era at the very beginning of the sixties, when vocalists seemed to spring from every street corner in America and nowhere more so than in the Chicago area, which produced such great groups as the Dells and the Impressions. The feeling was contagious; the music was thrilling and it was also a *way out,* a chance to get beyond the mean circumstances such tawdry towns imposed. "Everybody had a singing group in our neighborhood, everybody," Jackie told Hirshey. "There must have been thirty groups, always competing. There was always a big prize with money and stuff, and that's what really gave us the inspiration."

When his father went to work, Tito would lurk in the hallway, then steal into the closet in his parents' room, grab the guitar, and begin to work up some numbers with Jackie and Jermaine. His mother never told. "I didn't want to stop it because I saw a lot of talent there," she said.

Tito studied music at school—saxophone, violin, bass—which gave him enough knowledge of rudiments to pick up more as he watched his father's hands. He played until the guitar was damaged one day (maybe nothing more than a broken string) and his father learned what had been going on. "He caught me and tore me up," Tito later recalled.

"When he found Tito playing it, he whipped him, let him have it," said Michael. "Then he said to Tito, 'Let me see what you can do.' And he meant it. Well, Tito picked up the guitar and started *really* playing. My father was shocked, because he saw some special talent there. He was really surprised."

Who knows what thwarted hopes and frustrated ambitions Joe Jackson felt. Who knows how much he dared to dream of what his own offspring might accomplish, how much they might better their—and consequently, his own—station in life. With musical success could come many things, those that money could buy (space to live in, time to use it) and those that it could not directly affect (independence from the mill and the bosses, *respect*). And so what happened next is no surprise.

"One day, I remember my dad walking in the door after work," Tito said. "He was carrying something behind his back. It was a guitar—a red one. Man, I was really excited. I'd showed him I was serious about playing."

Joe set about teaching his sons a few songs, Ray Charles and James Brown tunes, rhythm and blues from the radio, only superficially far removed from the country songs their mother had taught them to love. His ostensible purpose was to divert them from worse—"It was one way of keeping the kids home and not roaming the streets of Gary. In our neighborhood, a lot of kids got in trouble." But Joe also worked with a keen eye toward building something bigger.

And he worked them hard. "When I found out that my kids were interested in becoming entertainers, I really went to work with them. I rehearsed them about three years before I turned them loose. That's practically every day for at least two or three hours. When the other kids would be out on the street playing games, my boys were in the house working—trying to learn how to be something in life," Joe told *Time*. "They got a little upset about the whole thing in the beginning because the other kids were out having a good time. I noticed though that they were getting better and better. Then I saw that after they became better, they enjoyed it more."

Surprisingly, that assessment is largely shared by his sons. "There are a lot of things I wish I had done growing up, you know, just be kids, running out with the fellas," Tito told Hirshey. "I think we spent at least sixty percent of our time in music. It used to drive me crazy: get home from school and rehearse. Kids from school would drop over, dance and have a good time. . . . I enjoyed doing it because I could do something no other kid could do."

But Tito also remembered that other kids came by to jeer. "They'd say, 'Look at those Jacksons. They won't get anywhere. They're just doing all that for nothing.' But we kept at it. I think a lot of our success now is because we got started so early." Michael also remembers teasing and frustration. "There was a big baseball park [the football stands] behind our house and we would hear the roar of the crowd and we would be inside rehearsing and this would get us mad."

It was 1962. For a time, the rehearsals included just Tito,

Jackie, and Jermaine. Marlon and Michael were both too young to participate. But after a few months, Marlon began to fill in on bongos. Then, one day, as Jermaine belted out another James Brown number, thumping bass all the while, his mother noticed little Michael aping him. He was singing the lyrics, however, in a preternaturally *adult* way. "I think we have another lead singer," she told her husband.

The family wasn't as surprised as it should have been, for Michael had been precocious since babyhood. "Ever since Michael was very young, he seemed different to me from the rest of the children," Katherine said. "I don't believe in reincarnation, but you know how babies move uncoordinated? He never moved that way. When he danced, it was like he was an older person." And Chrystal Johnson recalled that Michael began walking around humming tunes when he was three or four years old, long before most children can carry a tune. Tito remembered that Michael was "so quick that if my mother or father used to swing at him, he'd be out of the way. They'd be swinging at air."

Michael made an equally strong impression in 1963, when he began attending Garnett Elementary as a five-year-old kindergartener and sang "Climb Every Mountain," unbidden, to the class one morning. "Little Michael knew who *he* was from the very beginning," said Gladys Johnson. "When he had a little difficulty with arithmetic, in the fourth grade, he told the teacher, 'Oh, I don't need to learn those numbers. My manager will count my money.'

"One of our teachers won the Marian Anderson Award [for singing] in college. She recorded the school song and we put a tape of it on the intercom each morning. Michael *had* to find out who it was that was singing that song. And when he did, he told her, 'I'm going to marry you.' "

Finally, it was, as Katherine put it, "sort of frightening. He was so young. He didn't go out and play much. So if you want me to tell you the truth, I don't know where he got it. He just *knew*."

Michael wasn't just talented vocally. He had other natural abilities. "He was so energetic, he was like a leader," Jackie said. "So we said, 'Hey, Michael, you be the lead guy.' . . . The speed was the thing. He would see somebody do something and he could do it right away." From the beginning, he played a forceful hand in determining which songs the group would do, insisting upon James Brown and Sam & Dave numbers that were among the most sensual, hard-driving, and adult soul hits. Their ability to perform such mature material would give the Jackson brothers a significant edge over other teen groups in the local talent contests. That and Michael's dancing. He always loved to dance; the first record he bought was the Miracles' "Mickey's Monkey," sheer Holland-Dozier-Holland dance-floor groove.

Joe thought the five brothers looked good together, "the little ones on the side and the tall one [Jackie] in the center. And their voices blended well, because of the family thing. There's a basic tone quality that's common to all of them."

Joe spent months rehearsing the boys before he let them perform at a neighborhood talent show. The talent contest was a thriving Gary institution, and it produced other soul talents, notably Deniece Williams, a near neighbor on Jackson Street, and Kellee Patterson. At those shows, held at various high schools around town, the boys learned about competing.

"Every time there was a talent show, everyone on our block would go and try for a trophy," said Michael. "We learned at an early age that people don't just give you a chance—you have to win it. Everybody around us was trying to get into some type of show business. . . . We went to school, but I guess we were different even then, because everyone in the neighborhood knew about us. We'd win every talent show and our house was loaded with trophies." Thus began Michael's feeling that he was special, singled out by destiny (a feeling enhanced by the Witnesses' concept of themselves as the spiritually elect).

The talent contests were the major focus of the Jackson brothers. The group also appeared elsewhere, including a hospital at Christmastime, where young Michael was enchanted to be on the same bill as Santa Claus (even though the Witnesses disapprove of Santa). Michael once claimed that they played their first noncontest show at a Big Top supermarket. The idea, he explained with a straight face (he was about thirteen at the time), was that "then people would come and buy something— maybe some baby powder or something."

The Jacksons certainly didn't play any more elaborate gigs until after their first big break, which was winning Gary's first City Wide Talent Show (probably in 1964 or 1965). At this point, the group's potential, and especially Michael's, was fairly obvious to everyone. And so the family got serious.

Joe would travel to Chicago on his evenings off to check out professional acts in nightclubs for ideas about material and stage presentation, then spend the next few evenings drilling the moves and songs into his sons. Katherine was reluctant when Joe also decided to invest some of what little money the family had in buying musical equipment—guitar and amp for Tito, bass and amp for Jermaine, some microphones and drums—but she stayed up late sewing matching costumes for her sons. It's not entirely certain what the act was called at this point. One bit of evidence points to Ripples and Waves Plus Michael (as it is billed on an early local single), but if the band intended to call itself anything so cumbersome, those plans ended the day a neighbor lady, overhearing one of their incessant practices, remarked, "Listen to the Jackson Five!"

The family's money struggles continued, and the band added to the drain on funds. One reason drummer Johnnie Jackson was added in 1965 was that he owned his own equipment. Joe was making well under $10,000 a year working full time in the mill, and the family was still feeding eight kids. (Maureen had gotten married and moved back to the South.) Katherine was sometimes able to find part-time work as a clerk at Sears, but mainly it was Joe's job that put bread on the table. Musical success may have been the Jackson family's main chance, but in the part of the world in which they lived, any chance at all was a long shot.

For one thing, few groups lasted beyond their first talent contest victory. As Michael later said, "They'd all split up: someone would get married or someone would get mad at someone else. When you're brothers, it's easier." But even as brothers, to persevere long enough to win back-to-back citywide talent shows was an impressive feat. And it seems to have been the citywide shows that brought the Jacksons to the attention of Gordon Keith.

Gordon Keith was one of the chief characters on Gary's small music scene. His real name was William Adams, and while he worked at Youngstown Sheet and Tube, he had also been a performer himself. His career not blossoming into anything much, Keith parlayed some of his wages into opening Steeltown Recording at 10th and Washington, around the corner from City Hall and a few blocks from the mill. (The studio was torn down at the close of the sixties, when much of inner Gary was demolished for projected "urban renewal," which never took place.) It was anything but unusual for steelworkers to maintain a second job, often an entrepreneurial one, but at twenty-five Gordon Keith was well ahead of the game.

Steeltown was essentially a studio in which aspiring performers could cut crude (by professional standards) samples of their music, to be played for potential backers: record companies, agents, managers. Such places were springing up all over the country, the result of comparatively cheap tape equipment and a growing demand for recorded products, intensified by both the baby boom and the fact that there were three times as many radio stations in the United States as there had been prior to World War II. Between cutting songs and occasionally recording a local establishment's radio commercial, studios like Steeltown were becoming more and more viable. And it wasn't at all unusual for the owner of the studio, if he had any show business contacts or smarts at all, to spin off a record label from his little recording service. That's how Gordon Keith became the first record label chief to recognize the special quality of the Jackson brothers.

Joe later claimed that he was reluctant to push the boys into such early exposure. "At first, I told myself they were still just kids, that there was plenty of time for a career," he told *Rolling Stone* in 1971. "But the longer I tried to wait, the better they got. Their music got more complicated and they needed more and more direction all the time. I soon realized that they were very professional. There was nothing to wait for. The boys were ready for stage training and I ran out of reasons to keep them from the school of hard knocks."

Michael recalled his father's tutelage as exceptionally useful. "Though he had a group, he was never a real showman, but he knew exactly what I had to do to become a professional. He taught me exactly how to hold a mike and make gestures to the crowd and how to handle an audience. It's incredible how he could have been so right about things—he was the best teacher we children ever had."

Undoubtedly, there was in Joseph Jackson something of the stage parent, the frustrated mother or father who pushes the child into the world in which the adult has failed to succeed. But the Jackson brothers were genuinely talented, and Michael was truly something special, a one in a million child star, with the uncanny ability to project through his vocal mannerisms a kind of worldliness he couldn't possibly have known. "I'm still amazed at how my voice used to sound," Michael himself once said. "They used to tell me that I had the voice of a thirty-five-year-old when it came to phrasing and control."

Their pool of experience was being built up well before Gordon Keith came along with his Steeltown Recording deal. "After they started winning the talent contests, their little manager [a friend acting in that capacity] came to see me and wanted to put on a concert," Mrs. Johnson remembers. "So we arranged for them to put on their show at the school. Everyone loved it, and we took in a hundred and twenty dollars at ten cents admission per person. Out of that, we gave the family sixty dollars."

That was a major payday. Michael and his father have both recalled their first paying performance as one at Mr. Lucky's, a Gary nightclub, although their accounts don't square on the fee. It was somewhere between five and eight dollars—for the whole group, for an entire night. Michael said that at these early gigs they made their biggest money from coins and bills that the audience would throw to the stage floor: "Dollars, tens, twenties, lots of change. I remember my pockets being so full of money that I couldn't keep my pants up. I'd wear a real tight belt. And I'd buy candy like crazy." (His father says that Michael's favorite habit at this time was to buy candy for himself and the other neighborhood kids.)

Mr. Lucky's led them to other black nightclubs in Gary, even some of the smaller ones in Chicago. It was an experience that must have left strong marks on the boys. Jackie, the oldest, was only sixteen in 1966; Michael was only eight. Yet the clubs in which they performed—in which they had to perform, if they

were to have a chance at becoming known—were as likely as
not to feature, alongside the kiddie soul group, strippers and
worse.

"Some of the things I used to see from the stage!" said
Michael. "You'd probably think it was nothing, but this woman,
one of the stripteasers, would take her drawers off and men
would come up to her and they'd start doing . . . Aw, man! She
was too funky! That, to me, was awful." Yet Michael played
right into it, doing a version of Joe Tex's soul burlesque
"Skinny Legs and All," in which he'd enter the audience and
lift up girls' skirts and peer beneath them. It was the kind of
"cute" gimmick that got an act over in bars with crude jokes
printed on the cocktail napkins. And getting over was the goal.
When Michael and Joe talk about becoming "professional,"
they're referring to a set of credentials they eagerly sought not
out of creative pride but because only by becoming pros could
they ever get shut of Gary and all that that implied.

They came to Steeltown Recording with high hopes, a smat-
tering of knowledge, and sheer determination. They were still
performing cover material—black hits—in the stage act, so
they needed songs. The seven sides that Gordon Keith recorded
were all by writers outside the group (four written or cowritten
by Keith himself, including "Jam Session," which the group
probably deserved credit for composing spontaneously if in-
eptly). But that didn't seem to matter much at the time. The
Jackson 5 hoped to *get over,* and they must have known that
their most potent weapon for shattering the walls and hitting
the highway was the voice of young Michael. It's featured on six
of those seven tracks, and the seventh is an instrumental.

Steeltown released two Jackson 5 singles before the group
signed with Motown. "Big Boy"/"You've Changed," Steeltown
681, was picked up by Atco Records in New York for national
distribution on the basis of local rhythm and blues airplay of
"Big Boy." It didn't even make *Billboard*'s Bubbling Under
the Hot 100 chart, however, and as a result, the second Steeltown
release, "We Don't Have to Be Over 21 (To Fall in Love)"/
"Jam Session," never got a national release. (Indeed, Keith
never got around to *numbering* the release.) This is at least partly
because neither the song nor the performance was as good as on
"Big Boy."

After the J5 made it on Motown, Gordon Keith issued two more singles. One was a reissue of "We Don't Have to Be Over 21" with a new B-side, "Some Girls Want Me for Their Lover." This appeared on a separate label, as Dynamo 146. Keith also released another Jacksons track, but this one was billed as "Ripples & Waves Plus Michael." This included another pre-teen Michael vehicle, "Let Me Carry Your Schoolbooks," plus an amazingly sophisticated reading of a ballad, "I Never Had a Girl."

All of this music is recorded extremely crudely—whether because of primitive studio conditions or lack of good technicians is anybody's guess. In general, the records are all highs and lows, with very little midrange except for Michael's lead vocals. Everything else is not only less audible than it might be, but somewhat fuzzy and distorted.

The songs are not scintillating. As the titles indicate, Gordon Keith had already hit upon the idea of presenting Michael as a sexually precocious child performer. But each of the "kid"-based lyrics here is slightly off: "We Don't Have to Be Over 21" is wordy and strained; "Big Boy" is actually a witty lyric but doesn't quite pinpoint Michael's age group (it would have been better off in the hands of some late teen soul singer like Carl Carlton); "Let Me Carry Your Schoolbooks" veers too far in the direction of a white pop arrangement, with thin and reedy background vocals and a cold and unyielding arrangement that's all bass and percussion and brass.

A third problem was the presentation of the Jackson 5 as a self-contained band, that is, one that played its own instruments as well as sang. This had been the fashion in white rock since the Beatles, but the evolution of black pop had been quite different, and there the self-contained approach was still fairly unusual (although within a few months, Sly and the Family Stone would permanently change that). "Jam Session," an instrumental that opens with Michael reciting the personnel who are playing on the side, including his father on guitar, is clumsy, sounding more like a cautious living room electric guitar exercise than the "jam" it's supposed to be. And the other songs don't feature especially cohesive or imaginative playing.

The Jackson 5 wasn't really a band; it was a vehicle for Michael and his extraordinary vocal abilities. His singing here isn't great, but it is uncanny, strikingly similar to his early Motown hits and surprisingly confident, though some of his James Brown—style vocal interjections are a little forced and self-conscious. Given the weakness of his support, Michael is already pretty masterful on this first group of recordings. When he's asked to sing at the upper extreme of his range, as on "We Don't Have to Be Over 21," he sounds so nasal he might be the black Lou Christie, but most of the time, he's modeling a style that he will perfect on the first J5 singles for Motown.

The great triumph of the Steeltown sides is the Ripples and Waves Plus Michael ballad, "I Never Had a Girl." Its arrangement, with a beautiful slow soul bass line and featuring female and falsetto backing singers, is closer to the soul style developed in Chicago by the Dells, Jerry Butler, Curtis Mayfield, and the Impressions than to the harder Stax and Motown records the other Steeltown tracks emulate. It has a fairly mature theme, which also helps. When Michael says, "I really think I love ya so," it foreshadows the greatest moment in "I Want You Back"—"Sit down, girl, I think I love ya!" The contrast with the falsetto solo (possibly by Jermaine) is less than exquisite only because the recording is so poor—with a better mix, "I Never Had a Girl" could stand up well against many mid-sixties Chicago soul ballads.

At age nine or so, then, Michael Jackson was already confident and poised when standing before a microphone in the recording studio. He already showed an instinct for individualizing even ordinary material and a gift for soul ballad singing. The parts were falling into place. The Steeltown singles were more a parts warehouse than a production line, but everybody has to start somewhere.

The regional success of "Big Boy" gave the Jacksons the credentials to branch out in their live appearances. "It got so we could play nightclubs in Chicago, like the High Chapparral and the Guys and Gals Club," Joe said. "This was on the weekends. I had a Volkswagen bus and I bought a big luggage rack and put it on top and everybody on the inside of the bus. One day I noticed when I was coming out of the yard that the instruments on top of the bus were taller than the bus." Later, according to a handwritten bio by Joe soon after the J5 signed with Motown, they traveled in a 1969 twelve-passenger Ford Chateau wagon, with a professional driver, Jack Richardson.

The group's most impressive achievement in breaking into the so-called chitlin' circuit of black theaters and nightclubs around the U.S. was winning the amateur talent show at the Regal Theatre in Chicago three consecutive weeks. Aside from the weekly talent night at the Apollo in New York, the Regal shows were probably the most important in the country. Since the winners were decided by audience response, and since the audiences were tough and discerning, such a streak indicated serious commercial potential.

Even more so than today, the black touring circuit was utterly separate from the white one. Black acts played different houses and to different crowds with different expectations about entertainment styles and values. The laid-back, uncostumed demeanor of mid-sixties rock bands would not have survived the hook at the Apollo, and neither would the meandering, humorless music. In many ways, the chitlin' circuit (also known as the TOBA circuit, which stood for Theatre Owners Booking Association, but commonly read as Tough On Black Asses) was a relic of the vaudeville era, playing the same kind of two-to-three-thousand-seat theaters in downtown, inner-city areas, with large numbers of acts on the same bill in a variety show format that included comedians, dancers, and such novelty acts as jugglers and ventriloquists and usually a movie as well. The key points on the map were the Apollo in New York, the Howard Theatre in Washington, D.C., the Uptown Theatre in Philadelphia, the Greystone Ballroom or Fox Theatre in Detroit and the Regal in Chicago. There were other venues in other cities—the Jacksons played in St. Louis, Kansas City, Boston, Milwaukee, and various spots in Arizona, Illinois, Indiana, Ohio, and Michigan— but the Apollo, Howard, Fox, Regal, and Uptown were the key spots for any up-and-coming black group. This was where one could learn principles of stagecraft handed down over decades simply by staying in the wings and watching—as Michael says he watched James Brown on many, many nights. It was where one would meet the biggest soul stars and other up-and-comers, forming friendships, rivalries, lifelong enmities.

In other words, the chitlin' circuit offered the one advantage Jim Crow arrangements could afford, the chance for black people to bond together and forge from their unique and uniquely negative American experience a significant cultural style. As the margins of isolated black culture became smaller over the next decade, as more and more of the surface of black style was assimilated and expropriated by "mainstream" white America, that advantage withered until it is now all but dead. The Jackson 5 was one of the last groups to participate in the circuit while it was still pretty much in full swing, and like everyone else involved, they were deeply affected by it.

Playing in these theaters and nightclubs, they opened for all the names of the day: the Temptations, Etta James, James Brown, Gladys Knight and the Pips, the Chi-Lites, the Emotions, the O'Jays, Jackie Wilson, Jerry Butler, Joe Simon, the Five Stairsteps (another kid group), the Fantastic Four, Otis Clay, the Vibrations, the Esquires, Sam & Dave, Maurice and Mac, Bobby Taylor and the Vancouvers. Some of those names never meant anything outside the TOBA circuit; some were already stars to all of America; others were also awaiting their time. But all of them had something to teach the Jacksons, and their influence gave the group its firm, unshakable links to a black music tradition that could not be completely submerged in anyone's concept of "bubble gum." What Michael learned from experiencing up close and at such an early age performers as powerful as James Brown and as riveting as Sam & Dave, as utterly dynamic as Jackie Wilson and as coolly professional as Gladys Knight and Jerry Butler can only be guessed. (He has never been much for paying tribute.) But such surroundings might have filled a much less imaginative kid with gleaming dreams of greater glory, perhaps even the arrogant ambition of somehow fusing all of these styles into one that would, properly nurtured and presented, conquer not just the black scene and not just America, but the entire world.

If those thoughts crossed Michael's mind at the height of a performance or just before he drifted off to sleep in a hotel room he shared with Jermaine and Joe (who was called "The Hawk" because he always kept his eyes fixed on the younger boys), they must have been overwhelmed at other times by the sheer stamina it took to do the shows. The TOBA circuit lived up to its acronym.

"Everyone thinks we started at the top," Marlon once re-

marked in annoyance, "but we traveled around for years before
that crammed into a Volkswagen van. We'd get home at five in
the morning a lot of times, then get up the next day and go to
school."

"Of course, sometimes they'd be a little sleepy," Mrs. Johnson said. "Sometimes, like anyone in such a situation, they
would need a little more sleep than they had gotten." The boys
kept their grades in reasonable repair (though Michael had to
attend the school's reading lab for a spell), enough to keep the
Garnett Elementary staff enthusiastic—a few teachers would
drive over to see them perform whenever they were in Chicago.

Education was important to Joe Jackson, as it would be to
any schoolteacher's son, and he was to make sure that all of his
sons got their high school diplomas even after the group's move
to California. But whatever the risk to their education, he must
have felt (and not unreasonably) that the shot at breaking out
was worth it. And however great their exhaustion, all the boys
must have agreed with the thinking of Jackie, who once said,
"You work that hard every day, you think about that phone call
comin' every day, you know it's just gotta come sooner or
later."

Working in Chicago, they made an impression on the professionals who saw them. Freddie Perren, now a very well-known
record producer, remembers a nightclub date when he was
pianist with Jerry Butler, the smooth ballad singer who was a
hometown favorite. "When I saw these little kids opening the
show for us, I really felt sorry for them and hoped the crowd
would be kind to them. Michael was so little and innocent.
Well, they just destroyed the audience. He was just an amazing
performer. Hey, it was very tough trying to come on after that,
let me tell you." *Soul Train* impresario Don Cornelius, then
working as a Chicago disc jockey, also recalled being knocked
out by Michael at this time.

But Chicago was no longer an especially good town for
recording artists, and moving up in the music world absolutely
necessitated making records on a national basis. The important
Chicago record labels, Vee Jay and Chess, were both flounder-
ing. The former went bankrupt shortly after it had its contract
with the Beatles swiped by the much larger, conglomerate-
controlled Capitol. (It is nevertheless a delicious irony that

the Beatles were first widely presented to Americans on a black-owned record label that specialized in such blues primitives as John Lee Hooker and Jimmy Reed.)

Chess, on the other hand, had never quite made the transition from the harder R&B and urban blues sounds to the smoother and more elaborately arranged soul styles. Although it pioneered rock & roll and R&B with Muddy Waters, Howlin' Wolf, Little Walter, Bo Diddley, and Chuck Berry, among many, many others, Chess was on the wane by the late sixties, barely able to do a decent job for its few important soul stars—the Dells, Etta James, Billy Stewart—and recording albums of psychedelicized travesty with Wolf and Waters in an attempt to cash in on the hippie interest in blues. Chess was one of the great American independent record companies, but it was not able to modernize its sounds, and its marketplace was overtaken by Stax in Memphis and Motown in Detroit.

So Chicago was only a way station for the boys; staying there was a dead end as certainly as lingering for the rest of one's life in Gary would have been. For black performers in the mid-sixties, making it most often meant getting to New York. Not so much because the most important record labels were there—the recording industry was decentralized—but because New York was where the action was. Especially if you were young, barely known, but extremely good at winning talent contests.

New York had America's greatest amateur contest, and probably its longest-running one. It was held at the Apollo Theatre, the chief showplace of Harlem, every Wednesday night. Dozens of important black stars had gotten their start there: Dinah Washington, Leslie Uggams, James Brown, Ella Fitzgerald, Jackie Wilson, Dionne Warwick, the Isley Brothers, Gladys Knight and the Pips, Gloria Lynne, the Penguins, Sonny Til and the Orioles.

Half of the importance of the Apollo Theatre contest came from the fact that it was held in New York, the media capital of America. But the other half came from the Apollo's special nature as a unique institution in the heart of Harlem—it was located on 125th Street, in the center of the block between Seventh and Eighth avenues—the mecca of urban black America.

In the mid-sixties, and for several decades before, the Apollo was basically a dingy place, slightly decrepit with painful smells and the overall ambience of a hustlers' convention. Yet one could feel secure there, welcomed as if into a ritualized community that had no possibility of forming on the cruel streets outside. In the dim light, the audience forged a bond. It was known as the toughest audience in the world and on many nights (especially on Amateur Nights) it went to lengths to prove and keep that title.

The Apollo was a typical vaudeville house with two balconies, the second stacked so high above the first that its denizens looked upon the proceedings from the vantage of air traffic controllers. Which to a certain extent is what they were, since if a stage show was not to the liking of the second balcony, the performers were sure to hear about it, and from time to time, when someone was luckier in aim than usual, to actually feel a tangible piece of evidence to that effect in the form of, perhaps, some overripe vegetation. On the other hand, for a great performance (and the Apollo certainly saw more than its share of these), the second balcony was sure to lead the cheers. And Apollo cheers, like Apollo jeers, had a vigor that was utterly without peer.

The Amateur Nights probably did the most to establish the Apollo legend, not only because of the array of brilliant talents uncovered there over so many years, but because of the amazing ritual surrounding the talent contest. For instance, no amateur could simply walk off the stage of the Apollo. He must "truck" off to the tune of a song called "Christopher Columbus," sashaying sideways and shuffling, with one finger pointing to the air and circling endlessly, à la Cab Calloway. And such an exit must be made whether one had gone over with the Apollo crowd or whether one had fared so poorly that the Executioner had been summoned forth.

The Executioner was the perfection of the vaudevillian hook, a way of letting an addled amateur know that enough is enough, a *Gong Show* to end all *Gong Show*s. The original was sound man Norman "Porto Rico" Miller, short, fat, and profane. Wearying of a talentless boob one evening, Porto Rico grabbed a starter's pistol loaded with blanks and left his usual perch in the wings to take to the stage himself. There, in full view of the audience, and while the hapless amateur tried to carry on with his piece, then stopped dead and dumbfounded, Porto Rico circled him, as if he were dancing and stalking simultaneously. When the audience had reached the climax of its hilarity, Porto Rico "shot" the boob as a means of convincing him that the display of his amateurism had overstayed its welcome.

After Porto Rico's demise, other sound men took on the position. Always, they would circle their victim, usually with some silly prop. Always, they would "execute" them. Sometimes, if the victims were not cooperative, they would be "trucked" off forcibly.

Such humiliation was worth the risk, for the prize offered was not just a small sum of money and a week's paid engagement at the Apollo but notoriety or even fame itself, a very important leg up on the possibility of a full-scale show business career. Given the level of competition, the threat of execution, and the unflinching honesty of the audience response, winning the amateur contest was a genuine test of performance mettle. There aren't a lot of stories about stars who entered the Apollo Amateur Night contest and lost. To boast of such failure would be unbecoming, and anyway, the audience rarely called the wrong shot.

The Jacksons got their invitation to the Apollo Amateur Night toward the end of 1967, and they quickly, if nervously, accepted. As Joe already knew, "One thing about the Apollo Theatre, if you weren't good, you might get a few cans or bottles thrown at you. The kids were more afraid of that than anything else. We weren't afraid of losing the contest; we knew we had it. We just wanted the people to like us."

Of course they won, with a standing ovation from even the second balcony. That meant an invitation to return a few weeks later for their first *paid* engagement at the Apollo. Which made them professionals, done with amateur contests forever, determined to go out and succeed at whatever cost in the world of the entertainment business, reaping the highest rewards available. They were only a record deal shy of realizing all their dreams.

# F · O · U · R

Dear Michael,

I spent the other night reading the special issue of *People* devoted to you and went to bed feeling more strongly than ever how rootless your stardom really is. Albert Goldman's pretentious and overwritten essay blew smoke over the cloud it claimed to clarify. It only recited what was already known and avoided interpretation. In the end, only your mother suggested that you might have a life outside your career, and even she seemed confused about just what it is.

The contrast really leaped out from Gary Smith's opening piece about your brief encounter with Bruce Springsteen in a Philadelphia hotel. It purports to be a verbatim report and, because Smith is a fabulous writer and reporter, I trust it.

Smith's story takes place entirely in the Here and Now—no fantasy, no history, no context. Its premise seems to be that you and Bruce are the key stars of This Particular Moment and that the significance of your meeting is the absolute contrast between the ways in which you've accepted the roles thrust upon you. Those roles aren't as simple as those of previous pop idols can be, because they encompass the idea of the Symbolically Meaningful Individual—the artist who signifies, the entertainer who builds greater meaning into even the most trivial of his gestures.

In his stage show and on his albums (and always in his

meetings with the press), Springsteen edges warily around the Here and Now. He dwells a bit in the future and a lot in the past, not so much because he's self-consciously mythologizing or succumbing to nostalgia as because he is aware of certain historical patterns—in rock & roll as well as in ordinary life—and hopes to figure out how he fits in.

On the other hand, Michael, you've always seemed oblivious to where you're coming from, completely fixated on where you are and where you're going. When you exhibit a glimmer of historical awareness—dedicating a Grammy to Jackie Wilson, for instance—it always seems newsworthy for that reason alone. At the opening show of the Victory tour in Kansas City last June, a number of writers were struck by a couple of bits of gospel phrasing that you used. They'd never shown up before, and there was no real reason they should turn up now: You weren't raised in a Pentecostal church, and Motown was shaped by gospel only in its rhythmic accents, not in its singing styles. After asking around, it turned out that you'd come across a videotape of Mahalia Jackson from the mid-fifties.

"Michael apparently sits up all night and watches that tape over and over," a friend told me. "Just sits there and watches it and cries." (Crying, I've been given to understand, is a principal means by which you express enthusiasm.) To me, the most surprising aspect of the story was that you were even interested in things that happened thirty years ago. Much less that you were interested in a figure from history, rather than a fantasy character: Mahalia Jackson, I mean, rather than Mickey Mouse or Peter Pan.

I don't mean that as an insult, just as an observation. After all, if there's a systematically expressed Michael Jackson philosophy, it would seem to involve the elimination of all historical considerations. You can see the commercial consequences of an obvious mistake, like the Pepsi-Cola endorsement your brothers forced upon you, because it immediately hampers your career by upsetting the purity of your image and because it violates your own standards of healthful living. But at other times, you seem oblivious to consequences, as though for you history is not a stream of connected events but simply a bunch of things that happened to happen, without much relationship to one another.

A great example is that *People* special. You aren't in it—

there's no interview with you and, aside from Smith's piece, not a hint that you cooperated. The central articles are about your mother and your manager. Yet when I was watching TV the other day, I saw a commercial for the magazine that startled and stunned and saddened me. In the ad, which seems to take place at Disneyworld, the announcer talks about "Michael Jackson" in portentous tones while a figure very much resembling you (slouched shoulders, those clothes) walks with back to the camera. At the conclusion of the commercial, the camera pans around the figure and we see the face. It really is you.

Does it never occur to you that the implication of this ad is that the *People* special issue is your handiwork, or has your approval, and that people are going to feel cheated by you as well as *People* when they buy the issue and find not a single new quote from you in it? Not because quotes would make the issue better, but because your participation in the commercial is a *promise*.

If it doesn't occur to you, that would explain your otherwise unexplainable decision not to show up at the most important press conference of your career, the one in which "you" denounced homosexuality and the exploitation press, vehemently denied, in a statement read by your manager, that you had had any more plastic surgery than the nose job to which you admit, and generally tried to sweep aside the nastiest innuendoes surrounding your life and life-style. It does not seem to have occurred to you that by not being there, by having your manager read a prepared statement, by not making yourself (or even your manager) available to answer questions, that this press conference had the opposite effect: Rather than slamming the door on the leering snickerers, it allowed them to look upon you as a *weird* character (nudge, wink). Especially when you DID turn up at the next Hollywood event planned in your honor, the implantation of your star on Hollywood Boulevard. Apparently, it doesn't occur to you that many people will (consciously or not) remember those two events and compare them, and that the comparison will make you seem cold, arrogant, manipulative, and some sort of half-shrewd media hustler.

There are those who'd argue that your failure to see the connections comes from being involved in an almost antihistorical music world. As Gerri Hirshey remarks in *Nowhere to Run*

(Times Books, 1984), her adept survey of soul music history, "soul was a restless music that rarely set down to study on itself." There's no doubt that she's stating the plain fact of the matter, and that you're a product of the soul world to which she refers.

In fact, I'd say that the most striking contrast between contemporary black pop and white rock is in the two genres' relationship to their own pasts. White rockers, epitomized by Springsteen, seem continually to glance over their shoulders, doomed to compare their best efforts to fabled days of yore. Black rockers, like yourself, keep their eyes so firmly fixed on the present that it's as if you're afraid of being turned into pillars of salt by the searing story of your own cultural development. Bruce Springsteen wanted to grow up to be Elvis Presley. You say you'd never heard of Presley's "Heartbreak Hotel" until you wrote your own song of that name.

Why does it matter, all this yak about the past? Mostly because the music you make and the popular culture to which it speaks is an edifice constructed not on show tunes like your favorite, "Oh, What a Beautiful Mornin'," but on the blues and gospel and rhythm and blues and country and bluegrass of your forefathers. To understand how today's music really developed, you have to know what Berry Gordy learned from writing for Jackie Wilson; what Jackie Wilson learned from Roy Brown and Al Jolson; where what they all learned came from: the heart of American racial conflict. You have to know that just as the Beatles and Rolling Stones built a musical edifice from the foundation established by Chuck Berry, Muddy Waters, Elvis, Bo Diddley, Buddy Holly, and Little Richard—black and white performers, but mostly black ones—so did Chuck Berry come up with his style by drawing upon the jump blues of Louis Jordan and the nasal country harmonies of Gid Tanner and the Skillet Lickers' "Ida Red"; and Little Richard draw upon the great gospel shouting of Marion Williams and the Ward Singers and the flamboyant costuming and pianistics of Liberace; and Bob Dylan forge his style from Roy Acuff and Robert Johnson, Ma Rainey and Woody Guthrie. And that Bill Monroe's "Uncle Pen" was a black man and that Nat Cole had to have spent a lot of time listening to Bing Crosby . . . and that your own grandfather, a black man in Arkansas, where his skin color was an excuse and opportunity for humiliation and degradation all the livelong day, nevertheless tuned in "hillbilly" radio programs not out of perversity but because that music was "his" as much as it was "theirs." That is, because somewhere buried deep in American cultural memory is the story of your own rise and fall from public grace told over and over and over again as a continuing multiracial passion play. And without knowing where your music came from—not from magic and dreams alone, as you've been known to claim, but from hundreds of years of such interminglings and attempts to separate and segregate them— you will never, ever be able to make sense of what has happened to yourself. Maybe, like your mother says, "Michael just knew." But you have need and reason to know more.

The people I'm describing had access to a range of traditional music that was awesome, and each segment of that music was equally awesome in its capacities: In stumbling upon Mahalia Jackson, you found one of the grandest expressions of an important fragment of the whole picture. But without knowing that the whole picture exists, you're inevitably going to flounder. And it isn't easy to piece that picture together. Try getting Berry Gordy to admit that black pop existed before Jackie Wilson or maybe Nat "King" Cole. Try to find a course in American cultural history (or even black history) that accords the same respect to Mahalia and Muddy and Fats Domino, or, for that matter, Hank Williams, Bill Monroe, and George Jones, that it does to George Gershwin, Duke Ellington, and Frank Sinatra. (We're told that the latter group made music more complex and sophisticated than either of the others, as though only formal complexity was of consequence, as if only the developments of East Coast urban life were sophisticated.)

As a result, while you can find many descriptions of what happened at the Apollo and the similar places where your career began, you'll search long and hard to find attempts to explain what it all meant, why there was such a fantastic proliferation of styles of music, comedy, dancing, and all the other entertainments that formed the arts of black America for fifty years or more, and why those arts galvanized an entire community. This problem didn't exist only for black people and their culture. It exists for Southerners of all but the most patrician categories, and most especially for working-class whites everywhere in the

United States, and for Latins and Cajuns and almost everybody else who didn't immigrate to North America from western Europe. These people were encouraged to shut up, or if need be, to blend in as unobtrusively as possible. They were to know their place and keep to it at all times and at all costs. The result was the development of a series of all but secret strains in our national culture—gospel, blues, hillbilly, Cajun zydeco, salsa express only the grossest dimension of it.

After World War II, many of the barriers that kept these segments of America hidden away began to collapse. There are all sorts of reasons why this happened. The most important are probably the massive migration away from farms and the South toward the North and city life and the simultaneous economic expansion that made traveling with large bands or orchestras intolerably expensive but gave wide access to relatively cheap electrified and amplified musical instruments and tape recording technology.

The result was not only a recording boom but a flowering of an integrated American musical culture, which reached its climax in the rock & roll years of 1954–1958, bursting forth to captivate and excite not only the U.S. but wide swatches of the rest of the planet. In those days, each strain of American music was not sifted and separated but coagulated and brought forcibly together into a dynamic new noise. And so the most ungodly hordes of our nation, the most vulgar and barbaric citizens of the land, rose and spoke—momentarily—as if with one voice. And their voices roared strong and beautiful from jukeboxes and radios all over the country, and brought unease and ulceration and an urge to put the clamps back down to the regulators of normalcy and good taste.

The clampdown wasn't a complete success or neither of us would be here, but it worked well enough to divide the development of black and white popular music over the last couple of decades as thoroughly as it has ever been divided. Which means that even though black pop and white rock musicians draw upon one another's developments in rhythm and song structure, technique and technology, in consciousness they are as separate, maybe more separate, as ever before. Your grandfather and Roy Acuff used and thought about music much more similarly than you and Bruce Springsteen do.

It's tempting to say that the equation balances. Black pop has lost a sense of its roots, or a desire to know where it came from. White rock has lost a sense of immediacy precisely because it is so trapped in questions of what came from where. But both sides aren't equally hamstrung because at least the white rocker has some sense of what and to whom he or she is beholden, while the black pop attitude can cheat even the performer, much less the listener, of even that much information. The best black performers—yourself and Prince—continue to draw explicitly upon the tradition in which they are operating, but it is almost as if there is a taboo on digging too deeply. Which plays straight into the hands of those who'd like to see performers— yourself in particular, Michael—kept in line, who insist that what you do is just a disposable commodity or, to use your favorite term, "escapism." That is, that your work is destined soon to be forgotten, memorable only for "tonnage," the ability to move hard goods—records, tapes, jeans, tickets— and generate so much cash that the facts of the purchase will be permanently recorded, even if the content of what people bought is shunned or ignored or forgotten or dispensed with.

It wasn't always this way. In earlier years, performers stayed in touch with their past, and the work of their forebears as far back as could be remembered. In order to prosper and grow— and leave enough behind to make sure that the tradition itself was sustained, which was their only small hope of eternal survival—the performers felt (knew) they had to pay attention to what *had been*. So rituals and totems were devised and maintained, and new generations of performers were initiated.

At the Apollo, they stayed in touch physically. Do you remember what you did just before going on stage there for the first time? Your father once told the story.

"There was this object just offstage which resembled a tree trunk, which was supposed to bring good luck to first time entertainers, if you touched it just before going on," Joe said. "Although the object was onstage behind the curtain, it was positioned so that most of the audience could see you when you touched it. I remember the kids touching it before they went on."

As far as I can figure out, no one ever bothered to follow up on what your dad was talking about, what the object was or how it acquired its symbolic power. But the answer is anything but insignificant—and it's anything but hard to find. In his book *Harlem Heyday* (Prometheus Books, 1984), Jack Schiffman, of the family that owned the Apollo, wrote of its provenance: "On an island in the middle of Harlem—at Seventh Avenue just south of 132nd Street, to be exact—a plaque has been placed in the ground. Its legend tells the reader the 'Tree of Hope' once stood in that location. In terms of show business and Harlem, the plaque is a marker in history. For the Tree of Hope harkens back to the days of Bill 'Bojangles' Robinson, who gave it its name, and to the casting of *Green Pastures* [a long-running biblical Broadway hit that featured an all-black cast]. Hundreds of performers stood under its shade in the heat of summer and touched it 'just for luck' at any time of the year over a number of decades. Jack Johnson leaned against it; it was a witness to a real-life comic duel between Bill Robinson and Irwin C. Miller, producer of *Brownskin Models* (in which Bill's pistol was fired harmlessly in the air 'at' Miller); and Lord only knows how many scripts were born, deals were made and hopes were kindled under its sheltering branches."

According to Mezz Mezzrow, a wild white musician of the period who wrote a history of the scene, the Tree of Hope (which he terms "Harlem's Blarney Stone") stood across from an excellent rib joint, the Barbeque, above which were rehearsal halls used by the bands led by Louis Armstrong, Count Basie, Jimmie Lunceford, Cab Calloway, and Erskine Hawkins. The Tree stood directly in front of the marquee of Connie's Inn, where Louis Armstrong performed in the Harlem version of Fats Waller's *Hot Chocolates*. In the beginning, you could stand under that tree and listen to Louis Armstrong play Fats Waller, black American music explode into world consciousness for the first time. When the city decided to widen Seventh Avenue, it was Bojangles Robinson who arranged to have the tree moved out to the island in the center of the intersection.

Nevertheless, the Tree of Hope was eventually cut down. How it happened seems to be unrecorded: Was it hit by a car or felled by Dutch elm disease or some other blight? Burnt in a fire or collapsed of old age or cut down by some callow, careless city administration? I haven't been able to find out. But it is gone in any event, and all that remains on 132nd and Seventh is that plaque.

Half a dozen blocks farther south, a more substantial remnant was saved. The log you touched before racing onstage is the last known fragment from the Tree, "a small log mounted on a pedestal," as Schiffman wrote. When you touched it, you were participating in one of the fundamental rituals of Amateur Night at the Apollo. The dictum was "Touch the tree. Touch it for luck." But what you really contacted when you slapped that shiny piece of wood was the whole history of black entertainment, the rich and wonderful story of the most important part of American music, from field hollers and the minstrel show right straight through to Sly Stone and Miles Davis. By touching the Tree, you put yourself in a line of descent that begins in the mists of American popular culture, and through it you came into contact with Louis Armstrong, Bojangles Robinson, Bert Williams, the original blackface minstrel, Jack Johnson, and all the dozens and thousands who succeeded them, learning from some part of what they did and trying to carry it on. And I think that you also came into contact with all that preceded them as well, all that they learned from and attempted to carry forward.

Michael, you speak of your songs arriving in dreams as if by magic. That's a central tenet of your campaign to convince the world that you're a truly unique figure, genuinely larger than life—notwithstanding the fact that large-as-life would be rare enough, that campaign is as central to your public persona as any individual vocal stylization or dance step. It's also completely unnecessary, since one-of-a-kind is the least of your attributes.

The reason you shy away from the idea that you're connected to anything, much less history, is more intriguing. I wonder if you're a bit frightened of acknowledging such connections, even mythic ones, because you fear that they would limit you to being "merely" a black entertainer, rather than a universal one.

Well, you were taught by experts to avoid emphasizing the fact that you're black, taught to avoid making even casual references to the daily struggle anyone with dark skin must face in this culture. In a certain sense, that's the story of what Berry

Gordy tried to do at Motown: Bury the fact with sheer brilliance, obliterate them with musical genius and joy.

It led Gordy into the same dilemma you now face, the condescending and contemptuous statements that you aren't "really" black. As though you had your nose job for some other reason than that having a large, flat brown nose is a stigma in our society; as though the media is obsessed with the change in your facial features, most of which obviously resulted from the change in your diet to vegetarianism (a change whose effects were so radical that the bone structure of your face became visible), because, to unconscious bigots at least, those changes made you look "not black," as if you were "trying to be white"—that is, it made you violate the racial stereotype. In a certain sense, your bone structure is now taken as an implicit criticism of that stereotype and the kind of writing and thinking it produces. This does not make the people whose careers subsist on stereotyping happy, and when you make yourself vulnerable (partly by not sending down roots), they're happy to exploit the opportunity. It's not especially well thought out, a knee-jerk response, too sloppy to be termed revenge. But it's there.

Any black man who has ever "crossed over" into a predominantly white environment faces the same maddening set of expectations, which limit any opportunity to display individual humanity. Ralph Ellison's *Invisible Man,* one of the great American novels of this century, takes this situation as its premise. The rest of the book shows how it drives men—not just black men, either—completely mad. There is no black entertainer who hasn't faced this problem, from Louis Armstrong to Jimi Hendrix, and no one has ever solved it. You can quit, you can try to ignore it, you can rebel and refuse to play the game (which means you'll probably have to quit), but you can't win. That's the built-in racism of America coming to its nastiest head.

The problem is not unfamiliar even to your mentor, Berry Gordy, the king of crossover, the wealthiest and most prominent black businessman this country ever produced and a sorely underacknowledged musical artist to boot. Consider what Phil Spector, himself a great record producer, once said of Motown:

"I don't consider Motown black. I consider them half and half—black people making white records."

What does this mean? Mostly, in my view, that Phil Spector had no choice but to admit that Berry Gordy had made more hit records, with more different kinds of performers, for a longer period of time, than Spector himself ever had. But even though Spector is an egomaniac, not a racist, he was still unable to see "popular music," the broadest category, as anything but white. That is, Motown may be the most successful musical enterprise ever launched, but pop music still belongs to *us*. Not incidentally, Phil Spector made almost all of his best records and biggest hits while working with black singers.

Nevertheless, Berry Gordy, like you, tried to cut himself off from many aspects of his heritage. Motown put out a Martin Luther King, Jr., record once; it released and *promoted* Pat Boone records. And while the role that Motown played in smashing the chitlin' circuit was historically essential and has benefited every black performer since the late sixties, it replaced that circuit with nothing but a series of conventional performance styles derived from white show business: arena concerts, supper club revues. There is nothing distinctive and certainly nothing distinctively black about what Motown achieved in this area, no significant contribution that it made, and that's at least partly because Berry Gordy and company wanted it that way. (Records are another matter, of course. There, Motown was as original as it was influential.)

So you were taught by experts, Michael, to shun too close an association with black music's past. The goal has always been white show business success at its glitziest and corniest: Las Vegas, hokey TV specials (imagine the abomination of pairing Smokey Robinson with Linda Ronstadt, much less Adam Ant, as was done on *Motown 25*), the kinds of concert "production" that involve lots of glittering costume changes but very little *getting down* and as little intimate contact with the audience as possible, Hollywood movies with scores as mushy as their plots, Broadway plays that stand out not at all from the other entertainments designed to draw blue-haired ladies in from the suburbs on Wednesday afternoon.

That you have inherited this taste for kitsch and corn is undeniable—why else would you want to hang around with

someone as kitschy and corny as Liza Minnelli? But I wonder if
you know how much of a ceiling it places upon your imagination, your show-biz maneuverability, your ambition itself. There
are other ways of doing things: You can put on concerts that
reach much farther than mere costume changes (as George
Clinton and Prince regularly prove), you can make movies and
stage plays with *bite* (*Dreamgirls* was not a Motown production
in part because Motown would have wanted to softsoap the
story, to play down its rough edges). And as long as you don't
attempt anything so daring, you'll never know what you're
missing—but that doesn't mean that you aren't missing a lot.
Among other things, you're missing a chance to find out what
your success really means, how much of it belongs to you and
how much is just due to circumstances.

And you also miss the chance to set the story straight. Right
now, the world seems to believe that your triumphs in 1983
and 1984, when you united an audience of opposites and, for a
moment, rubbed out fundamental contradictions in our society,
were a triumph for that social system. Your failures, conventional wisdom seems to suggest, are your own.

The opposite is true. Your triumph was personal. Your descent
was, to an important degree, unavoidable, built into a star system
that thrives on planned obsolescence and sudden reversals in
fashion as surely as General Motors ever did. Just the same as
the miracle of Berry Gordy turning Motown into a long-lived
success is taken as proof of American capitalism's resilience and
adaptability, while the company's narrowness, stinginess, and
stuffiness is taken as some aberration of Gordy's personality.
Again, the opposite is equally true, but who's to tell the story?
Cut off from the resources of your own cultural history, how the
hell are you supposed to keep the details straight yourself?

The funny part is that you are connected whether or not you
want to be. As John Lee Hooker, whose own Detroit-bred
music is so primitive that it stands as the polar opposite of what
Berry Gordy achieved, once said: "It's not . . . that I had the
hardships that a lot of people had throughout the South and
other cities throughout the country, but I do know what they
went through. . . . It's not only what happened to you—it's
what happened to your foreparents and other people."

And it's not only about hardship, either. The greatest example happens to be your famous moonwalk, in which you seem effortlessly to move forward and backward simultaneously. The moonwalk is graceful and funny at the same time, but how original is it?

Well, take a look at this paragraph from Robert C. Toll's *Blacking Up* (Oxford University Press, 1974), a history of the nineteenth-century minstrel show. The topic is a dance step, "The Essence of Old Virginia":

> The "Essence" . . . was also characterized by the sliding steps of Afro-American shuffles. . . . "If a guy could really do it," ragtime composer Arthur Marshall said of "The Essence," "he sometimes looked as if he was being towed around on ice skates . . . the performer moves forward without appearing to move his feet at all."

Whether or not you know it, that great moonwalk move isn't new—it taps into something vastly older. (Older than the guy I read about the other day, who claims you picked up the moonwalk from steps he and his friends had been doing in the streets for years, that's for sure.)

I don't mean to suggest that just knowing that fact will get you anywhere. But it does suggest how much can be missed when you focus on the now and try to squeeze out the past. If you want a life of pure "escapism," a life of dream and magic, a life that denies everyday logic, that gaze will work well enough. But then again, reading between the lines of that *People* special, listening to what your mother, your manager, and others report about you, you seem confused and a little angry about why you've been inspiring some of the reactions that you have. I don't think it's any big mystery, but it is complicated, and many of the puzzle pieces can't be seen when you're looking straight ahead. Little as you may like it, the only way to tell this story right is to trample once again over the artifacts of your life and career. After all, as you'd be the first to say, your life is a great story. Like all such tales, it needs a beginning and a middle, as well as an end.

# F · I · V · E

The Jackson 5 had come almost as far as their wildest dreams. Winning the Apollo talent show assured them of additional successes: certainly some sort of recording contract, at least one with a specialized soul label, as well as more and better concert dates.

They had come this far on Michael's raw talent and Joe's unflinching determination. The other brothers did the best they knew how—Jermaine was using his teenage sexuality to best advantage on the occasional numbers he sang—but it was the inspired abilities of Michael, as lead singer and dumbfounding dancer, and the dogged hard work that Joe put into management, seeking out opportunities and making sure that the boys were ready to accept them, that spelled the difference between leaving the Gary small-time and remaining stuck in it.

Joe gave up just about everything for his boys, even the relative security of his job at Gary Works. He worked there only part time in 1968, bringing home $5100 rather than the $8000 to $10,000 that a crane operator working overtime during the Vietnam War boom years could have expected. Since he knew what he risked, and since he was guided by his own frustrations with the Falcons, Joe drove the boys, pushed them to the limits of their patience, endurance, and filial affection. "He wouldn't make it fun," Michael told Gerri Hirshey. "He would do it in a way . . . 'You're doing it wrong, you gotta do it like this.' Singing was fun, but he didn't do it in a way like, 'Oh that's nice'—jolly and happy-go-lucky and blah blah blah. He was more like, 'You gotta do it right' and whatever. And he'd be there really for us to get it, but we loved doing it. He told me how to work the stage and work the mike and make gestures and everything."

Like so many of Michael's statements, this one's conclusion is irrelevant to its opening. As gentle as his dad was rough, Michael was in deep and serious conflict with his father from the beginning of the Jackson 5. Whether the reason was jealousy, Michael's exuberance as it conflicted with stern discipline, a misunderstanding of motives, or something else, the struggle with Joe would be as essential to the development of the Michael Jackson story as any other single factor.

Because the Jacksons were a family group, they were split and factionalized by this conflict. (Michael and Jermaine's principal bond has been said to be that, of all the brothers, they're least like Joe.) Michael was indispensable to the group's success, while Joe's managerial limitations were obvious even to himself: He tried to sell a half-interest in the J5 to Sam Moore of Sam & Dave in 1968, and though Sam was a big fan of Michael's and the price was a bargain (five hundred dollars), he wouldn't do it. Moore remembers Joe Jackson locking Michael into the group's dingy dressing rooms so that the old man could go off and play cards or carouse. Michael would simply sit and tremble, a scared little kid despite his assurance in the spotlight. Whether that was why Sam said no to managing the group— maybe he just wanted to be a singer, not a businessman—is another question. At any rate, Joe continued seeking a partner after he was turned down by Sam.

In ordinary circumstances, the group might have simply sought more experienced direction. But while you can easily fire a personal manager, you can't fire your father, especially not if you're only ten years old and he's got the car keys to get you home. Besides, who knows what support Joe might have had from some of his other sons. If the older boys weren't envious of Michael to some degree, then their graciousness was so boundless it was barely human.

The Jacksons have long denied all reports of familial conflict— Michael's remarks to Gerri Hirshey are a rare and significant breach of Jacksons protocol. But during the Victory tour (and even before it, when Katherine finally filed for divorce), their phrases of solidarity grew progressively less and less meaningful as Michael's estrangement from his dad and several of his older brothers became more and more apparent. (That the family still tried to go on as if none of its feuding had occurred, much less been publicly reported, says a lot about the family.)

The Jacksons returned to the Apollo to play their first paid engagement there, on a bill with the great shouter Etta James, riding high with the gravelly hits "Tell Mama" and "Security"; Joe Simon, the sweet-voiced Nashville soulman who'd recently scored with a remake of the Supremes' "You Keep Me Hangin' On"; and another kid act, the Five Stairsteps and Cubie, then making a name for themselves with remakes of soul and R&B classics like Jimmy Charles's "A Million to One" and the Miracles' "Ooo Baby Baby."

The Stairsteps were from Chicago, where they had been discovered by Curtis Mayfield. Cubie Burke, the youngest of the six Burke brothers who formed the group, was only *two* years old! Though the Stairsteps would later record the magnificent "Ooh Child," the other brothers were more than a decade older than Cubie, and his inclusion in the group was a gimmick, nothing more. His position wasn't integral, as Michael's was, and the contrast must have made the J5 look even better.

Arriving in New York, Joe was sent to the American Federation of Musicians' hall, downtown above the Roseland Ballroom on 52nd Street, to fill out papers for the gig. There he met a young white attorney, Richard Arons. Arons was simply assigned to help Jackson with the paperwork for the Apollo performance, but before their meeting was over, Joe had asked him to help manage his sons. Arons held back. But when he went uptown to see them perform, he was persuaded. Arons left his AFM job and became Joe's partner.

Exactly why Joe Jackson selected Richard Arons as his partner isn't certain. It undoubtedly helped that Richard's father, Max Arons, was the head of the New York City AFM. But Jackson also probably felt that having a white partner with a law degree would give him some extra leverage in the business world. He was, and long remained, extremely sensitive to skin privilege.

Joe Jackson had already begun to make important music industry connections along the chitlin' circuit. He'd become especially friendly with Gladys Knight, who with her cousins, the Pips, was then hitting for Motown's Soul subsidiary with "The End of Our Road" and the original "I Heard It Through the Grapevine." Motown had resurrected Knight's career, which had faltered after two 1961 hits, and she encouraged Joe to contact the company in Detroit. Joe didn't need much persuading, since Motown was then the hottest record company, black or white, in the world. Berry Gordy was transforming all of black show business, bringing it into the mainstream of American pop culture in a big way for the first time.

"Joe used to talk to me and Taylor Cox," Knight recalled. "One night they had a talent show at the Regal and I told Joe we were going to get somebody down there to see them. So they went out, everybody loved them and the next thing I know—big headlines: 'Diana Ross Discovers the Jackson 5.' "

It wasn't quite that rapid, but Knight has certainly always had a better claim to being the discoverer of the J5 for Motown than Ross, who received the original and still semi-official credit. Joe Jackson later said that he'd been talking to Knight "for a year or so" before coming into contact with bandleader Bobby Taylor, who was the person most responsible for talking Jackson into taking his sons to audition in Detroit.

Taylor was a journeyman bandleader, whose group, the Vancouvers, had started in British Columbia and had once included both Jimi Hendrix and Tommy Chong (of Cheech & Chong). The Vancouvers never had any substantial hits, but they eked out a living, at least for their leader, by serving as an opening act on the chitlin' circuit and for appearances by various Motown acts. Taylor's role at Motown was supportive, and he understood it perfectly. It's also probable that like Ike Turner and Johnny Otis in earlier days, Taylor used his time at shows to scout the local talent, probably receiving a "finder's fee" from Gordy if he came up with anybody worth recording.

Joe Jackson had other offers, so he resisted Knight's initial advances. "I had sent Motown a few tapes and I never did get any reaction from the tapes," he said. "At the same time,

Gladys Knight was telling me to go to Motown with her. It took a year to be convinced, and finally Bobby Taylor convinced me."

According to Katherine Jackson, Taylor did his convincing backstage at the Regal in Chicago, only a few hours before the J5 was to leave for New York, where they would appear on the nationally broadcast David Frost show. "Instead, they headed for Detroit," she told *People*. "I didn't know where they were. Finally, I called Chicago and was told, 'No, Joe and the boys didn't go to New York.' I said, 'Well, where are they?' He said, 'They went to Detroit.' I said, 'Detroit? You mean to tell me they gave up that television show just to go to Detroit? What for?' He said, 'Motown.' "

The one-word explanation probably sufficed. Motown was something more than just the hottest record label in the United States; it represented a completely different vision of what blacks might aspire to within show business, and it represented a level of success (fame, money, glamour, respectability) that no other black-owned firm had come close to achieving.

As much as any institution can ever be said to be the product of one man's vision, Motown was the personal creation of Berry Gordy, Jr. Born in 1939 to a middle-class Detroit black family (middle class marking the difference between life in the slums of the east side and the relatively more comfortable existence in the ghetto on Hastings Street, a mile or so west), Gordy had been around. He'd fought in the Golden Gloves, worked briefly in an auto plant, and, like all of his brothers and sisters, kept his hand in the family enterprises from adolescence. Gordy was a jazz fan, and in the early fifties, he started a jazz-oriented record shop in Detroit. He was quickly wiped out, not by shoddy business practice or lack of musical acumen, but by the advent of rock & roll.

From this experience, Gordy learned much, including the interesting facts that retail stores were not where the action and money were in the music business; that you can have the greatest eloquence and hippest taste in the world but unless you are speaking to a great mass of humanity, you are not gonna pay the rent with it; and that, despite it all, music was where he belonged, for he did indeed have a gift.

He wasn't cut out to be a performer. Short and chunky, Gordy never sang professionally, and though he played mean and rhythmic piano on many of his records, he was hardly virtuosic. He was not intending a career as anyone's sideman, anyway. So he set himself up as a songwriter, and soon wrote a string of hits for Jackie Wilson, the Detroit-based singer who had fronted Billy Ward's Dominoes and was just then starting off on his own. The Wilson hits were a string of R&B and pop successes, crossing over into the white market effortlessly: "Reet Petite," "To Be Loved," "Lonely Teardrops," "That's Why (I Love You So)," "I'll Be Satisfied," simple dance rhythms with teen romance lyrics that Wilson put across brilliantly. On the best of them, "Lonely Teardrops," he bridged the gap between the zoot-suited shouters and evangelical wild men who started rock and R&B and the more suave yet still reckless types who would perpetuate that music for the next few decades.

By 1960, Gordy had written (or cowritten, often with his sister Gwen) eighteen songs that made *Billboard*'s Hot 100, the *pop* chart, not just the R&B ghetto standings. Six of those had gone into the Top 20, and four had reached the Grail, selling over one million copies.

Gordy studied and learned from each experience. What he found, working with Wilson, was that he was limited and frustrated operating solely as a songwriter. Wilson was saddled with arrangements that were dated, too "swinging," and he was handled by people of limited vision, who would just as soon have turned him into another saloon vocalist, rather than let him pursue the potential breakthroughs implicit in his singing style. So Gordy determined to do more than just write the songs; he would also produce the records, controlling the music to the last possible stage.

He made a couple of hits with Marv Johnson in this fashion, notably "You Got What It Takes," but Johnson was but a shadow of Jackie Wilson. And he worked on a couple of singles with a Detroit harmony quartet, the Miracles, led by Bill "Smokey" Robinson, who became his best friend and greatest student. The Miracles made a pair of singles that were picked up for national distribution by Chess and End, but neither "Bad Girl" nor "Got a Job" did more than graze the charts. Gordy was again frustrated: He controlled neither promotion of the record to the indispensable radio station disc jockeys nor distribution to the network of wholesalers and retailers. Without the former, no one would be aware of a record's existence, and without the latter, no one would be able to find it in order to buy it. And even if everything went right, he learned the hard way that getting paid was another matter. As an independent producer, you simply didn't see significant amounts of money, no matter what handsome figures might be spelled out on paper. There were "provisions for returns," and getting paid on 90 percent of net sales, and records that were pressed off the books and ruses without end that labels could use to diminish the sums they actually had to relinquish. The situation was revolting.

So Gordy seized the means of production. His sister Gwen had married Harvey Fuqua of the Moonglows ("Sincerely") and they had formed a record label, Anna. In February 1960, Gordy released his latest production, Barrett Strong's "Money," through them. Gordy wrote the song and it spoke directly to what he had learned in the music industry so far. Over a pounding, primitive beat—drums, piano, a thud or two of bass, and the rattle of tambourine composed the whole sound—Strong and his female accompanists chanted "Money don't get everything, it's true / But what it don't get, I can't use." It spoke to the pink Cadillac imbedded in the heart of every true rock & roller's heart and became a Top 30 hit.

Gordy's relatives did pay him, and with the gelt he got, he started his own label—two of them, Motown (first release: "My Beloved" / "Sugar Daddy" by the long-lost Satintones) and Tamla (originally Tammy, until that name turned out to be owned by the movie), which reissued "Money." Eight releases later, Tamla put out its first single by the Miracles, a Smokey Robinson homily entitled "Shop Around," which went through the roof: It hit number two on the pop chart, higher than any of the songs Gordy had written for Jackie Wilson, and sold way over a million copies.

After Smokey, the deluge. Gordy and his minions uncovered an unbelievably rich seam of talent, more than any other record label has ever discovered so rapidly: Marvin Gaye, Diana Ross and the Supremes, the Temptations, the Four Tops, Martha and the Vandellas, Little Stevie Wonder, Tammi Terrell, Junior

Walker and the All Stars, Jimmy Ruffin, the Marvelettes, Mary Wells (and those only the major names) all leaped out of the Hitsville, U.S.A. studios on shabby-genteel West Grand Boulevard in a five-year period from 1961 to 1966.

And Motown's greatness wasn't only the acts. The songwriting was superb, particularly the tunes written by Brian and Eddie Holland with Lamont Dozier and various combinations of staff writers including Mickey Stevenson, Clarence Paul, Barrett Strong, Janie Bradford, Norman Whitfield, Harvey Fuqua, Ivy Hunter, Hank Cosby, and Johnny Bristol. (That's not counting the writer/performers: Gaye, Robinson, Wonder, Walker, Brenda Holloway.)

There were also half a dozen formidable, state-of-the-art producers at Motown: Brian Holland and Lamont Dozier, Smokey again, Whitfield, Bristol, Stevenson, Paul, Fuqua. Motown records were the hottest sounding on the radio, and the best of the producers—Holland-Dozier and later Whitfield, especially—made sounds as distinctive as any vocalist or instrumentalist. The pounding gospel piano riffs and basic drum pattern of a Holland-Dozier record were as much a signature as Smokey's falsetto and Diana Ross's whispery soprano.

Supervising all of it, often participating, was Berry Gordy himself. For the most part, Gordy collaborated or merely oversaw his company's production; he believed in teamwork, with himself as a not-quite-dictatorial central authority. When called upon, he could step in to galvanize songwriting or even come up with a winner himself (he wrote "Do You Love Me," a classic piece of dance rock, for the Contours) or do the same behind the board. It's safe to say that there has never been a record executive as musically gifted as Berry Gordy. He was so talented that he almost justified the paternalism and autocracy around which Motown was built.

Almost every artist, writer, and producer at Motown was a Detroit resident (not necessarily a native of the city, since the Motor City had experienced the same surge in black population that transformed Chicago and Gary). Several were related: Both Fuqua and his protégé, Marvin Gaye, married Gordy sisters, for instance. Working together in the quickly antiquated, cramped quarters of Hitsville, U.S.A., conquering a world many of them had had only an inkling of before, there grew an almost familial closeness among the stars and their coworkers. Even the girls who ran the telephones aspired to more and pulled together, for hadn't Martha Reeves of the Vandellas gotten her start just that way? Motown was a living embodiment of the American dream, the warm corporate family where everybody eventually got rich.

Gordy did much more than record his artists. He controlled their personal management, their touring and club appearances, frequently their personal finances (as business manager) as well. Motown was a full-service company, and it developed strict rules of procedure as part of its pattern of talent development. The very idea of career development was unprecedented among black-oriented record labels, which had previously had neither the interest nor the resources to provide the kind of services Motown insisted upon as a matter of course. Motown took live performance and table manners, costuming and good grammar as seriously as the bedrock groove of its hits. It hired not just a staff choreographer but Cholly Atkins, of Coles and Atkins, the great black vaudeville tap dance team, and he taught much more than the great dance steps epitomized by the Temptations' uncannily elegant routines. Atkins trained his charges to *move*, so that the act of replacing the microphone in its stand became a fluid gesture of gracious simplicity, not a clumsy, mechanical maneuver. Other Motown tutors instructed kids from homes where there were barely enough knives and forks to go around which spoon to use first at dinners on white damask tablecloths, made certain that tuxedos were spiffily tailored (and pimp-eleganza costumes generally eschewed), did their best to saw the rough edges off ghetto-bred vocabulary and speed up mid-South drawls.

Motown was justifiably criticized for keeping too much control over the lives and careers of its stars; many felt that the company was patronizing in its subjection of its performers to bureaucratic dictates, perhaps with pecuniary motivation. At the very least, having the same entity write royalty checks and provide financial management, which should have meant scrutinizing those royalty statements and renegotiating the recording deals, was an undesirable conflict of interests.

Yet consider the alternatives. In the early sixties, when most of the Motown stars were making their names, there was barely any career support structure for white pop singers, let alone black ones. Personal managers were too often grifters, and anybody presenting himself as a financial adviser was most likely a shark. Booking agencies regarded singers as either potential movie stars (which meant moving them out of music as quickly as possible, even if music was their most significant skill) or as human hula hoops, to be sucked dry as quickly as possible before the fad passed on to someone new. Motown established its own talent development system because there was no alternative. The fact that it worked can be measured by how many Motown talents prospered for ten, fifteen, twenty years or more: Stevie Wonder, Smokey Robinson, Diana Ross, Marvin Gaye, Gladys Knight. Contrast this with the record label to which Motown is most often compared, Atlantic, which was not even able to sustain the career of its most broadly talented star, Aretha Franklin, for so much as a decade. That doesn't deny or excuse Motown's paternalism, but it does explain a lot of how it came about.

It also explains the familial feeling that lingers, sometimes even for years after stars have left the label. It is as hard to imagine so many stars who left a record company returning to honor it as did for the *Motown 25* TV special as it is to imagine any other label being honored with such a show on prime-time network TV in the first place. Performers who've left Motown may hint at their dissatisfaction with some of the label's practices and policies, but they're usually reluctant to spell out their grievances, not necessarily out of fear (several, including the Jacksons, have been quite explicit without retribution) but through their sense of solidarity with what the institution gave to them. Loose lips never sank a Gordy ship because, cumbersome and unfair as some of Motown's behavior could be, it was also a marked improvement over most of the alternatives, and veteran performers can't help but know it.

Berry Gordy did not build an entertainment empire—the most successful black-owned corporation in American, and probably world, history—out of good-heartedness. He was able to accomplish as much as he did in part because he began Motown under very favorable historical circumstances. Between the end of World War II and the end of the sixties, operating in a generally overheated economy, the record industry increased annual sales more than ten times, from just over $100 million to more than $1.5 billion in 1969. Much of the expansion represented sales to blacks and other working-class groups newly integrated into the urban consumer economy. And this left a great deal of room for entrepreneurs who understood black and other working-class tastes better than the East Coast businessmen who controlled the "major" record labels (RCA, Columbia, and Decca) that accounted for almost all of the 1945 sales.

It's true that most of these entrepreneurs were white, not black. But Motown was hardly the only black-owned R&B label of significance: Vee Jay Records in Chicago, owned by Vivian Carter and Jimmy Bracken, a husband-and-wife team; Bobby Robinson's Fire and Fury labels in New York; and Don Robey's Duke/Peacock in Houston were all black-controlled labels that had long strings of hits. Neither was Motown the only black label to break many of its pop acts. Vee Jay, in fact, had two major white pop groups, the Four Seasons and the Beatles, and might have had as long and glorious a run as Motown itself had not the multinational corporation EMI brutally (and possibly illegally) snatched the Beatles away for its Capitol subsidiary.

At any rate, many of the white-owned independent labels were run by various brands of outsiders, Jews or immigrants (Ahmet and Neshui Ertegun of Atlantic were Turks) or both (Phil and Leonard Chess, whose Chess and Checker labels ruled Chicago blues and R&B). Others were just plain strange men, like Sam Phillips of Sun in Memphis and Syd Nathan of King in Cincinnati. You had to be an outsider or an eccentric or a fanatic (or all three) to make your living as a white man trafficking in black culture.

And then, as black music began to be absorbed and assimilated into America's white cultural "mainstream," you had to be plenty shrewd to just stay afloat. Mostly, the independent labels of the fifties and early sixties sold out to larger corporations: Atlantic to Warner Communications, Chess to GRT and a host of successors. The unlucky—Bobby Robinson, the Vee Jay folks—went belly-up. Only Berry Gordy gobbled discreetly at the same trough as the bigger players, because his staff and performers and support teams were so tightly knit. Just a few of Motown's performers and producers were wooed away in the sixties, and of those who left (Mickey Stevenson, Mary Wells, and Kim Weston, most notably) none succeeded in equalling their Motown track record. Later defections cost the label more heavily—particularly grievous was a hostile split with Holland-Dozier-Holland—but by then Gordy and Motown had already become entrenched in the American show business establishment. There was always talk of him selling out, and from time to time rumors of financial catastrophe surfaced, but it was twenty-five years before Gordy even hooked up with a major label for distribution.

In part, Gordy was able to prevail and persevere because he was in Detroit, which had an awesome pool of talent and had long had it, going back to the early fifties when not only Wilson but also Little Willie John, Hank Ballard, Della Reese, La Vern Baker, and Johnnie Ray (a white singer) emerged from the city's black clubs. More important, Detroit had no other hometown record company of significance.

Gordy was able to snatch up some additional Detroit singers by buying smaller labels—acquiring Ric Tic and Golden World got Motown Edwin Starr and Brenda Holloway. In other cases, the Motown "production line" process was able to re-vive the careers of veteran rhythm and blues singers. Before coming to Motown, neither the Isley Brothers nor Gladys Knight had had hits in several years. While there, they had the biggest records of their careers up to that point. And both left with a clearer picture of what they wanted to achieve and had their biggest records of all after completing their Motown apprenticeship.

In many ways, Gordy and Motown were interchangeable. The company's vaunted "quality control," in which paid listeners screened and rated all recently completed tracks, boiled down to weekly meetings at which all potential new releases were played and criticized. If the reviewing process seemed to bog down, becoming too polite or political, Berry Gordy himself would most likely cut through, with a trenchant examination of a record's flaws or overlooked potentialities. From time to time, Gordy would just take matters into his own hands. Smokey Robinson tells the story of being awakened in the middle of the night to rerecord "Shop Around," after the first pressings had already been released, because Gordy had figured

out a way to do it better. The resulting session, with Gordy
not only producing but playing piano, gave Motown its first
Top 10 hit. Gordy wasn't that driven all the time, and he
did display a lot of faith in his house producers. But he
gazed over their shoulders constantly and with a lot more
credibility than most record company owners because everyone
was aware that he could do the job himself (as he sometimes still does).

By 1966, Motown was already the most successful black-
owned record company in history. Berry Gordy was wealthy
beyond any ordinary reckoning, since he owned the vast majority of the company's privately held shares. Just the holdings of
Jobete and Stein and Van Stock, the music publishing companies that handled all the Motown song copyrights, would have
made him a multimillionaire.

Gordy had not only wealth but power. Within his realm,
that power was vast, and his realm included not only Motown
itself, where the pleasure and displeasure written on his counte-
nance could determine the future of an act, but the entire record
business. Retailers, wholesalers, and other record labels paid
strict attention to his every move and scrutinized his rare public
and semipublic utterances. Gordy was a retiring man and a
guarded one, and his reclusiveness, his reluctance to grandstand
and pontificate, made him seem that much more oracular and
contributed to a building legend of toughness and near omni-
science. Even outside the music world, Motown was beginning
to make its presence felt . . . including in politics, as poli-
ticians like Richard Hatcher in Gary and Carl Stokes in Cleveland began the first successful black mayoral campaigns in
major cities and turned to Gordy for support, money, and
counsel.

Yet Gordy didn't follow the usual pattern of entrepreneurs
who get what they wanted—mass recognition of their talent
and ideas, and the wealth that comes with it—but lose what
they had—the vigor and inspiration behind their ideas. Neither
did he dissipate his ideas in a spectacular way, eschewing drink
and drugs, and he never used Motown as a vehicle for personal
whims. Berry Gordy may have remained a jazz fan, but you'd
never guess it from the label's artist roster. When Motown
needed horn players, it ignored Detroit's many fine jazz players

and called the same place that provided the string players, the Detroit Symphony Orchestra.

Which provides a meaningful index of what continued to drive Berry Gordy, Jr. What he really wanted was, in one cold word, respectability. "Motown success hasn't just been a matter of making a fortune, it has also been having its fortune *legitimized,*" wrote British critic Simon Frith, "i.e., acknowledged and honored by the world of (white) power. So in the days of the Supremes and Four Tops, Motown was 'The Sound of Young America'—patriotic not black. . . ."

Because Gordy was the quintessential parvenu, rather than overturning the standard format of popular culture fame and glory, he determined to take over the existing show-biz structure. As soon as possible, Motown talent was directed away from the TOBA circuit and package show tours and into "classy" supper clubs, the kind of high-class niteries still somewhat reluctant to book most black talent (much less eagerly recruit black customers). Motown's acceptance in those precincts was revolutionary in its impact on black entertainers.

But that impact wasn't felt in the white niteries, which easily absorbed black talent and uneasily accommodated upscale black audiences without changing very much in orientation (or even repertoire). Where Motown's "making it" in the white nightclubs was most profoundly felt was on the circuit of black clubs and theaters. As Frith wrote, once Motown broke the color line, "never again would black performers be confined to the fabled chitlin' circuit." Within a decade, that circuit was dead, taken down not only by the rot and desolation of the urban centers in which the TOBA theaters and clubs were located but also by the elimination of a need for such a circuit. When the Supremes could play Vegas and Al Green the Copa, the chitlin' circuit had become as redundant as Negro league baseball after the arrival of Jackie Robinson.

Berry Gordy took his acts not only into Las Vegas and the supper clubs, but onto TV: Motown was the subject of two prime-time specials, and its acts were given a widely disproportionate share of the time devoted to contemporary black music on the network variety shows. He was willing to pay a creative price for such access. Motown acts recorded albums of middle-of-the-road standards, like *The Supremes Sing Rodgers and Hart*; live, they featured blaring "big band" arrangements of hits and sang the most overworked chestnuts (a medley of "Yesterday" and "What Now My Love" on the *Temptations Live!* album is typical). As critic Jon Landau wrote, "The head of the Motown corporation picked up some pretty perverse notions as to what constitutes success, somewhere along the line."

If Motown artists had displayed any particular affinity for singing standards or working with big band arrangements, Landau's criticism (which is a distillation of the basic criticism all white rock critics directed at this aspect of Motown) wouldn't have much validity. Marvin Gaye and Diana Ross, after all, were *singers*, not devotees of any particular musical cult—there was no abstract reason for them not to sing any particular kind of music. But none of Motown's stars displayed any gift for or evidenced any desire to sing standards or to be backed by supper club charts, not even Ross, the label's most light-headed pop voice, or Gaye, its most versatile stylist. Motown itself confirmed this judgment by continuing to release grittier, bluesier material as potential (often actual) hit singles. Aside from Stevie Wonder's reworking of "Alfie" as a harmonica instrumental (which is in this context a kind of perverse musical joke), it's impossible to think of a Motown act that ever hit with a show tune or a standard. (In contrast, one of James Brown's biggest hits was "Prisoner of Love," a radically reworked standard originally written in the thirties.) Although Gordy could claim as late as 1965 that Motown's music expressed "rats, roaches and soul," the ugly, unchanging conditions of ghetto life, part of that condition, as historian Charlie Gillett noted, "was the determination to get out of it, which Gordy expressed with infallible accuracy."

The notion persists that Gordy somehow forced Motown artists to conform to peculiar black bourgeoise standards when the performers themselves would have preferred something rootsier, more "authentic." This is nonsense; there's no evidence to support it and much that refutes it. When artists left Motown, it was almost always for a more mainstream "pop" label. (This is true from Mary Wells signing with 20th Century-Fox in 1963 to Diana Ross leaving for RCA in 1982.) Generally, those singers adopted styles that were more "pop"—a word much more racially ambiguous today than it was when Motown began—than the styles they had used at Motown.

Even more interestingly, as Motown edged closer and closer to the mainstream of American musical taste, as it came to *define* a certain period of that taste, the label never lost its black following. This is one of the most striking qualities that marks Motown artists as different from the black musical artists who worked in cabarets or sang pop: Josephine Baker and Nat "King" Cole, Sammy Davis, Jr., and even Mahalia Jackson abandoned or were isolated from a substantial quantity of the black community in the process of "crossing over" (to use the contemporary phrase). Motown's stars never did, and that says a lot about the times in which Motown's breakthrough was created and about why that breakthrough was possible.

Motown music was not born in the kind of struggle that characterized the blues, jazz, or even early R&B. It wasn't born out of struggle at all, in a certain sense, and its lack of acknowledgment of the struggle against feudalism and segregation in the South and Jim Crow restrictions in the North is striking. Not until 1968, with the Supremes' "Love Child," did a Motown hit speak of ghetto life in specific terms. Throughout the era of the civil rights movement, black power, and urban insurrection, Motown singers commented only upon the ecstasy of the dance floor and the rigors of love lost and found. True, in 1966, Stevie Wonder recorded Bob Dylan's metaphoric freedom song "Blowin' in the Wind," but that was a controversial record—at least, it was within Motown, where the bosses (from the top down) saw no reason to rock the boat. Outside of Hitsville, U.S.A., everyone had already heard stronger, more explicit words from pop singers and "Blowin' in the Wind" made the Top 10 without a struggle.

Berry Gordy's goal was not just to sing "the sound of young America" but to embody it. Motown wanted and needed to be *completely* assimilated as the very definition of young, affluent America. And that meant seeing America not in terms of race and class privilege and miserable poverty but in terms of wealth, leisure, perpetual youth, and eternal "fun."

A new generation of black Americans, like Gordy raised in Northern urban cities, had also made its way to the fringes of the "middle class"—that is, the middle rungs of the employed working class. Better educated and more sophisticated, comfortable in the Northern cities as their parents and grandparents had never been, prospering (at least in relative terms) during the boom times engendered by the Asian wars, this section shared Berry Gordy's vision of America as a consumer paradise. They, too, wanted to be accepted in the white middle-class palaces of entertainment, the legitimate theaters and nightclubs, the casinos and showrooms of Las Vegas. They shunned, as Motown shunned, shabby blues bars and the reeking theaters of the chitlin' circuit. Or rather, as soon as a classier, more prestigious and comfortable place to see their favorites was provided, they shunned such places. Until then, until the Motown stars had upset the hegemony of white stars in the cosmopolitan boîtes, blacks had been almost as uninterested in the entertainment such spots offered as the venues were in having black customers.

So Gordy had it both ways. Unlike any other black showman in history, he reached the white middle-class constituency that made him a fortune and kept the black audience, too. That's an essential ingredient in what made Motown such a spectacular success, and why the label's rise created the downfall of the chitlin' circuit, spurred the rise of the most integrated radio broadcasting America ever knew, and helped initiate a short-lived but thrilling cycle of black-oriented TV shows and movies. In creating and exploiting such opportunities, Motown and its artists weren't selling out; they were making a deal in which they kept their identity and got the material things they wanted, which is a very good deal indeed.

Motown was such a success that it was bound to spawn imitators, and while it took a few years to understand that Gordy's methodology wasn't as cheap and quick and careless as previous methods of producing black hits, by 1968, the rest of the music industry had begun to catch on and catch up. From San Francisco, Sly and the Family Stone emerged, led by Sly Stone, a former soul disc jockey who was prepared to go Motown one better: He'd use even hipper dance grooves, driven by a bedrock bass inspired by Motown's great James Jamerson, to speak his piece in the kind of explicit terms the Gordy groups feared. Even on a major label (CBS-owned Epic), Sly and the Family Stone were an immediate sensation, making records that revolutionized what black pop could accomplish. Meanwhile, in England, Jimi Hendrix, a TOBA show band veteran, remodeled white rock innovations, taking the technological and production ideas of British rock and the literary lyricism of Bob Dylan and applying them to blues and soul. Hendrix never got a chance to finish the job, but what he started transformed black record making, liberating it from the three-minute dance-'n'-romance format as surely as Motown had lifted black shows out of the chitlin' circuit.

Shrewd as ever, Berry Gordy knew he had to respond. He set about allowing producer/songwriter Norman Whitfield (working with Barrett Strong) to produce psychedelic soul singles such as "Runaway Child, Running Wild" and "Cloud Nine" with the Temptations. But Gordy was sharp enough to know that he'd never be able to alter the image of his established acts enough to conform to this more than minor and temporary shift in style. In order to keep Motown alive, he needed an act that could maintain the label's presence on the charts while making a version of the new black pop that was as palatable across the board as his earlier stars had proved to be.

Gordy also needed a group that could be fitted into the Motown production team concept. Sly and Hendrix achieved their new music by obtaining the kind of creative leeway given to the new white rock stars—they spent huge amounts of studio time (which was nothing new at Motown), but they were self-contained, writing and producing their own material, running their own bands, calling their own shots, releasing many abstract or loosely structured tracks with controversial lyrics on their albums, pushing the record industry process as wide open as it would ever get.

Gordy was not at all interested in making such concessions to artistic liberty. He wasn't attracted to Jimi and Sly for the risks they had taken, just for the new marketing necessities and possibilities they had unearthed. So he needed an act that could be controlled, that would allow the new musical procedures to be applied *to* them, rather than trying to run the show themselves. What could be better suited for this purpose than a group led by a ten-year-old?

*        *        *

The Jacksons did their Motown audition at the famous Hitsville, U.S.A. Studio, actually located in the basement and back rooms of a huge old house, the front of which was devoted to Motown offices. The Motown session musicians, the label's roughneck workingmen, found playing with this children's group highly amusing, James Jamerson later said. Partly it was their name, "jackson jive" being an epithet in local argot, but mostly it was their act.

The Motown crew had worked with kids before; many of the Motown performers—even prima donna Diana Ross—had started working at Hitsville, or at least hanging out there, before they left high school. Little Stevie Wonder had arrived at age twelve and this strange blind child was almost immediately befriended by drummer Benny Benjamin and James Jamerson, the great drummer and bassist, who were the most talented players and hardest drinkers of all. But Stevie was a prodigy; blind prodigies are a staple of the blues and gospel tradition, Ray Charles being only his most immediate precursor.

There was no precedent for Michael's mimicry, his unearthly ability for capturing adult nuances, the skittering dancing that propelled him across the stage at an almost hysterical velocity. (Many believed that he danced so fast and furiously not because he was enchanted with James Brown, but because he had been told that you never knew who might be out there in the audience—maybe *a man with a gun*—so the best policy was to present a constantly moving target.) The Jacksons' audition was not only taped, it was filmed, and in the footage later shown on the *Motown 25* TV special, the musicians are playing with looks of stunned hilarity upon their faces, as if they cannot believe the comedy of what they're seeing.

The Jackson 5 audition was filmed as well as recorded for several reasons. Berry Gordy has said that the practice was usual, and by then, maybe it was. Motown, with its extensive interest in exploiting all aspects of an entertainment career, wanted to know how an act looked, as well as how it sounded. A screen test (as it were) offered an opportunity for the company's choreographers and costumers to assess the performance. But just as important, auditions in Detroit weren't seen by Berry Gordy, because he was, by then, spending very little time in Detroit.

In his search for legitimacy and respectability, Gordy had set his sights on Hollywood. Beverly Hills was a much more pleasant place to live than even his mansion on Detroit's Boston Boulevard, and being in Los Angeles gave Gordy access to the movie industry, on which he was training Motown's hopes for expansion. Since he remained Motown's autocrat, even in his absence, audition tapes and films were regularly sent west to him.

The Jacksons' discovery by the label was not just lucky. Like any label that hoped to stay in business, Motown spread its net wide in looking for new talent. It would have been more surprising if Motown hadn't had at least an opportunity to sign the group. On the other hand, the signing *was* fortuitous. The J5 was given special treatment from the beginning—soon after the recorded audition, the group was invited to play at a party for all the Motown staff, which was being held at Gordy's Detroit home.

Diana Ross *might* have been the reason. Sometime during this period, Ross and the Jackson boys played on the same bill at a benefit for Richard Hatcher, then campaigning to become Gary's first black mayor. According to the official Motown version of the J5's "discovery":

> The Jackson 5 tore through songs, giving each one all they had. "More!" "Fantastic!" The crowd was jumping with enthusiasm. Pushing through the crowd to the foot of the stage completely unnoticed in all the excitement was Gary's mayor, and with him none other than Diana Ross! Diana was rocking back and forth, clapping her hands and saying, "Right on!" with the rest of the crowd. The mayor was smiling and moving in time to the music. "See Diana? These kids are great . . ." The mayor shouted above the J5 sounds. But Diana didn't need to be told; she was sold.
>
> When their numbers were over, the J5 smiled at the applause, waved and ran right for the bus. They were shy but happy about their performance. "Let's go; let's get out of here!" they said to their dad. Before they could pull away from their parking spot,

a voice called to them, "Don't go, Mr. Jackson, don't go!" The Jackson family looked. Their mouths dropped open. Who should be yelling and running toward the bus but the mayor and Diana Ross herself.

Both Michael Jackson and Diana Ross have repudiated this story—but their repudiations came years later. It says something important about the credulity of the press that the Motown version was repeated for several years, until Gladys Knight asserted her claim as the J5's discoverer.

Diana Ross was certainly instrumental in the Jacksons' early career. "Let me put it this way," Joe Jackson said. "We were at the gate. To me, it seems—there was an iron gate in the entertainment field. And there just had to be a way to open that gate before you could get through. We sorta had one foot in and then along came Diana Ross. What she did for my boys was to open that gate." Surely, Ross's memory of the first time she saw Michael Jackson perform remains indelible: "I looked at this little kid whirling around up there and I thought I was looking at myself. I couldn't believe it . . . I saw so much of myself as a child in Michael. He was performing all the time. That's the way I was. He could be my son."

Former Motown executive Tom Noonan clarified the issue somewhat by telling Nelson George, "Bobby Taylor had been talking about the Jackson 5 before this, but it wasn't until Diana called Berry full of enthusiasm for these kids that Berry got interested. If anybody else had called I don't think it would have happened. Diana is the reason he got excited."

At any rate, something made Gordy sufficiently enthused to fly the Los Angeles Motown staff back to Detroit and to throw a party for the whole company at his huge house. Originally built for an auto magnate, "it was the biggest place we had ever seen," Jackie recalled. "His backyard was like a golf course and he had an indoor pool."

The Jacksons set up back near the pool house and played for an audience that included the Temptations, Diana Ross, and the Marvelettes. "A lot of performers who we admired were there, but it wasn't much different performing for them than it was getting on a stage in front of an audience of people we didn't know. Being on stage is the thing; that's the exciting

part for me, so it really didn't matter if we performed before ten or twenty celebrities or twenty neighbors," Michael
claimed. "Maybe I was too young at the time to realize
what the audition meant. I knew it was important and that
it meant a lot to our careers. But I didn't feel any pressure
to perform any differently than I had any other time, if you
know what I mean." But Jackie remembered it differently.
What really scared the boys, he said, was that "we were up
there doing their songs," hits made famous by members of the
audience.

All fears proved groundless. "They just killed us with
their energy," Noonan said. And Michael remembered that
afterward, Ross came up to the group and gushed about their
show. "She kissed us each one of us," he said. "She said
she loved what she saw and she wanted to be a part of what
we [did]."

The Jacksons returned to Gary to wait while the contracts
were signed and negotiated. (The contract they eventually signed
was virtually Motown boilerplate, however.) The family was
still hardly able to believe what was happening. Jackie recalled
"not being able to use the phone for two months while we
waited to hear from Motown. We wanted to keep the line
clear."

When the call came, it contained unusual instructions. The
Jacksons would relocate to California. Jackie, Jermaine, and
Michael left immediately, driving out with Joe; the rest would
follow with Katherine some weeks later.

When they hit Hollywood, Motown split the family up.
Half stayed with Berry Gordy at his place, half with Diana
Ross at hers. It was freezing when they left Gary, and the
boys were amazed at what they found when they got to
California: "the sun, the swimming pools, a whole other image,
a whole other life," Michael said. "It was magic. It was
like paradise. We went to Disneyland, we had fun every
day. This was a whole other thing from Gary, Indiana. And
we went into the studio and came up with 'I Want You
Back.' "

# S · I · X

Dear Michael,

For such a ubiquitous fellow, you're sure hard to pin down. Trying to get a firm fix on your image is like trying to bottle smoke. It sort of makes me wonder if you can get your image to hold still when you gaze into a mirror. And even though, way back at the beginning, I gave up trying to distinguish between the "real" you and the mythological Michael, I never expected the puzzles to keep piling up so far into the story.

Of course, you came into the music business living out a batch of fables and tall tales. The Diana Ross discovery story is only half of it. I would have thought that kind of press agent's fabrication went out with the old movie studios—it's like finding out that Michael Paré wasn't a salad chef or something. What was important about the Ross story, though, was that people bought it—not just the public, but the press, too. After all, Diana Ross was there in the flesh, hosting your coming-out press party at Daisy, the Beverly Hills disco, in the summer of 1969 and then introducing you as her special guests on her TV special that fall. Or check the liner notes to your first album (titled, wonderfully enough, *Diana Ross Presents the Jackson 5*). They appear over Diana's signature, though I would never go so far as to accuse her of actually writing them.

"Honesty has always been a very special word for me," they begin, "—a very special idea. I don't necessarily mean the kind of honesty that our history books tell us Abraham Lincoln practiced—although that's fine.

"But when I think of my own personal idea of honesty, I think of something being straight out, all there, on the table— the way it is. . . . That's how I feel about the JACKSON 5. . . ."

It was?

I mean, forget about the fact that Diana's not exactly living up to old Abe's pragmatic idea of truth-saying herself in these sentences. That's to be expected, and you could run through the whole gamut of epistemological, dialectical, and teleogical disputations on whether there is truth and whether you or I or Diana Ross will ever know it, this side of Heaven or Godhead, anyhow. I don't care. Famous person wants to make a fool of herself in public, forgetting that *these things linger* and some sucker is likely to drag 'em out in a couple of decades and make mock, feign disbelief and whatnot, that's her problem. I'm hip to the wiles of show biz. You do what you gotta do, even if it means sweeping up after the elephants. (Though if I were sweeping up after elephants at that point in my career . . . oh, never mind.)

No, what is absolutely confounding about what Diana Ross writes here is this: She is writing about hearing *honesty* coming from your mouth, and as far as I can make out, that is the one thing that it is absolutely, positively, finally certain that your singing has never expressed.

To start with, that first album is built upon a series of cover versions—mostly of Motown staples, such as "Who's Lovin' You," "My Cherie Amour," and, lamentably, "Reach Out I'll Be There," but including Sly and the Family Stone's "Stand!" Each of these is reproduced with an arrangement that directly lifts from the original as much as possible. This is not dishonest, true, but it wouldn't stop Diogenes in his tracks, either.

Even more obviously, there's "I Want You Back," your first hit. Now, at the start, let me make something clear. I think that "I Want You Back" is not only your greatest recorded performance, but that it is one of the glories of Motown, period. In *The Book of Rock Lists* (Dell, 1981), when

I had to choose the greatest debut records of all time, "I Want You Back" topped the list. The record is almost perfect. (The Four Tops' "Reach Out I'll Be There" *is* perfect, which is why I resent your messing with it.) But "I Want You Back" is based not upon honesty, certainly not upon emotional honesty, but on a deception, an illusion, a trick of perspective. An eleven-year-old sings a song in a voice that begins in a childish whine and then quickly grows in knowing assurance of its own carnal cravings, expressing niceties of desire that would be beyond any adolescent and almost all adults. And this is characterized as "straight out, all there, on the table"? Thrilling, yes. Honest, no.

Yet this idea, that you show all your cards whenever possible, is the center of your public image. What a myth! Now, it's true that this fable serves many purposes, justifying both those who believe that your rather limited and halting expressions, your inability to come to terms with so many details and issues, reflects a deck that's a few cards short and those who believe that you simply retain so much natural innocence that what you found simple to evoke at eleven, you find impossible to even acknowledge at twenty-six. But that doesn't mean that it's right; that doesn't make it true. I'd say that (unless you've pulled off a feat of psychological retrogression otherwise unknown in human history) this disparity actually reveals a consistent sleight of hand.

That makes you no more dishonest than any other artist of this age of uncertainty, needless to say. Maybe it even makes you typical. After all, Picasso himself said, "We all know that Art is not truth. Art is a lie that makes you realize truth, at least the truth that is given us to understand." Here, epistemology once again rears its ugly face. Unable to give it the smack it deserves, let's let Picasso conclude: "The artist must know the manner whereby to convince others of the truthfulness of his lies. If he only shows in his work that he has searched and re-searched for the way to put over lies, he would never accomplish anything."

Now, I don't raise the specter of Picasso in order to further burden you with an artistic comparison the mere suggestion of whose weight would break the fragile back of your creations. I raise it, to tell you the truth, because it's quoted in John Berger's *The*

*Success and Failure of Picasso* (Pantheon, 1980), in the midst of a discussion of what it means to be a prodigy. "The distinction between object and image is the natural starting point for all visual art which has emerged from magic and childhood," Berger writes. "To exaggerate this distinction, as Picasso does here, until lie and truth are reversed, suggests that part of him still believes in magic and has remained fixed in his childhood."

I'm not sure just why Berger limits his contention only to visual art. Undoubtedly, what he says here applies also to your work, which certainly has its basis in childhood. And, however much the Jehovah's Witnesses request that you deny it, you consistently attribute your creations to magic and dream states. At the recent plagiarism trial, in which a Chicago songwriter accused you of stealing "The Girl Is Mine" from his melody, you entered a cogent and eloquent defense of the process by which you craft your songs. But the genesis of the song, you insisted, as everyone to whom I spoke predicted you would, was that the song had initially come to you in a dream. And to say that something is "magic"—as you did of your stay at Diana Ross's house—is the highest praise you can offer. And there is also no doubt that this is precisely a result of your fixation upon childhood, your refusal (I am not at all sure that it is an inability) to leave it behind for the worries and responsibilities of adulthood.

Berger recounts one of the most famous stories about Picasso. Just as you were a natural born singer from infancy, Picasso drew before he talked, and by the time he was ten, he was, like you, as good as any journeyman in his field. Picasso's father was an artist, also, a provincial art teacher—more successful at his work than your dad ever was with his music, but in a parallel relationship with his son, at any rate.

When Picasso was fourteen, his father gave him his brushes, saying that he would paint no more because his son had already surpassed him. Soon thereafter, Picasso took the entrance examination to the Barcelona Art School, the Apollo of his world. He did a month's worth of drawings in a day and was immediately admitted. At sixteen, he was admitted with honors to the Royal Academy of Madrid, which was kind of like being signed to Motown.

Berger makes two points about this. First, he tries to imag

ine what it is like to be a prodigy, reminding us that the prodigy has always been associated with magic and the supernatural: Paganini, he says, was supposed to have been taught to play his violin by the Devil. But this is only how the prodigy appears to us. To himself, Berger says, the nature of his genius is also inexplicable and irrational because he does things without effort and without much comprehension of what his effects really signify. "He obeys what is the equivalent of an instinctual desire. Perhaps the nearest we can get to imagining the extent of the mystery for him is to remember our own discovery of sex within ourselves. And even when we have become familiar with sex and have learnt all the scientific explanations, we still tend to think of the force of it . . . as something outside ourselves, we still tend to project its force onto nature, to which we gladly submit." (Well, we know that not everyone submits, and certainly not gladly, don't we? Nevertheless . . .) Berger says that Picasso's attitude is this: "Understanding has nothing to do with it—indeed understanding is a hindrance, almost a threat." This is not a statement you would repudiate concerning your own work. And Berger goes on to build an elaborate and well-grounded case for why this concept held back Picasso, the most immensely gifted artist of our age, except in those few periods when he established a fertile relationship with a community of his peers.

Second, Berger says some interesting things about the story of Picasso's father and the gift of the brushes. He takes this as an unusual variation on the Oedipus myth, which in Freudian terms we all act out with our parents, attempting to overthrow the father figure and assume his position, sexually and socially. But in Picasso's case, his father surrendered—the young boy won a clear-cut victory, being told that he *deserved* to take his father's place. "Since this is what every boy wants to happen, is he not more likely to believe in magic?" asks the critic. "Yet at the same time, and again because he has wanted it to happen, is he not likely to feel guilty? The most obvious relief from his guilt is then to tell himself that his father's patience and slow development and experience do not, by the very nature of things, count for anything: that the only thing which can count is the mysterious power he feels within himself. But this relief can only be partial: he will remain frightened of explanations and of discussion with and between other people of the way he overthrew his father."

Now, Michael, this story does not directly apply to you. In your case, your father surrendered his brushes grudgingly, if at all, and proceeded to instruct you to paint what he could not. Nonetheless, when you did those paintings, and with so much success, your guilt must have been no less intense than Picasso's, for your victory was no less complete.

Worse, you've been condemned to replay this scenario throughout your life and career, with various antagonists: sometimes your father (with whom you made a clear break when you dismissed him as your manager and publicly chided him for making racialist remarks), sometimes father figures (most obviously when you split with Berry Gordy and quasi-parental Motown in 1976, though at times it seems that any old authority figure will do, even the press).

Like you, Picasso was often praised for his eternal youthfulness. This was a myth, as the horror of death and loss of potency reflected in his final paintings attests. Similarly, you have been celebrated as the repository of eternal pop music youthfulness. You seem to believe in this particular myth rather wholeheartedly yourself, so much so that you've been known to identify with Peter Pan. "All boys but one grow up," begins J. M. Barrie's awful classic. But, Michael, you're not that one. Without the resources of a Picasso (it is no shame to lack them), your work stays young, but its youth is an anomaly, not a confirmation of anything, but a denial of many things. It leads to confusion, nothing better. And while it may lend you and your work an immense appeal at any given moment, that appeal will be superficial and fleeting. It's meant to be outgrown.

This is the fate of the teen star in the media age—to be not just a prodigy but a commodity, something to be bought and sold. Just as you allowed your one really mature song, "Billie Jean," to be turned into a Pepsi commercial, so you yourself are converted into an object of spectacle, celebrated today, derided the moment the party's over. It's hard to think of a torture more complete.

As hard as you've worked to make yourself unique, then, your situation is anything but unparalleled. But what to compare it with is not so obvious. It's tempting to equate what

happened during the *Thriller* period and the Victory tour with
the similar splurges of public attention devoted to Elvis, Frank
Sinatra, and the Beatles. But that's superficial. Even though
you, like them, symbolize contemporary cool, in the final
analysis your stardom is quite different. Sinatra, Elvis, and
the Beatles all represented musical leaps forward: Sinatra was
the quintessence of the saloon singer, really the culminating
figure of a whole style of music. It would be ludicrous to try to
claim that *Thriller* has such stature in regards to soul and
dance music. Even at the moment of its release, it was outstripped in audacity of conception by Marvin Gaye's *Midnight
Love.*

Both Elvis, as a performer, and the Beatles, as writers and
performers, made significant stylistic breakthroughs in popular
music. *Thriller* was less revolutionary in its approach and performing style than *Off the Wall*, although it did contain a
significant expansion of black pop to include hard-rock guitar
playing, thanks to the Edward Van Halen solo on "Beat It."
This hardly ranks with the dazzling formal fusion Elvis accomplished, or with the revitalization of rock & roll that the Beatles
achieved. And judging from your productions and songwriting
since then—the work you've done with the Jacksons, Diana
Ross, and your sisters—"Beat It" was a one-shot gimmick, not
an approach you're especially interested in pursuing. (The real
follow-up to "Beat It" in the musical sense was Run-D.M.C.'s
heavy-metal/rap concoction "Beat Box," the special dance mix
assemblages of producer Arthur Baker, working on Bruce
Springsteen's guitar-heavy *Born in the U.S.A.*—and Prince's
*Purple Rain.*)

To tell the truth, Michael, you don't seem very interested in
the content of your songs. There's that "Billie Jean" Pepsi
commercial—a rewrite that was your own idea. For someone
who wants honor as badly as you seem to desire it, for someone
who hopes to be appreciated as an adult artist, this is self-
contradictory behavior.

But, especially after last summer's concert tour, it's pretty
obvious that you are not particularly interested in what your
songs might be saying: The banalities of "The Girl Is Mine" are
of a piece, in this sense, with the more message-oriented "Beat
It," the marvelously metaphoric "Wanna Be Startin' Somethin',"

and the raging "Billie Jean." For Michael Jackson himself, the only meaningful measure of success and respectability would seem to be sheer size: gross quantities of records shipped, dollars earned, people fascinated (not necessarily moved).

This obsession with bigness obliterates the issue of what's best, buries it under the banner of Biggest Ever. This was epitomized by your remark at the Epic Records ceremony honoring the inclusion of *Thriller* in the *Guinness Book of World Records* as the largest-selling record album ever made. This was, you said with a straight face, "the first time in my life I really feel that I've accomplished something." Michael, if that's true (and folks behind the scenes tell me that it is), you're on a disastrous course. Maybe you're convinced that to be biggest is necessarily to be best—that delusion is pretty widely held among pop performers. Yet it's also false and finally self-defeating. To start with, you aren't in the *Guinness Book of World Records*—*Thriller* is. And before *Thriller,* that book listed *Saturday Night Fever,* and before that, Peter Frampton's live album, and before that *Tapestry* by Carole King, and, who knows, before that *Bridge Over Troubled Water* or *Sgt. Pepper's Lonely Hearts Club Band* or *50,000,000 Elvis Fans Can't Be Wrong*—who knows? Who remembers? No one does, because being biggest is a setup for being eclipsed.

There's another way to look at such questions: What's best? But that issue has been lost in the current splurge of media spectacles that arise and depart with such shattering rapidity. Let me offer a few examples, ones skimpier on content than anything you have ever done. A good place to start might be with 1983's so-called second British Invasion of rock groups, since it was the only other interesting musical fad of the *Thriller* period. There was indeed a spate of new British bands, making music considerably different from their (white) American counterparts, who had U.S. hits during 1983. Such groups as Duran Duran, Culture Club, the Eurhythmics, Human League, Naked Eyes, Spandau Ballet, Thomas Dolby, and Dexy's Midnight Runners did have Top 10 hits in 1983. Combined with the marginal success of such bands as ABC, Big Country, U2, Re-Flex, and the Thompson Twins, plus the successes scored by veterans David Bowie, the Police, and the Pretenders, there was some justification for spotting a trend. But to inflate a commercial trend into the status of a movement, as even such astute observers as *Newsweek*'s Jim Miller and *Rolling Stone* did, was to make an ultimate confusion between size and importance.

True, the British Invasion groups of the eighties made records that sold millions. But the groups of the first Invasion— the Beatles, Rolling Stones, Animals, Who, Kinks, Yardbirds— revolutionized the way records were made and concerts were conducted, changed the very grounds on which rock was played, heard, and discussed. The eighties' pseudo-invasion had no such aspirations; most of the male models who led those groups had barely an inkling that any such revolution could be possible, and anyway, they lacked the creative resources to make even an effective series of hits. The result, barely two years later, is that most of those acts are dead in the water, neither making amazing music nor selling astonishing quantities of records.

This confusion between biggest and best is all-pervasive among the cultural phenomena of our time. Look at the video-game business: A billion-dollar invention at Christmas 1982, such games were said to be luring youngsters away from movies and rock & roll records, maybe even regular TV. By Christmas 1983, the major companies in the industry were reporting losses nearing two *billion* dollars. Or consider the 1984 presidential election: During the campaign, both candidates and all the major press reports discussed Ronald Reagan's candidacy on the premise that he had restored American prosperity. Nobody widely visible in American public life seriously questioned this "recovery" . . . yet the day after the election—not twenty-four hours after Mondale's concession—the financial-page headlines were filled with reports of huge deficits and other economic weaknesses.

Such events have their entertainment business parallels: the disco boom of the late seventies, blockbuster films like the *Star Wars* cycle and *Ghostbusters*. More strikingly, these grandiose spectacles more and more frequently take place outside of show biz. The 1984 Olympics and presidential election are obvious examples. *Star Wars* and *Ghostbusters* are celebrated for their numbers far more than for their quality of production. Mostly they are devices for manipulating the same people over and over into the theaters on their way to becoming the biggest-grossing pictures of all time. Similarly, the sheer scale of the Los Angeles

Olympics was used to overwhelm the fact that the Soviet bloc pullout impoverished the competition; Mary Lou Retton became a heroine for winning her gold medal even though she wasn't competing against the best gymnasts in the world because they were absent.

The other unifying feature of these faddist phenomena is their startlingly short lifespan. Disco was a craze in East Coast working-class and gay neighborhoods as early as 1974 or 1975; in 1977, thanks to Studio 54, it became a craze among the elite; in 1978, it became a national boom on the heels of *Saturday Night Fever*, another biggest but not best hit movie. By 1979, disco was passé, finished except for a hard-core cult. Mass success had made it seem interesting and exciting in the first place. This short half-life is again quite similar to the "recovery" and Reagan's 1984 election campaign.

The magnitude of *Thriller*'s success and the backlash against it must be measured against such events. In contemporary myth-making, what happened to you and your album was not nearly so extraordinary as we believed at the time. What made it exceptional, to a degree, was that you were black and androgynous in appearance and that the most innovative marketing devices used in packaging and selling *Thriller*—the videos— were virtually brand-new.

Could you have controlled the process more carefully and escaped the worst consequences of the spectacle environment? The question is important, if only because it would be unfair to expect you to entirely evade the consequences of a process that permeates almost every social ritual in our society. After all, the other blockbuster spectacles didn't crop up in every area from movies to politics to children's toys by accident. They are emblematic of a general deterioration of judgment, a widespread inability on the part of everybody—consumer and producer alike—to discern the difference between biggest and best. This is an especially knotty problem in a mass society, where reaching a great many people potentially has enormous significance, whatever the quality of the specific artifact that attracts that attention.

Then again, it's impossible to say that you attempted to make the story come out differently. In your interview with Gerri Hirshey, conducted well before *Thriller* was released, you outlined your plan to make it the biggest hit of all time. The complete alacrity with which you entered the myth-making process is partly your best excuse: It indicates that you weren't fully aware of the consequences of having your plan carried out.

When you get what you wanted and lose what you had, to paraphrase Little Richard, all complaints became unseemly. Skeptics will always say that you set yourself up to take a fall, and in the narrowest sense, they'll be right. Once again, it comes down to whether you consider the essence of this story that Michael Jackson's personal triumph was destroyed by social forces or whether you see your success as a victory of society's best impulses in which what one manchild did was easy and simple.

Michael, I believe that you and I both know that the latter idea is untrue and unfair. But in order to prove the point, it's necessary to know quite a bit more about how you became a star and what alternatives to bigness have been offered to you as a method of calculating your success. If there even were any . . .

# S · E · V · E · N

Brian and Eddie Holland and their partner, Lamont Dozier, left Motown in 1968. It was the first really serious defection in the label's history. The issue was money and credit. Holland-Dozier-Holland didn't figure they were getting enough of either, considering that they'd been responsible for almost all the hits of the Supremes and the Four Tops as well as many by Marvin Gaye, the Temptations, and the Miracles.

Holland-Dozier-Holland were so successful because they were so good—although their approach was widely imitated, no one else ever got as much out of the relatively simple musical patterns they used. Their records were the funkiest—the blackest, most gospelly and soulful—records that Motown released. Their absence created a huge gap for the Gordy group to fill.

Typically, Gordy decided to replace Holland-Dozier-Holland with a similar setup, but granting himself fuller control. To ensure that the new production and songwriting team would never leave the label, it would be called The Corporation, its membership remaining anonymous to the public. And it would not flout Berry Gordy's principles and ideas because he made himself one of the members. The others were Freddie Perren, Lawrence "Fonce" Mizell, and Deke Richards. (Not to be outdone in establishing themselves as a budding bureaucracy, Holland-Dozier-Holland had their first post-Motown hits with the Chairmen of the Board.) But The Corporation never developed as a permanent alternative to Holland-Dozier-Holland. In fact, it had only one really important act to work with: the Jackson 5.

The Corporation may have been Holland-Dozier-Holland's designated successor but within the Motown system, they had no track record and consequently little clout, despite Gordy's titular membership. Like almost everybody else at the company, they had to compete to bring their work to the attention of the top stars. As a result, they targeted their composing for specific talents. Their first really outstanding song, "I Want to Be Free," was written for Gladys Knight. But Perren, Mizell, and Richards were so impressed with what they'd done, they decided to shoot for the top: Diana Ross.

"We took it to Berry," said Perren, who went on to become an important dance music producer of the seventies with hits like Gloria Gaynor's "I Will Survive" and Peaches & Herb's "Reunited." "We played it and he liked it. But then he said, 'I signed this group of kids out of Gary, Indiana, and if you rewrite it this would be good for them. Direct it to kids so they can identify with it. A Frankie Lymon type thing.' " It was at this meeting that Perren realized that the Jackson 5 was the same group he'd seen in Chicago, when he was playing piano for Jerry Butler.

They rewrote the song and titled it "I Want You Back." Rather than the story of a singer shackled by love, it became a song of yearning, in which the singer is trying to hook back up with his lover. They recorded it with the Motown band, which included many of the Detroit stalwarts, and came up with a track that Perren has justifiably characterized as "one of Motown's greatest performances." Opening with a piano glissando, attacking guitar supported by strings, and a popping, propulsive bass, the track perfectly combines the essential aspects of Motown with the advances pioneered by Sly and the Family Stone.

Taking the group to Deke Richards's apartment, they rehearsed them throughout a Friday evening. Michael held the lead, but there were group harmony parts based on the nonsense chants in Sly's "Dance to the Music" and a feature spot for Jermaine. The next day, they went into the studio and cut the vocals, created a rough mix, and rushed over to another studio, where Gordy was working. Pridefully, they played it for the boss, expecting he'd be as enthusiastic as they were.

"You guys are getting ready to blow a hit," Gordy said and then, in his inimitable fashion, he proceeded to dissect the record, changing the arrangement, the lyrics, fine-tuning it. Then he sent them back into the studio. They worked until almost two in the morning, until Michael and Marlon were staggering with weariness.

For Perren, the most impressive part of the experience was Michael. "I would have him do the song, and by the time we got to the end, it sounded so good, he had improved the performance so much, that I'd have him go back to the beginning," Perren told Nelson George. "This would go on. First the beginning was better. Then he'd keep on and the ending was better than the beginning. With every take he got better."

The result was glorious, a performance in which every note seems perfectly placed for maximum excitement. There was nothing profound about it; there was nothing particularly unprecedented about it either—Frankie Lymon and Stevie Wonder were only the biggest among many previous prepubescent soul and R&B singers. Michael sounded more mature than any other preteen singer, but in general, the greatness of "I Want You Back" is derived from its perfect expression of the Motown sound. As *Rolling Stone*'s Jon Landau wrote of it, "The arrangement, energy and simple spacing of the rhythm all contribute to the record's spellbinding impact. Surely the coupling of this group with the Motown production staff is one of the most fortuitous events in the recent history of pop music."

"I Want You Back" departed less radically from the Motown prototypes than records such as "Cloud Nine" and "Runaway Child, Running Wild," which Norman Whitfield had been producing for the Temptations for the past several months. It never even came close to revolutionizing the Motown sound as did the Temptations' "Ball of Confusion," which was a hit a few weeks after the Jackson 5 made their chart debut. In a sense, then, "I Want You Back" is both the debut single of the Jackson 5 and the Motown production mill's last grasp at modernizing its original format.

"I Want You Back" didn't take the pop charts by storm. Released in October 1969, it charted on November 15. It wasn't until ten weeks later that it made number one, displacing B. J. Thomas's "Raindrops Keep Falling on My Head" on the January 31 edition of *Billboard*'s Hot 100. (A week later, "I Want You Back" was itself supplanted by Shocking Blue's "Venus.") "I Want You Back" spent nineteen weeks on the Hot 100, which is a comparatively long time and accounts for its estimated U.S. sales of two million copies and worldwide sales of over four million. (The record didn't "go gold" because Motown refused to submit to an accounting of the number of discs it had shipped the Recording Industry Association of America, the trade group that issues the gold record awards. No Motown records were eligible for gold and platinum record awards until the mid-seventies, when the company's policy on allowing the audits was changed.)

But no amount of statistics can fully capture the excitement that the initial appearances of the Jackson 5 created. They debuted on ABC's *Hollywood Palace*, in a show hosted by Diana Ross and the Supremes on October 18, 1969. The show was also the final appearance of the Supremes with Ross—their breakup was announced two weeks later. But, the buzz from the show was about the kids from Gary, Indiana. They performed two songs, the first a rather undistinguished soul ballad, "Can You Remember?" followed by "I Want You Back." It was a great send-off for Motown's latest pet project, and it inspired millions of teenagers and preteens with a passion to know more about Michael and his brothers.

"The Jackson 5 were then a very timely group for black Americans," longtime Jackson retainer Steve Manning said. "It was the time of the Afro and black pride. Never before had black teenagers had someone to idolize like that . . . The kids identified with them not as stars, but as contemporaries fulfilling their fantasies of stardom."

Berry Gordy knew exactly what he was doing. As Nelson George has written, "he saw a unique opportunity to develop an act that was perfect for tapping the lucrative teenage market." Gordy understood that the increasing assimilation of the black middle class into American consumer culture and the new affluence of the highest level of black workers (the kind of guys who had union jobs in the steel mills of Gary and the auto factories of Detroit) had created a black teenage market with amounts of surplus spending money similar to those of white teens. But nobody was marketing to the black kids—there was no category of teen idols to appeal especially to *them*. "What Gordy had realized," wrote British critic Simon Frith, "was that out there was a generation of black kids with money to spend and feet to dance and walls to hang pictures on. And there had never been soul idols for clean black teens before (only sportsmen and Martin Luther King). Motown was going to give them idols and music and posters and fan magazines and tee shirts and lockets and TV shows and everything."

The move was especially shrewdly timed to coincide with the rising of "black pride," in which a strong, new sense of black cultural self-respect and intense identification with black-originated culture asserted itself for the first time in mass terms. Just as processed hair gave way to the "natural" Afro 'do, America's blond, blue-eyed teen stars had to give way. That meant the Jackson 5 dressed in bright costumes with flared slacks and loose, wildly patterned shirts that were antithetical to Motown's usual conservatively tailored look.

"In most respects," Frith wrote, "Motown has achieved [the Jackson 5's success] by following the lessons of the fifties white exploitations of white teenagers: even if Michael Jackson has got a better voice than any other teen idol, he's still had to sing 'Young Love'. . . ."

But the most important tips Motown picked up from the white teen idols and their handlers had nothing to do with music. Although some of the Jackson 5 records after "I Want You Back" went after preteen lyrics with a vengeance ("ABC," the immediate follow-up, is the obvious example), the group was never used exclusively to purvey wimpy sentiment. ("Young Love" was an obscure album track.) The music remained solid Motown stuff: "ABC" played off the Sly Stone riffs even more strongly, "I'll Be There" was a ballad (but a *soul* ballad). To me, some of the other material was relatively slight, but the Jackson 5 earned their four number-one hit singles of 1970 by making records that had across-the-board appeal for lovers of soul and dance music.

No, what Motown learned from the teen idols was how to merchandise a teen success. To that end, the label (whose contract with the group gave them control over all such subsidiary merchandising) hired Fred Rice, who had worked for the Beatles and the Monkees. Rice was to create spin-off items for department stores and five-and-dimes around the world and to help coordinate the publicity blitz that created the follow-the-leader demand among preteens for everything from Jackson 5 lunchboxes to cutout Jackson 5 records on the backs of cereal boxes.

"This is the first time in my twenty-four years in the business that we've had anything like this," Rice told *Time*'s Tim Tyler. "I call 'em the black Beatles. . . . They're heroes, it's unbelievable.

"Of course, we tested the market with paper first, you always test the paper first. Posters and decal stickers with pictures of the kids, and if they go, then you do the toys, clothes, buttons, the hard stuff. We're just now getting out the clothes, and we're negotiating for a Jackson 5 hairspray and a Jackson 5 watch.

"All their stuff has their logo on it—Jackson 5 with a heart growing out of [the number 5] and some of 'em have a heart in a circle, that means soul. And I'm putting out the Jackson 5 magazine—we call it TCB . . . that'll come out quarterly. [It] has all their vital statistics, color pictures, song lyrics—we're doing everything.

"The kids just grab this subteen market, the twelve- or thirteen-year-old girl, she just flips over Jermaine and that Michael's coming along: It's a whole subteen adoration . . . that used to come in the movies, now it's records, because movies are too expensive a way to develop new young talent. Music is the most economical way to do it."

"We're labeling it 'soul bubblegum,' " said Berry Gordy. "It's a style that appeals to the young teens." But because the Jacksons had to get their start in the black pop market, which is traditionally more adult in its taste than the pop market (particularly in taste for lyrics and rhythms), the Jacksons couldn't churn out the kind of processed wimpiness in which the typical teen idols of the period—the Partridge Family, Bobby Sherman—specialized. And even though Michael was the musical focus of the group, he couldn't be the center of its teen appeal; he was the same age as that audience, but that made him too young. Young girls, the target of teen idol marketing, fantasize about boys slightly older than themselves. So the teen idol marketing strategy was centered on Jermaine, with Michael, in Rice's words, "coming along." Nevertheless, on record, Jermaine's biggest hit, "I Found a Girl," still took a backseat to its flip side, "The Love You Save," which Michael sang.

Which only reinforces a crucial point: The creation of teen idols, even those who are singers, has very little to do with music, even hit music. Generally, teen idols have been established through visual images: movies or TV shows. This was even true of Elvis, the Beatles, and Sinatra, and in order to establish the Jackson 5 as the first black teen idols, it was necessary to exploit such opportunities.

The company Motown had been could never have done this, mostly because it lacked the economic resources to mount its own films and programs. Also, until the early seventies, blacks had almost no access on any consistent basis to either TV or the movies. Producers simply weren't interested.

Gordy hoped that Motown would become a company devoted to exploiting its chances in these fields. That was the real point in making the transition from Detroit to Los Angeles. So Motown concentrated not on pumping out a steady stream of hit singles, which was comparatively easy (or at least, a task the company understood), or on concert tours, which were delayed for about a year after the first hit, but on getting the Jacksons on television. (A feature film or a series was too much to hope for in the case of an act both black and unknown.) In addition to appearing on the Diana Ross special, the Jackson 5 appeared on the Miss Black America beauty pageant telecast (actually before "I Want You Back" came out); *The Ed Sullivan Show; The Andy Williams Show*, home of their soon-to-be archrivals, the Osmonds; *The Sonny and Cher Comedy Hour;* and a special called *One More Time* with the Mills Brothers and Pat Boone. By 1971, they were hosting their own special, *Goin' Back to Indiana*, built around their January 31, 1971, "homecoming" to Gary, at which Mayor Richard Hatcher gave them the key to the city. Their guests were Tom Smothers, Bill Cosby, Bobby Darin, Elgin Baylor, and, of course, Diana Ross (as "the pregnant lady"). So important was this exposure that Jackie later remembered "breaking" the record on the Sullivan show, even though their first appearance on that program took place after "I Want You Back" was already a million-seller.

By the fall of 1971, the Jacksons had their own series: a Saturday morning cartoon show, which they had nothing to do with except that their records were used on its sound track. (The dialogue voices were overdubbed by actors.) The show ran for only twenty-three episodes, but its very existence symbolized how far the Jackson 5 had come in two years. After all, the only other pop music idols ever granted their own cartoon show were the Beatles. "The audience, black and white, is going to see black kids on Saturday morning. It isn't going to be all white faces [anymore]," a Motown executive told *Time*'s Tim Tyler.

That quickly, Motown's marketing men had successfully converted the group from five impoverished kids from Gary into a cute commodity. In this regard, Motown's assault was total; its hard-sell tactics blunt. Buy a Jackson 5 album and out spilled an inner sleeve covered with merchandising come-ons, an opportunity to become the "soul-mate" of your favorite brother.

The copy itself gives the full flavor of the tactics used: For only two dollars, for instance, a Michael lover could receive:

- Your own Michael Jackson Personal Soul-Mate Poem Poster! Written by Mike!
- Your Michael Jackson Personal Soul-Mate wallet-size ID card. It has a photo of Michael and his autograph!
- A giant (12 × 18!) Personal Soul-Mate Poster of Michael!
- A portrait-size (5 × 7!) signed photo of Michael!
- 9 different wallet-size photos of Michael!
- 65 (just count them!) Official Michael Jackson Soul-Mate letter seal stickers! All 65 have Michael's photo! Great for all your letters to Michael and *The Jackson 5!*

Plus! A Personal Letter from Michael Himself! 79 things In All! For only $2.00! Don't Wait!

## YOU'LL LOVE BEING MICHAEL'S PERSONAL SOUL-MATE! SEND AWAY NOW!

The inner sleeves also offered "Giant-Sized Photo Posters," photo stickers, a "private" photo album and "autographed" pictures, the official concert poster, and other assorted junk, destined to be lost, broken, forgotten, and later to turn up in comparatively minute quantities on an overpriced collectors' market.

The teen idol marketing wasn't directed solely at black kids. In fact, the Jackson 5 was so popular across the board with teens and preteens that MGM Records' straitlaced Mormons, the Osmonds, were retooled, with Donny Osmond as their Jermaine and Little Jimmy as their Michael, and former Motown staffer H. B. Barnum hired as producer to replicate the sound and substance of the Jackson 5's appeal. (The union had at least one moderately happy result, an imitation-Michael single, "One Bad Apple." Needless to say, even though the playing and songwriting were a pretty fair Motown approximation, the ecord fell down in the area of vocal performance.) The Jacksons "crossed over" bigger than any black act ever had: They made the cover of the bible of the teen scene, *Sixteen* magazine, although its astute editor, Gloria Stavers, had to fight to put them there the first time. And the group graced the cover of *Life* in its 1971 special issue, "Rock Stars at Home with Their Parents," in which they were featured along with David Crosby, Grace Slick, Elton John, and Frank Zappa. Coverage also came from *Time, Look*, and (much less comfortably) on the cover of the rock rag *Rolling Stone*.

The success of the Jackson 5 also inspired black imitators, such as the Five Stairsteps, and assisted in the rise of black-oriented *Sixteen* equivalents, such as *Right On!* The group was also granted the NAACP's prestigious Image Award for 1970, as well as being honored as *Billboard*'s Top Single Artists, after scoring four consecutive number ones, the heftiest string since the Beatles and the Supremes.

Jermaine recalled being told by Berry Gordy at one of their first meetings that they would have several hits before the public ever saw them, and that's how it was. They did a few isolated dates in the summer of 1970, at the Philadelphia Convention Hall and San Francisco's Cow Palace for instance, but their first major tour didn't begin until just after the shooting of *Goin' Back to Indiana* was completed, by which time they were a nationwide sensation—worldwide, given their reception in London, where Tito was stranded atop a Rolls-Royce, surrounded by screamers. The Dick Clark–promoted tour covered fifty cities, from New York to Honolulu. On and off through 1972, they traveled, hitting England, Japan, and West Africa (principally Nigeria) as well.

There was only one noticeable negative result: Black concert promoters complained that Gordy was doing them out of business that was rightfully theirs. That the first black teen stars were in the stable of Clark, who had specialized in promoting the tawdry, trivializing R&B reductions of Frankie Avalon and Fabian, was high irony indeed.

If black promoters were unhappy, they were about the only ones. Vince Aletti, the sharpest critic of such sounds, reviewed the Jacksons' Madison Square Garden debut: "[They were] astonishing . . . First of all, visually; the five brothers are beautiful or perhaps only cute, but they have complete control. There's none of the embarrassment of child stars, but the stunning assurance of young men. When Michael punctuated his rendition of 'Who's Loving You' with a graduated series of forward crotch-thrusts—a standard R&B crowd-pleasing gesture— one was struck not so much by his precocity as his perfection, his professionalism." In Cincinnati, girls fainted when Jermaine, singing "Mama, I Found a Girl," sang, "Won't you take me with you."

As for the Jackson brothers themselves, all was not so well. However professional they may have seemed, they were still a bunch of kids, tinkering with forces well beyond their control. "Basically they were pretty shy little kids," Mary Wilson of the Supremes recalled. And Tito confessed, "I was fourteen on the first major tour and I was scared to death—having your clothes torn off at airports and all that. I knew what was happening, but I wasn't used to it . . . Michael was being pulled every which way on that tour in London, he just seemed to disappear and it was scary."

And scary not only to his brothers and his parents. Michael himself was shaken. "Being mobbed *hurts*," he once exclaimed. "You feel like you're spaghetti among thousands of hands. They're just ripping you and pulling your hair and you feel that [at] any moment you're just going to break."

The entire Jackson family was transplanted to California before the end of 1969. Their first home there was in one of the cañons in the Hollywood Hills; set on the side of a hill, with a huge asphalt driveway, it reminded *Time*'s Tyler of nothing so much as a dinky motel. Well protected by a guard dog who doubled as a pet, the house was luxurious next to 2300 Jackson Street. But by the end of 1970, Joe and Katherine had located the house in Encino, where Michael and his mother still reside. It already had a swimming pool, badminton court, basketball half-court and archery range, a separate guesthouse, and servants' quarters. There were six bedrooms, which meant Michael, Marlon, and Randy would share, at least for the first year, until Tito married Dee Dee Martes and moved out, though it probably wasn't until Jackie and Jermaine were also married that each of the younger boys had a separate room.

Encino is one of the wealthiest communities in Los Angeles County; during the early seventies, it became known as a bedroom community for celebrities such as Dennis Weaver, Dick Van Dyke, and Aretha Franklin—singers and middle-level TV stars. The really big names still resided in million-dollar mansions in Beverly Hills or even more exclusive enclaves: Bel Air, Brentwood, Malibu. Still, the Jacksons' house—more properly, their estate—was a major investment; it cost around a quarter of a million dollars, even before the addition of a hundred-thousand-dollar recording studio and twenty-five-thousand-dollar darkroom (photography was a hobby for both Michael and Marlon).

One reason for the relocation was the inclusion of the Hollywood house on the Map to the Stars, sold to tourists visiting the area, which meant that strangers were frequently popping up. "They'd come around with cameras and sleeping bags," Michael said. "They'd jump the fence and sleep in the yard and try to get inside the house. It really got crazy." The Encino house had walls and a huge iron gate, a closed-circuit television system for added security, and it was a long time before it made the map.

But even without the intrusion of frenzied fans, the transition from life in working-class Gary to posh southern California was difficult. "California's a funny place," Tito said as late as 1984. "It's not like Gary or Detroit, where you know your whole block, you know who lives next door to you, you know who lives down the street. Here, you won't even know your next-door neighbor unless you make it your business to go knock on their door . . . because everybody is in their own domain here." Yet it was also Tito, in many ways the most sober of the brothers, who understood what happened most clearly. "Had we stayed in Gary, there wouldn't have been any alternatives whatsoever." Since the Jacksons moved just as smokestack industries such as steel went into an almost terminal decline, the older brothers, maintaining some contact with old friends back home, must have had a sense of having escaped just in the nick of time.

But that wasn't all. The Jackson family was estranged both from the world and from each other by the rapid ascendance of the group. It was hard to say which was most disorienting, or whether they would have been any less affected had they been less insular—as Jehovah's Witnesses, as blacks, as the progeny of a particular and arrogant patriarch—to begin with.

"You know," Jermaine said several years later, when he had spent a long period estranged from his parents and siblings, "when we first moved out to California we were very close—we did almost everything as a family. I saw that changing after the whole family got out there. We all lived in one really big house, but it wasn't like it had been in Gary. Back there, there were two bedrooms, one for my parents and one for the kids. There was a closeness there, a warmth I remember. That's what kept us together and got us so close as a family. But in that house in California, everybody had their own room, their own TV . . . It wasn't a warm place. Everyone was doing things on their own, losing touch with one another. We were growing up, but we seemed to be growing apart."

It isn't even all that certain that they were growing up by any normal standards. The fallout from their 1984 tour alone is convincing evidence that the Jackson brothers grew up to be eccentric, one and all. Michael's oddness is more exaggerated, more unabashed, but his brothers are also without many of the socializing inhibitions a more conventional youth might have given them. Given the bizarre confluence of parental strictness—Joe still insisted that telephone calls be limited to five minutes and he had no compunctions about taking the strap to any of his children when they got out of hand—and the inevitable indulgences granted to (and expected of) pop stars, maybe the resulting arrogance and greed shouldn't be all that surprising.

Which doesn't mean they were bad kids. Said Regina Jones, editor of *Soul*, "the Jackson children [were] some of the best-mannered, well-behaved I've ever met, in or out of show business. They had been well-trained, had great manners. If anything, you sometimes thought they were too nice, that they didn't have enough freedom."

Most estranged of all was Michael. For a start, even he couldn't miss the discrepancy between his former home and his new environment. ". . . In Hollywood, it was different," he said. "As our popularity grew . . . it seemed as if we had fewer friends. It seemed as if there was less contact with people not involved in the business. . . . It's kind of a shame we couldn't grow up doing what the other kids did. Even after we moved to California, we'd go to Disneyland or visit a Hollywood studio, which was sheer fantasy for me. But it was like we couldn't have any personal contact. Like we had to keep our distance from other kids. It was hard to get close to anyone outside the family or outside people we worked with every day. And even then, it seemed like most of the time it was business."

More than anything, Michael seemed confused about his life, unable to decide whether it was as strange as it might be or pretty much normal after all. An interview he gave to *Jet* in 1973 sums it up: "We don't get out of the gate much. All we need is right here. When we used to live in another house, we would go to the park and play basketball and volleyball. But we have all that here. Everything is here." Yet a few moments later, he claimed, "I live pretty much of a normal life and do all the things other kids do. I don't know why everyone thinks I'm so much different."

In fact, beyond whatever hormonal stirrings the Jackson boys unavoidably felt, it is hard to see what their lives during this period had in common with those of any other kids their age. Beyond the obviously increased degree of attention and availability of possessions, there were even more fundamental divergences between their existence and what might be described as "normal" in this time and place.

The lives of most kids are organized around school. The Jacksons' lives could not be. To start with, they worked: That first year, Motown released four singles and three albums, followed by two albums and five singles in 1971, four albums (counting Michael's solo material) and six singles in 1972. Beginning in 1971, there were steady concert tours. In addition, there were magazine interviews, photo sessions, TV appearances.

When they first moved to Los Angeles, the boys attended a public school. But that couldn't last long. "We'd be in our class and a bunch of fans would break into the classroom or we'd come out of the school and there'd be a bunch of kids waiting to take pictures and stuff like that. We stayed in that school a week. One week!" Michael said. "That was all we could take."

They were moved to a small, exclusive private facility, the Walton School, with five classrooms, the student body made up entirely of show business kids or the children of wealthy families. The older boys still hung around Hollywood High School and Beverly Hills School (where Berry Gordy sent his own children), making friends there with Berry Gordy's son, Berry III, and Diana Ross's brother, Chico Ross, and such other black celebrity spawn as Ed Eckstine, Billy Eckstine's son. None of them seems to have had much social life at the Walton School. Michael described it as "like a jail. There are only two or three people in each class."

When they were working, California law required that they must be taught a minimum of three hours per day. Their tutor was Rose Fine, a white woman accredited by the state as a children's "welfare supervisor." Fine would often conduct classes in hotel rooms, all the boys together but with separate lessons, as a kind of Little Red Schoolhouse with room service.

"The Jackson 5 went to school all day and were serious about it," wrote former Motown promotion man Weldon A. McDougal III. "During school hours in their hotel rooms, they wouldn't talk to you. . . . They started classes at nine, like regular school. When we traveled they had to follow lesson plans. They would read on the plane in the morning and answer questions and take tests in the afternoon. They were in school, believe me, when they were on the plane. When they got to the hotel, a lot of times they had to go right to their rooms and study." But McDougal added that, on days when they had concerts, "they usually didn't have school because it took all day to prepare for the show." Since very few days off are booked into tour schedules (because it's too expensive to have all that man- power lying idle while the hotel and room service bills rack up), that must have meant a minimum of learning went on while touring. And since the boys were frequently working just as steadily back in Los Angeles—they had to be, to record so much music—there's reason to wonder how much concentration could have gone into any of their schooling. All of the brothers got high school equivalency diplomas, which Rose Fine was empowered to grant, but then, there are millions of illiterate Americans with high school diplomas of almost every sort.

That doesn't mean that Michael Jackson is illiterate, as has often been rumored (and as a particularly scurrilous 1984 col- umn in *The New Republic* asserted). He certainly is not, even though his taste in reading material runs to relatively indiscrim- inate juvenilia. (L. Frank Baum and Og Mandino are one thing, but Michael's all-time favorite, *Peter Pan*, is possibly the most arch and prissy "classic" ever published.) On the other hand, there is no doubt that neither Michael nor his brothers ever acquired the kind of intellectual sophistication required to deal with the intricacies of wealth and fame. After all, if Michael was already attending remedial reading classes in fourth grade, he certainly wasn't going to develop much intellectually with just three hours of lessons a day, even if he was tutored that briefly only part of the year. What remains is native intelligence— by any standard, Michael possesses a great deal—and a certain unprocessed shrewdness and cunning, areas where (on the evi- dence, once again, of the 1984 tour) he may be considerably outstripped by others in the family.

Of course, the Jacksons were also receiving another kind of education, this one from the staff of Motown Records. Al- though the Artist Development department came to an end as a formal entity with the move to Los Angeles (neither the great choreographer, Cholly Atkins, nor the able music and voice coach, Maurice King, made the move), the Jacksons were given very careful grooming. "They covered every aspect of our life and behavior," Jermaine said. "A team worked on our career development. They told us what to say, what we shouldn't say, how to be polite." Among the most important figures involved was Suzanne DePasse, initially their choreographer, later their tour manager, eventually Motown's executive vice-president.

That education went far beyond standard music technique and working up a stage show. The Jackson boys were already well bred, but Motown made sure that their grammar and diction were at least passable. The company insisted, as strongly as their parents ever had, on strictly decorous behavior. There are no tales of hotel room trashing, gang-bangs, and drug taking to mar these years. Above all, and at all times, they were to present the proper image of respectable Motown stars—and this just at the time when such Motown stars as Marvin Gaye and Stevie Wonder were creatively undermining that image.

There were few signs of rebellion. As the eldest, Jackie probably felt the tug of misbehavior most strongly. At any rate, it was he who articulated the situation most clearly: "It's necessary for it to be this way," he said. "But I don't like the private life. . . . Being good is part of the business. . . . It's my job. My work is entertaining people." Others found ways of tuning out. According to *Soul*'s Regina Jones, "Michael could be in a crowd at their house with groups of people around and just sit there with his sketch pad drawing. You could see he was a thoughtful, sensitive child." And perhaps one who deeply resented being onstage even in his own home.

Still, the degree to which the brothers reined it in was striking, especially in that heyday of derelict celebrities, particularly derelict pop music stars. It was a time when Sly Stone was almost as famous for not showing up at sold-out gigs as for making great music. Yet those who knew the Jacksons in high school all say that they were almost always in control. "Neither Jackie nor Jermaine was obnoxious or loud as you might expect from young stars," journalist Frank Brown, who attended Beverly Hills High School, told Nelson George. "Tito was more boisterous. He was always walking around in big hats and gangster-styled clothes." (Tito was also nearly framed on a charge of receiving stolen property in 1973; the charges were later dropped, in what was probably just another instance of the notoriously racist Los Angeles police snatching the first young black punk they thought they saw.)

Within the family, alliances were sometimes uneasy. The older boys teased Michael, calling him "liver lips." Maybe they wanted to put him in his place. And there were unquestionably many conflicts between Joe Jackson and several of his sons, most notably Michael and Jermaine. But in general, the boys followed their parental and corporate dictates far more faithfully than could have been expected.

The principal effect of the training they received, though, was not just to make the Jackson brothers a group of uncommonly well-mannered adolescents. It was to make them think of themselves as a commodity, a product to be packaged, bought and sold. That's not unusual—it's the process that all stars have to accept as part of the price of fame.

The problem is that popular artists literally become the commodities they sell, at least to the extent that what they're selling is completely identified with them: Not *Thriller* but "the Michael Jackson album," not *The Natural* but "the Robert Redford movie," not *The Hotel New Hampshire* but "the new John Irving novel." The extent of that identification is greater than anyone usually admits, because it exists not only in the minds of marketing men and the public, but even in the minds of the performers themselves.

When you get down to cases, even though it's almost always in the interests of the people who do the selling to keep stars from becoming too conscious of this process and its consequences, in the long run, lack of awareness is deadly. Unless they grapple with the way in which their life has been altered, stars lose track of their own lives and fall by the wayside, discarded for a more contemporary product that speaks more clearly and cogently to their audience.

Since almost all popular culture entrepreneurs lack the ability to think beyond short-term results, the few performers who escape this cycle do it almost accidentally, often due only to an accident (Richard Pryor's nearly fatal burning is the perfect example). More often, performers create around themselves a sealed-off environment. When the real world outside does intrude, the results can be explosive. If the performer is challenged to present himself as a regular guy, or if he or she is subjected to criticism as a commodity, the results can be ugly. So Frank Sinatra specializes in bullying reporters.

The most likely force to intrude on the performer's hermetic dreamworld is the press. Print journalists try to breach the gap between product and person deliberately, but even radio and TV interviewers have to do it sometimes, if only because it's so dull to talk to a Coke can with lungs. Most celebrity-commodities can only interpret even the least probing questions as either insulting or threatening.

Given an atmosphere as institutionally defensive as Motown's the problem was compounded. Motown stars were virtually obligated to hold questioners at bay, to obfuscate and blow smoke, to fudge facts and avoid even half-truths wherever possible, above all to short-circuit any line of inquiry that might lead to controversy. Gordy instilled his clients with the attitude that the press was out to get them. Nothing could have been further from the truth—almost any journalist is just out to get a story and will settle for good copy. But somehow, Motown never figured this out and not one of the stars it developed has ever established a cordial, much less comfortable, relationship with the press.

At the time the Jacksons were being processed, Motown's fears were doubled by the same swell of black consciousness that the Jacksons records tried to exploit. A fairly large proportion of black cultural awareness was explicitly political. Yet too close an identification with their blackness would limit the Jackson 5's appeal, and Motown still was primarily crossover-oriented.

So wearing huge Afros was a necessity for the Jacksons, but when an *Ingenue* interviewer, asking questions for what should have been a harmless story in a mainstream magazine for young women, asked why they wore them—"Does it mean something politically? Has it got something to do with Black Power?" —the Motown representative chaperoning the session immediately butted in, for the first time all afternoon.

"Come on now," he said sternly. "These are children, not adults. Let's not get into that."

But Jackie was twenty years old and eligible to vote, the lady from *Ingenue* pointed out.

"Well certainly, he has convictions," said the Motown man. "But he's a commercial product, too. He may very well be doing things behind the scenes that you'd never know about because he believes in them. But he's got to be making money, too. So let's stay away from controversial issues."

At the end of this humiliating scene, Jackie could offer only a small, wincing shrug. The interview clearly over, the reporter packed up her tape recorder, preparing to leave. Michael made sure to say good-bye with a soul shake and a big wink.

By making a mountain of this particular molehill, the Motown PR man had made a classic public-relations mistake, converting a question that was innocent to the point of naïveté into the centerpiece of the reporter's story. He didn't bother to make his comments off the record or even try to phrase them diplomatically. (Calling someone "a commercial product" to their face is pretty insulting.) His only instinct was to close the door on any such thoughts, to deny even the most superficial and unavoidable connection between the Jackson 5 and the world in which they lived. The reporter used this anecdote as the bang-up conclusion of her story, letting it make points she most likely would never have ventured on her own, but the Motown staff did not learn from its mistake. Such incidents only confirmed a long-standing paranoia about the press.

And the *Ingenue* incident wasn't isolated; it was typical. In his *Rolling Stone* cover story on the Jacksons, reporter Ben Fong-Torres reported that Motown's preconditions for the interview were "no questions about drugs or politics. They aren't into that and we'd rather lay off it." By laying off the topic of drugs, Motown was probably asking only that the boys not speak about things they knew next to nothing about. But by asking that they not be questioned about politics, the company was reflecting a desire to segregate its performers from what was happening in the world outside of recording studios, concert halls, radio stations, and nightclubs.

This was the atmosphere in which the Jacksons were reared; it led to an unquestioned assumption that the wealth and privilege they had achieved were not only their due but beyond criticism. And that led to the even more dangerous assumption that anybody who raised such issues was "out to get" them.

It's ironic that Motown adopted this position even though

one of its biggest hits of 1970 was Edwin Starr's "War" ("What's it good for? / Absolutely nothin'."). It held this position tenaciously, despite the fact that the Jackson 5 were asked to speak directly to black kids, who were dying in unprecedented numbers in the jungles of Vietnam, numbers out of all proportion to their representation in the overall population. It kept to this stance even though the Jackson 5's musical style was consistently poached by the all-white Osmonds (who belonged to the segregated Mormon sect), something that would not have been possible if not for institutionalized American racism. And it stuck to its guns even though Berry Gordy, Jr., even then was preparing, as his first movie venture, the life story of Billie Holiday as a vehicle for Diana Ross, and in the process was converting that story into one that was about heroin addiction and the consequences of racism—that is, a story about drugs and politics.

What's worse, in the long run, is that the Jackson brothers were led to believe that such questions were only marginally relevant, always subordinate to their prime function as "a commercial product." This was the truest education that Michael and his brothers received. As a blueprint for the public-relations catastrophe of 1984, it was infallibly accurate, offering everything but a written guarantee that the Jacksons not only would not be able to fend off even the most obvious criticisms, but could only respond to them in confusion, befuddlement, and by feeling "picked on." As preparation for life beyond teen idolhood, Motown's education was worse than useless—it was a liability.

# E ◆ I ◆ G ◆ H ◆ T

Dear Michael,

My biggest problem in trying to get a handle on how you feel about things is that I'm a writer—a journalist and critic. The clearest feedback one gets from you about anything at all is your fear and loathing for people who do those jobs. Your mistrust and suspicion are so complete that it overrides even using the press effectively. When it comes to what are now called "media relations" in order to accommodate radio and TV, you're so hapless that it's like you have an allergy to ink, but are condemned to swim in a sea of it.

Your latest *faux pas*—that's French for "fuck up"—is the way you chose to appear in the USA for Africa video. Your participation and leadership in this project is one of the most admirable things you've done. "We Are the World," the song you wrote with Lionel Richie, isn't one of your better efforts (and it's not one of Lionel's, either), but hey, you guys never claimed to be expert at writing message songs for choirs, right?

It's the video that's the problem, Michael. You're appearing with other stars who are your peers and progenitors. Ray Charles, Smokey Robinson, Bruce Springsteen, Diana Ross, Stevie Wonder, Hall and Oates, Paul Simon, Billy Joel, James Ingram, Cyndi Lauper—forty-six of the great living voices in American music. Each of these stars had subordinated his mammoth ego to the needs of the cause in order to make a record and a video (and later, construct an album) that will raise funds for famine relief in Ethiopia. For the video, all of you were filmed during the recording session. There's a kind of rough equality about the presentation, which lends it a spirit of tremendous unity and makes USA for Africa less of a standard charity hype, brings it closer to being a true pop music event.

On the record, this unity is almost perfectly established by a brilliant Quincy Jones arrangement that leads one from Willie Nelson to Al Jarreau to Bruce Springsteen to Kenny Loggins without a hitch. In the video, there is a single moment of grandstanding. It belongs to you: a shot, from the toes on up, made outside the studio setting. It's beyond me what you thought you were going to achieve by arranging this, Michael, except to emphasize the fact that you consider yourself "special." Which is a point that has been made perfectly well previously, I should have thought.

What the "special" shot actually does is make you look like a knave—the only performer in the crowd who simply can't control his egomania, no matter what the cause. Instead of contributing something extra, you've detracted from the event. And ultimately, that's how your behavior will be seen and interpreted. You can blame the messenger that brings you these unwelcome tidings—the press—but if you had any public-relations sense at all, if you had stopped a minute to imagine the consequences to your reputation, you'd know that there was no one at all to blame except Michael Jackson for the criticism, and maybe mockery, sure to ensue.

It would be unfair to pick out this example, if it weren't absolutely consistent with other examples of your public behavior. To me, the one incident that remains continually fascinating is your September 5, 1984, Los Angeles press conference. The ostensible purpose of this affair was to denounce rumors that you were gay and that your altered features were the result of plastic surgery. By any reasonable standard, merely raising such issues in front of an audience that would include many writers and broadcasters who would otherwise not traffic in such scurrilous innuendo was unwise. According to your press agent, the old Hollywood hand Norman Winter, and others in your entourage to whom I spoke, you were repeatedly talked out of making such a statement for exactly that reason, until you finally prevailed in the midst of the tour. "He was undaunted," Winter said. "He's been wanting to do this for a long time. He just decided he was going to once and for all come out and address these crazy charges." The bottom line, Winter maintained, was that you were "just fed up with the lies." Not coincidentally, I guess, the press conference was held only a few days after a *New York Times* article that contained the line "thanks to plastic surgery and cosmetics" your features "have become more 'white' and more feminine."

The press conference had no chance of dispelling such ideas. All it could do was make you look like a man withering under not especially heavy fire. But the way that you handled the meeting itself reflected either unbelievable arrogance or a lack of PR sense bordering on idiocy. In the first place, the two-page press release was poorly written, simply blatting out denials of the rumors: "NO! I have never had cosmetic surgery on my eyes. NO! I have never taken hormones to maintain my high voice. YES! One day in the future I plan to get married and have a family. Any statements to the contrary are simply untrue." Of course, it is impossible to offer evidence that proves you have *not* done something, but the release offered no explanation of why such rumors had been spread, indicated nothing about your own assessment of them except that you felt picked upon. Worse, by making the statement "cosmetic surgery on my eyes," but not frankly stating that you *had* had nose surgery, you left yourself wide open—if you were hedging your bets here, what about elsewhere in the statement? After all, you say that you "plan to get married and have a family." You don't say "I don't make love with men." As a whole, this press release was a less honest and direct statement of your situation than what your mother had told *Time* the previous March. Katherine acknowledged your nose surgery and got right to it about sex: "Michael isn't gay. It's against his religion."

There was only one added touch necessary to turn the press conference into a complete travesty, and you found it effortlessly. Rather than attending the press conference—the most minimal expectation one might have had—you had your manager, Frank DiLeo, read the press release. Rather than having you, or at least himself, available for questions after your statement had been read, DiLeo split and left it up to Winter. This automatically increased the frustrations of journalists who were expected to show up back at the office with the goods. The net effect was to make you seem arrogant, a little sneaky, way out of control, maybe even giving the impression that you were a guy with something important to hide.

Even more important, at least from your point of view, the press conference subverted its stated purpose. Rather than dispelling the rumors, it circulated them more widely than ever, without doing anything significant to dissuade those who believe whatever they want to believe anyhow. About the only part of the press conference that worked was its final threat to "prosecute all guilty" of spreading "new fantasies" about you. And that was only a winner if you consider that it might be a good idea for a pop star to threaten the press. A writer who was seriously interested in libeling you might not be dissuaded nearly so effectively by this bark as by an actual bite, prosecution of someone who had wronged you by claiming you were gay.

Well, we can chalk most of that up to fallout from your lack of effective training in how to handle the media. That leaves us with what the press conference was really all about, which raises the really big question: Why the hell were you so upset by a bunch of stupid rumors, anyhow, Michael? As I've said before, anybody could see that you'd had a nose job but that the other changes in your features were most likely the result of having become a vegetarian, which tends to streamline anyone's body, especially people who already are as adverse to eating as you are. Who cares about people too dumb to figure that out? As for homosexuality, it really doesn't make a damn bit of difference if you sleep with everybody, nobody, or Louie the Llama. What counts is what people think you do, and that is something dictated a lot more by your mannerisms and a century or two of conditioning about how to read such mannerisms and the like than by anything you can do or say. (For the record, I believe your denial. But see? Who cares?)

One reason you might have been legitimately concerned about the rumors about your changed appearance is that the particular changes you made—the shape of your nose, especially—seemed to deny pride in your blackness, which was very dangerous, because it threatened to alienate your black audience. Unfortunately, the way you use cosmetics to heighten the relative lightness of your skin and diminish the thickness of your lips has the same effect, and you can't exactly trumpet those cosmetic decisions as a triumph of black pride. Those particular alterations in your appearance almost had to stem from a desire to appear less black. Pretty understandable, given how people with black skin get treated in America.

But I don't think that race had much to do with why you called that press conference or felt so strongly that the rumors needed to be denied. Sex was the real motivation for what you did, just as it was the real thrust behind even the most outlandish rumors. Rumors that you'd taken sex hormones to heighten the pitch of your voice (a dumb, unscientific idea in the first place) were really a way of saying that you weren't a real man. Similarly, "cosmetic surgery" is often used as a euphemism for "sex change operation." (Again, stupid, unscientific, and pretty unknowing about the world, too, since it presumes that all gay people would really like to be members of the opposite sex.) For a variety of reasons, people had decided that you must be homosexual, and for your own reasons, you'd decided that you had to get rid of that thought.

Where did the idea that you are gay begin? It's pretty easy to pinpoint the time—in 1976 and 1977, just as you left post-adolescence. That was when the stories first went around linking you with Clifton Davis, who wrote "Never Can Say Goodbye." The rumors spread fast; according to what you told one interviewer, they even appeared in *Jet*, which is a pretty respectable publication. There were also stories that you were taking hormones and considering a sex change. Then you were offered a role in *A Chorus Line*, a starring part but one that provides the show's climax because it concerns the one dancer who finally leaps out of the closet, revealing his homosexuality and all the pain that concealing and revealing it has caused him. You told the gossip columnist Marilyn Beck: ". . . if I do it, people will link me with the part. Because of my voice, some people already think I'm that way—homosexual. Though I'm not actually."

At that time, your explanation—the public one, at least—was that "people make up those things because they have nothing better to do. Some people let rumors like that get to them and have nervous breakdowns and stuff like that."

There are reasons other than your voice that people imagine you're gay, you must know that. As Jay Cocks wrote in his *Time* cover story: "His high flying tenor makes him sound like the lead in some funked-up boys choir, even as the sexual dynamism irradiating from the arch of his dancing challenges Government standards for a nuclear meltdown. His lithe frame, five-fathom eyes, long lashes might be threatening if Jackson gave, even for a second, the impression that he is obtainable. But the audience's sense of his sensuality becomes quite deliberately tangled up with the mirror image of his life. . . . Undeniably sexy. Absolutely safe. Eroticism at arm's length." The unstated implication is that you have every reason to keep the public manifestation of your sexuality at a safe distance.

The *Time* story spent a lot of space dwelling on the issue of your sexuality, quoting your vocal coach Seth Riggs and your mother. The incident that stands out is less direct: the scene in which reporter Denise Worrell is brought to your Encino home by your dad and comes to the door of your room with him. You're in there in the dark, watching TV not just with a friend. Worrell's description is a classic of fag baiting: "Michael in a very quiet voice introduces his friend to his father, giving only one name. I cannot hear it. Jackson introduces me to Michael . . . Michael and I shake hands. His hand feels like a cloud. He barely says 'Hi.' His friend extends his hand, which is damp. He seems nervous. Michael stares with his almond eyes for a long minute and turns to the television. There is silence and I feel that Joe is uncomfortable. It is so dark I cannot see anything. We back out of the room and Joe shuts the door."

There we have it: the sweaty palms, the furtive glances, the light touch, the dark room, the anxious parent. Or, as Cocks wrote in the main story, "The power of gossip is such that it has penetrated the iron gates that surround the Jacksons' never-never land out in Encino. It takes no effort of imagination to calculate what talk like that must do to a proud father and a mother who is a devout churchwoman. . . ." That is, there is no way that parents can maintain their pride and respect if it turns out they have raised a . . . queer.

In other words, Michael, people think you must be gay because you conform to a long-standing stereotype of what gay men are like. This stereotype of the limp-wristed, reclusive faggot persists even after two decades of the gay liberation movement, even after the Village People have come up with alternative stereotypes, long after urban dwellers at least have had to accept that there are gay firemen and cops, lumberjacks and bikers, athletes and plumbers, as well as the dancers, painters, musicians, and child molesters of lore.

People think you're gay, in a word, because you're pretty. This can inspire many resentments. As Gore Vidal has written, over the past hundred years, "physical ugliness tends to be highly prized on the ground that it will not only be cruel but provocative for, let us say, a popular performer to look better than the plainest member of the audience." One of the epithets pretty boys like you are attacked with is that they're faggots. The accusation remains an epithet. Millions of people still hate homosexuals, and, I suppose, millions of parents *would* feel humiliated if it turned out that their child was gay. Or at least, that's what they think they'd do. Actually, what they'd probably do is begin to accommodate themselves to Vidal's idea that "there is no such thing as a homosexual person, any more than there is such a thing as a heterosexual person. The words are adjectives describing sexual acts, not people. Those sexual acts are entirely natural; if they were not, no one would perform them."

But because we live in what Vidal calls a "heterosexual dictatorship," in which homosexuality is often made humiliating, we also have to acknowledge one other truth: "the majority of those millions of Americans who prefer same-sex sex to other-sex sex are obliged, sometimes willingly and happily but often not, to marry and have children and to conform. . . ." In other words, homosexuality isn't what one *is*, and it isn't even what one does. It's a matter of one's preference, which means that there are millions of "gay" dads and moms, who would probably feel more confirmed than humiliated if their children came out of the closet. Or something like that.

Why bring all this up now? Well, first, I figure you don't read a lot of Gore Vidal, but on the other hand, Vidal being on the best-seller lists and talk shows and all, he might be some-

body you at least know about. There isn't another theorist of
homosexuality about whom that can be hoped. And second,
because, as near as I can tell, you're as stuck in rigid categoriza-
tions about sexuality—not just homosexuality—as any human
being alive in this licentious time could ever be. Here is the
story you told Seth Riggs when he told you, "You know,
everybody thinks you're gay":

> I know. The other day a big, tall, blond, nice-
> looking fellow came up to me and said, "Gee, Mi-
> chael, I think you're wonderful. I sure would like to
> go to bed with you." I looked at him and said,
> "When's the last time you read the Bible? You know
> you really should read it because there is some real
> information in there about homosexuality." The guy
> says, "I guess if I'd been a girl, it would have been
> different." And I said, "No, there are some very
> direct words on that in the Bible, too."

So what you're doing, in essence, isn't just denying an
interest in homosexuality; you're denying the need for *any*
sexual expression. You'll admit, I hope, that if this is not
abnormal for a twenty-six-year-old human being, it is certainly
highly unusual. And it kind of calls into question your statement back at the press conference that "YES! One day in the
future I plan to get married and have a family." Unless . . .

In 1979, around the time *Off the Wall* came out, American
journalist Stephen Demorest came to your house to interview
you for the British music weekly *Melody Maker*. The interview
was, to say the least, extremely odd. As a precondition for
talking, you insisted that your sister Janet stay in the room and
that Demorest direct all his questions through her. So for
several hours the three of you sat, Stephen asking questions,
Janet relaying them. Then there were your answers, which were
bizarre enough by themselves.

One of the things that you told Demorest and Janet was that
you would have a family "in the far future." You also said that
you would not procreate (the word is Demorest's), but would
adopt your kids. "I don't have to bring my own into the
world," you said.

You also told him, "Who says at a certain age you have to get married? Who says at eighteen you've got to leave the house? Who says at sixteen you have to drive? I didn't drive until I was twenty, and I still don't want to. Quincy [Jones] doesn't know how to drive, he doesn't know his way around at all. That doesn't make him dumb, that just makes him not want to drive."

That was just another one of your tirades about why Michael Jackson, the most special guy in the world, should never be asked to conform about anything; why he should never be asked to do anything except his absolute heart's desire. Needless to say, the rant is childish and its logic stinks. (It's also exactly the kind of gossip about somebody else's life [Quincy's] that you resent about yours.) Count on this: when you choose to act eccentrically—and living in L.A. and refusing to drive is eccentric, at least—people are going to gossip, blow the facts out of proportion, distort them, cast all kinds of aspersions.

Then again, there is more than that going on in your little discourse. It begins with the topic of sex and family, but by the time you're finished, it's become a statement about personal freedom and the right to remain infantile in adulthood. Somewhere along the line, the subject has been neatly, sharply deflected. What you're really saying is what you started to go into before the cover-up about "growing up." The question that remains really interesting is what you said about "in the future" and "have a family," the reason you reject procreation as a means of acquiring children. Those terms are awfully close to the ones used in your press release. I suspect that they are coded references that don't refer to the immediate future or a contemporary biological family so much as to the coming of the Time of the End in the near future, to the time beyond that end, and to the human family. In other words, you're alluding to the apocalyptic prophecies and expectations of the Jehovah's Witnesses, the religion to which you belong.

There can't be a dozen people who've paid close attention to the Michael Jackson story without coming across the seemingly anomalous fact that you belong (as do your mother and sisters) to this unworldly church. We have all heard the stories about how you went out on door-to-door calls, even while you were touring, trying to place copies of the Witness publications, *Awake!* and *The Watchtower*, in the homes of unbelievers. I'm told you also regularly do such "publishing," as the Witnesses term this work, when you are at home in Los Angeles.

What else does the unwashed public know about the Jehovah's Witnesses? Not very much. Before doing some studying up in preparation for this book, about all I'd ever heard were the usual superficialities: that Witnesses do not believe in blood transfusions; that they reject the authority of the secular state to such an extreme degree that they are automatically registered as conscientious objectors to the military draft and do not stand to pledge allegiance to the flag; that they reject Easter and Christmas as "pagan holidays." And, of course, as anyone can attest to who has ever answered their door, bleary-eyed on a Sunday morning, to the sight of a cheerful Witness holding magazines in hand, that Witnesses believe in the imminence of the End but that "millions now living will never die."

Why the Witnesses believe such things is less easy to understand. I'm not sure any outsider can grasp it, because unless you're an initiate, there are several leaps of logic that are awfully hard to make. But let me try to lay out what I've learned, not so much for you, Michael, as for those looking over our shoulders here. Basically, the Witnesses base everything on their faith that Armageddon is just around the corner, and that it will be so directed that God's most beloved believers—Jehovah's Witnesses one and all—will be the only survivors. One hundred forty-four thousand of these will be transported to heaven, where they'll rule in consort with Jesus for a thousand years while the other Witnesses rebuild Earth as a paradise, preparing it for the eventual resurrection of everybody else who ever lived. During that time, everybody gets one last shot at either Satanic temptation or sticking with Jehovah. At the end of the millennium, the good guys get to live in eternal bliss while the rest of us hit the brimstone furnaces.

These apocalyptic beliefs encourage an extremely repressive attitude toward sex and even procreation. Until 1944, the Witnesses all but forbade marriage, regarding it as "selfish" because married members were kept from full-time service to Jehovah and because they were more often subjected to "tribulations of the flesh" (i.e., a sex life). Even today, marriage is regarded as "somewhat foolhardy" in a "dying world." While the post-Armageddon resurrection proceeds, there will be plenty of children to be taken care of. No need to spawn brats of your own.

So the Witnesses discourage not only all oral and anal sexual activity, homosexuality and extramarital intercourse, but holding hands, kissing, and passionate gazes. All are regarded as either perversions or as potentially evil occasions of sin. Furthermore, writes Barbara Grizzuti Harrison in *Visions of Glory*, her celebrated book about the Witnesses, "you don't have to perform a homosexual act to qualify as a homosexual: If you have homosexual fantasies, you are a homosexual in your heart and God sees your heart."

Elements of this kind of sexually repressive teaching pervade Christian religion, of course. The Witnesses merely take it to a bizarre extreme. What really separates the Jehovah's Witness sect from other Christian groups is the other things that members are denied. For instance, the society forbids any "fellowship" with outsiders, except in the process of conversion. Persisting in "outside" relationships can result in being disfellowshipped, and that means that no proper Witness—not even a mother or a father—can even speak to the disfellowshipped person.

Which kind of puts you in a bad situation, since your whole life is wrapped up in associations with non-Witnesses. Neither Quincy Jones nor any of the well-known members of your recording and touring bands are Witnesses. Don King and Chuck Sullivan sure aren't members; neither are any of the upper level executives at Epic or Motown. Even your brothers and father aren't Witnesses. And it would be ludicrous to presume that the essence of your relationship with any of these people consists of you trying to convert them.

In general, I'd guess that you get along by doing what all members of irrational cults do with the rules that make it next to impossible to live in the modern world: you ignore what you have to ignore and do your best with the rest. But it's not quite so simple, because it isn't so easy anymore for the leadership of the Witnesses to ignore you.

No other Witness has ever become a pop star, but even if there had been a precedent, your fame would have eclipsed it. And as you became more prominent, aspects of your beliefs became more prominent. For instance, in April 1984, you attended the T.J. Martell Foundation's dinner honoring CBS Records president Walter Yetnikoff. You were the top-billed attraction, but as the thousand-odd tuxedoed guests arrived and the dozen or more celebrities and executives took their places on the dais, the seat reserved for you remained conspicuously empty. Only after Monsignor Vincent Puma delivered the invocation and the crowd was led in the pledge of allegiance to the flag and the national anthem did you appear, with Emmanuel Lewis ("Webster") sitting in your lap.

No one made a fuss about the fact that you had arrived as if through a trap door and hardly anyone speculated about why you showed up late. I doubt that very many understood that you were not only forbidden to stand during the pledge and anthem (pretty silly exercises for a fund-raising dinner anyhow) but that Msgr. Puma's very presence should also have been an abomination to you, since Catholicism is often represented in Witness demonology as the Whore of Babylon itself.

None of this kept you from attending or from making an exceptionally generous contribution to the Martell Foundation: It was announced that evening that you had contributed a nineteen-bed unit at Mt. Sinai Medical Center in New York. (Later, the Martell Fund was made a recipient of one-third of your profits from the Victory Tour.) From my point of view, with my dad just then dying of leukemia, this was just about the best thing you did all year.

But Michael, how the hell are they gonna do leukemia research and treatment at the Michael Jackson Research Center without blood transfusions? Leukemia is a cancer that directly affects the blood, after all.

I'm not trying to make fun of you or the situation in which you find yourself. But you've got to wonder how anyone can balance such a huge contradiction between the tenets of his faith and the actions that result from his best instincts. You also have to wonder what kind of pressure the Witnesses can apply when you step out of line.

We know about one example. In the "Thriller" video, you dabble dangerously with what the Witnesses outlaw as "spiritism," which can roughly be defined as messing around with anything that smacks of mysticism or the occult. You tried to sidestep the problem with an opening disclaimer: "Due to my strong personal convictions, I wish to stress that this film in no way endorses a belief in the occult. [signed] Michael Jackson."

What a fairy tale! "Thriller" was unmistakably made by people who love the occult, delighted in being scared out of their wits by ghosts and ghouls and goblins. And you can't be scared if you don't believe. Even if you and the others who made that video argue in the light of day that such beliefs are primitive and pagan, at night, I bet you all like to sleep with the lights on. Unfortunately, the Jehovah's Witness leadership lacks much sense of humor at the best of times. They placed you on the spot and forced you to recant. The May 22, 1984 issue of *Awake!* was probably the single most widely quoted number of any Witness periodical in history, for it contained a rare set of new quotes from you, appearing as the centerpiece of a three-page article on music video.

"I would never do it again! I just intended to do a good, fun, short film, not to purposely bring to the screen something to scare people or to do anything bad. I want to do what's right. I would never do anything like that again."

Why not? asked *Awake!* "Because a lot of people were offended by it. That makes me feel bad," you said. "I don't want them to feel that way. I realize now that it wasn't a good idea. I'll never do a video like *that* again! In fact, I have blocked further distribution of the film over which I have control, including its release in some other countries. There's all kinds of promotional stuff being proposed on 'Thriller.' But I tell them, 'No, no, no. I don't want to do anything on 'Thriller.' No more 'Thriller.' "

It's hard to believe you'd say that—partly because the sentences sound like they were drafted by a lawyer (or a parson), although goodness knows, stranger utterances have spewed from your lips. Given the size of your ambitions, it's difficult to imagine that you'd go so far as to disown the "Thriller" video. After all, in addition to it being the longest, most expensive and best-selling music video ever created, it was also the impact of the "Thriller" video that sent the *Thriller* album soaring into the thirty-million-unit stratosphere, guaranteeing its status as history's Biggest Best Seller for a long time to come.

On the other hand, "Thriller" was the only Top 10 hit from your solo career that you didn't perform on the Victory tour, so maybe you have disowned it. Either way, the *Awake!* article and the video controversy symbolize the dangerously contradictory position in which you and the Witness organization have now been placed. As James Penton, a religion professor, told *U.S.A. Today*, "If they don't discipline him, a great many youth in the organization will say, 'If he can get away with it, why can't we?' " On the other hand, Penton said, "if they go too far [it would] make them look like fools, because he's apparently a very moral individual."

Around this time, the rumor began to spread that a cult within the Jehovah's Witnesses had formed around the idea that you were an incarnation of the Archangel Michael, a symbol of the arisen Christ, and perhaps the Messiah come again. (Biblical theories, for some reason, are like academic literary theories, always interpreting one thing as another, never letting anything stand for itself.) The fantasizing must have struck you as exceedingly bizarre and all but impossible to cope with.

In your day-to-day life, Michael, I'd guess you're like most people, letting your religious beliefs inform what you do, but not allowing them to dictate it. That wouldn't make you any less "moral," clean-living and decent and it probably wouldn't get too much in the way of surviving Armageddon, either, one way or the other.

So why are you a Jehovah's Witness? Maybe just to make your mom happy. Maybe because it's easier to stay in than make a break—after all, the "Thriller" video was already a well-known and widely distributed hit, so your remarks to *Awake!* weren't very costly. Yet it strikes me that the next-to-last paragraph in that article seems to strike out directly at you and your fame: "While not condemning all videos, don't you agree that genuine Christians should rightly reject any videos (and *any other* form of entertainment) that feature sex, violence, occultism or any other theme that is clearly contrary to the principles set forth in God's Word, the Bible? And why put on a pedestal those who produce such things?" Given the Witnesses' peculiar interpretation of Biblical principles, living up to those words would just about stop you from making popular music at all.

It's not surprising that you're the only celebrity who remains a Jehovah's Witness into adulthood because the tenets of this faith, which so adamantly denies the importance of this world's rewards, appeal most heavily to have-nots. That's one reason that 20 percent of all American Witnesses are black even though virtually the entire hierarchy of the organization remains white. (Founder Charles Taze Russell was a segregationist and while the Witnesses have been very successful in black Africa, they refuse to fight South African apartheid or to support anti-racist movements in the U.S.)

But why do you remain in the church? How do you reconcile your life-style with such pie-in-the-sky beliefs? Is it just fealty to your mother or have you been granted some great personal revelation?

The most interesting possibility is that the doctrines of the Jehovah's Witnesses appeal to your lust for the supernatural and irrational, your driving desire to find reasons beyond logic to explain the way things are. As a Jehovah's Witness, you're able to disregard many things you find inconvenient—your own sexuality chief among them—while satisfying these superstitious impulses.

That you are essentially superstitious, bound by a belief in magic and the power of the unknowable, is all but beyond question. Over and over, your faith in the supernatural is expressed, almost uncontrollably and unconsciously in the public record of your statements. Time after time, your highest term of praise is that something is "escapism" (by which you mean, not just a means of leaving behind everyday cares and woes but beyond the bounds of rational knowledge and science—escaping the need or ability to use your brain) or that it's "magic." For example, take your taste in literature, which runs to (escapist) fairy tales and children's stories of the most infantile variety, the kind that deny there is any logic or order to the way that the world works, or else that that logic and order is hidden from us in the secrets of some sect (whether adults or the Jehovah's Witnesses makes little difference) that will not share it unless we submit.

"[M]agic is easy if you put your mind to it," you've said. "[W]e *can* fly, you know. We just don't know how to think the right thoughts and levitate ourselves off the ground." And again: "That's what's great about show business. It's escapism. You pay your five bucks to get in and sit there and you're in another world. Forget about the problems in the world. It's wonderful! It's entertaining! It's magic!"

Even your songwriting, about which you are justifiably proud, must be associated with the supernatural, the dream state, not something that can be produced by the conscious mind in an orderly fashion. "I wake up from dreams and go, 'Wow! Put this down on paper!' The whole thing is strange. You hear the words, everything is right there in front of your face, and you say to yourself, 'I'm sorry, I just didn't write this. It's there already.' That's why I hate to take credit for the songs I've written. I feel that somewhere, some place, it's been done and I'm just a courier bringing it into the world. I really believe that. I love what I do. I'm happy at what I do. It's escapism."

At times, you grow almost drunken with such speculation; it's easy to understand why you avoid interviews—occasions on which you seem hardly able to restrain yourself from saying dizzy things. Most of the time what comes out is blather, a diatribe of nonsense, but every once in a while some minor revelation slips through. For instance, consider this statement from the Demorest interview. "I really believe that each person has a destiny from the day he's born and certain people have a thing that they're meant to do," you told him. "There's a reason why the Japanese are better at technology and a reason why the Negro race [are] more into music—you go back to Africa and the tribes and the beating of the drums." It's hard to conceive of a black American millionaire, living at the tag end of the twentieth century, who fails to comprehend the racist implications of such a statement. Demorest reports no levity in your tone, no ironic awareness that this is exactly the idea that has been used to oppress blacks on this continent for hundreds of years. Here, you don't just succumb to the stereotype; you wallow in it. And all because of a silly hope to believe that you have been especially outfitted by destiny.

Thus the Jehovah's Witnesses strengthen their appeal to you with every convolution of theology. All their twisting, turbulent attempts to explain away the facts of evolution in preference to their own complicated and chaotic biblical chronology simply make them more attractive to you. It's their illogic that sucks you in because it gives you the room for such studiedly childish pronouncements as (to choose yet another example from the

Demorest interview), "Science is so silly sometimes. The sun has been up there for ages and ages—what holds it up? I don't care how many scientific explanations they give me, it ain't enough for me." So much for gravity.

All of this, mind you, for the sake of showing off, as you show off in the "We Are the World" video. Maybe because you felt safe with Janet doing the interpreting, Demorest was even able to get you to define and justify that obsession with escapism:

"But, uh, Michael . . . don't you think it's possible to appreciate escapism a little too much?"

"No, I don't," you answered. "There's a reason why God made the sunset red or purple or green. It's beautiful to look at—it's a minute of joy. There's a reason why we see rainbows after a rain, or a forest where deer come out. That wonder, that's escapism—it touches your heart and there's no danger in that. Escapism and wonder is influence. It makes you feel good and that allows you to do things. You just keep on moving ahead and you say, 'God is this wonderful—do I appreciate it.' "

Well, Michael, if all that touches the heart is safe, then what about Hitler's appeal to the heartstrings of the German people? They had ovens heated up for all those talented singing and dancing Negroes you were talking about earlier.

More interesting, maybe, is the idea that religious faith is, for you, an almost purely utilitarian concept: *"It makes you feel good and that allows you to do things."* This belief in God as the agent by which all things occur is not Christian but pagan or, more precisely, barbaric. In *The Golden Bough*, his mammoth study of the correlation between myth, ritual behavior, and modern society, James George Frazer wrote, "A savage hardly conceives the distinction commonly drawn by more advanced peoples between the natural and the supernatural. To him the world is to a great extent worked by supernatural agents, that is, by personal beings acting on impulses and motives like his own. . . ." Of course, you're too sophisticated to believe that willpower will ensure good crops for farmers next year. (Unless we define prayer as a form of willpower.) But it appears that you're not sophisticated enough to understand the comparison between such outrageously superstitious beliefs and your confidence that "we *can* fly, you know." As a result, when bad things happen, you're immobilized—you *can't* do things. That is the Devil's work. When all goes well, you feel capable of anything. That is the hand of God showing itself. One way or another, it's all out of your hands.

Maybe you're simply drawn by cosmic forces toward the power of what the Jehovah's Witnesses teach as truth, but since I don't share your faith, other explanations present themselves. I'd say what you like about the Witness worldview is the same thing you find in children's literature and cartoons, both forms of "escapism" for which you express unbounded enthusiasm.

From *The Wizard of Oz* and Bugs Bunny to *Peter Pan* and Tom & Jerry, you're head over heels about all things childish. "They're not childlike at all," you've claimed. "They're really, really deep. You can rule your life by them." Following their lead, you have discovered within yourself unparalleled capacities for mush and sentimentality.

That's not all bad. Just as a degree of savagery is a necessary component for making great rock & roll songs, the ability to succumb to weepy sentiment is essential for singing the kind of maudlin love tunes—"She's Out of My Life" heads the list, but there are many more—that you put over with such tremendous conviction. But to "run your life by" such undigested emotional goo is to be swamped in meaningless tears, sobbing pitifully over all life's predicaments without ever summoning the energy and conviction to do anything about altering them. Since everyone swoons at you when you express these sentiments, you naturally conclude that you've won. But what we're swooning over, Michael, is how engulfed you are in your own fantasy—we're not buying the emotion itself because it's too superficial to fool anybody but you. We're just dazed at the intensity with which you mouth hogwash.

This is the appeal of your religion, too, I think. It asks nothing of you as an adult. It lays out rigid rules and regulations, a complete story of how the universe has unfolded, and a blueprint for what happens next, with heroes and villains and a happy ending for those who really deserve it. In its grip, you become a perpetual child, not responsible for anything that occurs, overawed by all of it. In this scheme, even backsliding has a ready-made excuse. It's the ultimate in escapism, all right—an escape from any possibility of shaping your own life.

# N · I · N · E

Between November 1969 (when "I Want You Back" first made the charts) and December 1971, Motown issued eight Jackson 5 singles, one Michael Jackson solo single, and five albums, containing fifty-four songs. Even presuming that some of this material had been stockpiled while the group was woodshedding, the output was prodigious, even by Motown's standards—and Motown was the most prolific record company in the world.

Such rapid-fire release schedules had been commonplace right up through the end of the sixties. (Capitol Records re-leased fourteen Beatles singles in their first two years on the U.S. charts.) But starting in the early seventies, labels stopped force-feeding the market. Taking advantage of more sophisticated marketing techniques and the ascendance of the LP over the single, the labels waited considerably longer between releases. In order to exploit the LP market most effectively, they needed to give the record a chance to be heard—releasing one album right on the heels of another prematurely stalled the old record's life cycle.

But Motown was not an album-oriented record company, not even after the massive successes it scored in 1971 with Marvin Gaye's *What's Going On* and in 1972 with Stevie Wonder's *Talking Book*. Partly this reflects the fact that the black pop audience and black-oriented radio stations had not yet made the transition to buying and playing LP cuts as well as singles. It equally reflects Motown's inherent conservatism, however. Singles are cheaper to make and sell than albums, and besides, singles were what the company knew. The Gordy record companies were never known for their willingness to abandon a successful approach, no matter what newfangled notions came along.

With the Jackson 5, there was an additional complication. Since the essence of its appeal was as a teen idol group, most of its fans had only spare change to spend. Albums sold for four or five dollars; singles were still about a buck. Relatively speaking, that could make a big difference in adolescent budgets, as reflected in the fact that, while the first four Jackson 5 singles made number one on the pop charts, their first three albums, which contained those singles, made only the middle rungs of the Top 10, a pattern consistently repeated throughout the group's Motown tenure.

The reputation of Motown albums also comes into play here. The company's policy of releasing anomalous hodgepodge LPs, containing show tunes and filler, while exaggerated in latter-day hagiography, had long been the bane of its fans. What was surprising about the early Jackson 5 albums was their consistent quality. The material was generally well selected, including not only the hits and predictable covers from the catalogue of Jobete and Stein & Van Stock, the Motown song publishing companies, but also intelligently chosen covers of recent soul hits, such as the Delfonics' "La La Means I Love You" and the Parliaments' "I'll Bet You" (the first incarnation of George Clinton's master project emphasized group harmony). There were even a couple of R&B oldies, such as the Crests' "Sixteen Candles." The only pop standard the J5 was asked to sing on any of its early albums was perfectly suited to its style: Paul Simon's magnificent, pop-gospel "Bridge Over Troubled Water."

The majority of the songs on these albums were written either by The Corporation or by other well-known Motown writers. So were all the hits, except Clifton Davis's "Never Can Say Goodbye," which certainly doesn't lack quality. Everything was produced by The Corporation, with the later assistance of Hal Davis. A stable production relationship is important to many artists, but it was especially crucial given the internal politics of Motown, where gaining and sustaining the attention of the label's top behind-the-scenes talent was the *sine qua non* of success. In this system, working consistently with the same producer symbolized the company's commitment, since it meant that the producer wasn't being shuttled in and out to work haphazardly with whoever was cutting a song, but had time to help develop a sound.

It would be a mistake to claim too much for any of these albums. For every "Oh How Happy" (a scintillating remake of the 1966 hit by Shades of Blue) there was filler as mediocre as "Reach In," whose only discernible virtue is the fact that it was published by Stein & Van Stock and therefore further filled the Gordy coffers. In general, the albums were well made and they've held up better than might have been expected, but outside of the singles, there's little on them that is revealing of personal involvement, much less anything that adds up to a group or collective personality.

An individual personality does begin to emerge through these early recordings: Michael Jackson's. The earliest Jackson 5 records are truly group affairs—even "I Want You Back" is arranged to give a sense of a group, not a solo, performance, although the lead vocal blows everything else aside. "ABC" and the other follow-ups were very much collaborative efforts. Motown's initial intention must have been to make a contemporary black Beatles of the J5, a group in which each member had near-equal weight, distinguished by some obvious personality trait. Marlon was the quiet one, Jackie the jock, Michael the cute kid brother, Jermaine the sex symbol, Tito the clown. Naturally, since Michael and Jermaine sang most of the leads, they drew more attention, but the idea was to spread out the overall adulation.

However, none of the other Jacksons had a really captivating presence. Jermaine was cute, but his voice lacked the expressiveness of Michael's, and since he was not much of an instrumentalist and the group wrote none of its own music, it was difficult to present him and Michael as black analogues of John Lennon and Paul McCartney. As time went by, it became more and more evident that if Motown and the group hoped to sustain interest in the J5 beyond the brief life expectancy of a teen idol phenomenon, the act would have to center almost exclusively on Michael. Jermaine was later to claim that there was a heavy element of luck in Michael's massive success, that "it just as easily could have been me." But as early as 1971 it was obvious who the really exciting member of the group was going to be.

This was immediately evident from the pattern of the Jackson 5 single releases. With the exception of "I Found That Girl," which was backed with a Michael lead, "The Love You Save," not a single one of the group's early hits was sung by Jermaine. On *The Jackson Five's Greatest Hits*, issued as the group's 1971 Christmas release, "I Found That Girl" is the only lead he sings. While Jermaine remained an important part of the group's stage show, capable of projecting a tough-but-tender sensuality Michael didn't have, musically he took a decided backseat.

Michael's dominance of the group sent it in specific directions; it was as much limiting as liberating. Since he was so young, there was a natural tendency to emphasize his upper register, but since he was also on the edge of puberty, there was also a tendency for that register to get a bit pinched and squeaky. On "Maybe Tomorrow," the result is jarring. It was the only single of the first two years not to make Top 10.

Besides, even though Michael had an easy way with rhythm numbers, his real forte was ballads. This was first evident on "I'll Be There," a mushy tune and, after "I Want You Back," by far the best of the J5 hits. Not asked to add any grit to his breathy vocal, Michael simply turned in a stunning, airy tour de force (ably abetted by Jermaine, who could handle slightly earthier inflections).

"Just look over your shoulder, honey!" Michael exclaims near the end, as wrapped up in the corniness of this moment as he had been in the horniness of "I Want You Back." The result is chill and perfect, right down to the final squeals of "Ooh, ooh, ooh."

Given Michael's propensity for stealing the show, the temptation was to give him one of his own. Motown didn't resist for long. Shortly after the group's *Goin' Back to Indiana* TV special was aired, the label issued Michael's first solo single. "Got To Be There," a beautifully produced, stunningly performed midtempo ballad, was an immediate smash, bigger than the

Jackson 5 hits that preceded and followed it. It was simply the finest track Motown had come up with for Michael since "I'll Be There." And the follow-up album, released in February 1972, was more consistent and less padded than any of the J5 releases ever had been. It produced two other Top 20 hits, a remake of Bobby Day's "Rockin' Robin" and the more upbeat "I Wanna Be Where You Are."

As a result, the Jackson 5 spent 1972 as a group suffused with identity crisis. Sandwiched between the chart runs of "Rockin' Robin" and "I Wanna Be Where You Are" was the group's biggest hit of the year, "Little Bitty Pretty One," another recast oldie. (The original was by Thurston Harris.) But that record only made number thirteen on the *Billboard* chart. So Michael's solo success came along at just the right time. As critic Pablo Guzman commented several years later, "The basic problem of teen idolatory, you see, is that teens grow up; and subsequent waves usually consider last year's model passé."

Nineteen seventy was by far the greatest year that the Jackson family, as a group, ever knew. By 1971, the wave had crested. Neither of the J5 albums released that year cracked the Top 10; none of its four singles made number one, and "Maybe Tomorrow" failed to get past number twenty. The concert tours still sold out, but the cartoon show folded after a single season. They appeared in a feature film, *Save the Children,* but it was a documentary (about Jesse Jackson's Operation PUSH organization in Chicago) and they were simply one more group in a lineup that included Gladys Knight and the Pips, the Temptations, Sammy Davis, Jr. (harassed for his Republicanism), Marvin Gaye, Isaac Hayes, James Cleveland, and a dozen other black show-business luminaries.

If 1971 was rocky for the group, 1972 seemed conclusive evidence that they were on the wane. The decline could have been predicted, since two years is about the standard run for teen groups. Then their audiences grow up and want something more, or at least something different.

That year's recordings were few and unimpressive. "Little Bitty Pretty One" was followed in June by the group's eighth album, *Lookin' through the Window.* Ominously, it was the first Jackson 5 album not to have the full services of Hal Davis and

The Corporation. Instead, tracks were also made by veterans Johnny Bristol and Willie Hutch and a pair of apprentice hacks, Jerry Marcellino and Mel Larson. (Larson and Marcellino also wrote songs but were not especially skilled at that, either.) Whatever it meant in terms of music, the move to multiple producers was a sure signal that the group's relationship with Motown was sinking.

"The age of innocence is gone, there is no more exquisite trash," wrote the group's biggest critical fan, Vince Aletti, in his *Rolling Stone* review. "[T]he Jackson 5's boyish brashness has been polished to a fine semi-gloss." Aletti was willing to call both "Little Bitty Pretty One" and an enigmatic cover of Jackson Browne's "Doctor My Eyes" "perfectly natural [and] actually inspired choices," but even he couldn't find much good in the rest. Although the title track (a piece of noisy jive penned by Clifton Davis) made number sixteen in *Billboard* and the album itself scraped into the Top 10, as a whole, the album was by far the sorriest music the group had made since the Steeltown singles.

For the rest of the year, Motown focused on the solo careers of Michael and Jermaine, releasing only one more Jackson 5 record, the Top 20 single "Corner of the Sky." The song came from the Broadway musical *Pippin,* of which the company was a principal backer. It's entirely possible that at that point Motown had more faith in the song than the group.

Motown was undergoing a rocky transitional period. The production line had just about disintegrated. Black pop styles were changing, and as FM radio became increasingly dominant, white rock separated itself almost entirely from black sounds, relying much more heavily on British influences. The Motown style was to play both ends against a very broad middle. But that middle was fast disappearing as a market category. The result was that during 1972, Motown had only two number one hits, "Ben" and "Papa Was a Rolling Stone," where even the year before it had had four.

Motown's difficulties at this time were especially ironic because black music was having one of its most interesting and prolific seasons ever. The Temptations' "Papa Was a Rolling Stone" was merely the finest of a flood of potent black singles: Curtis Mayfield's "Superfly," the O'Jays' "Back Stabbers" and "992

Arguments," Al Green's "I'm Still in Love with You," War's "Slipping into Darkness," "If You Don't Know Me by Now" by Harold Melvin and the Blue Notes, "Starting All Over Again" by Mel and Tim, "Could It Be I'm Falling in Love" by the Spinners, great harmony records by the Stylistics and the Chi-Lites, revitalized Southern soul by Luther Ingram and Timmy Thomas, the pop gospel of the Staple Singers' "I'll Take You There."

Black pop was reforming itself. The old models of soul were having a grand last gasp before disintegrating in the face of new, darker, more specifically danceable music suggested by the styles of Mayfield, War, and a new production team out of Philadelphia led by Thom Bell (who produced the Spinners) and Kenneth Gamble and Leon Huff (the O'Jays). Such radical developments would have been impossible without the pioneering of Motown both as a production company and in the person of its rebel acts, Stevie Wonder and Marvin Gaye, but for the moment, the company's bureaucratic entropy immobilized it and most of its artists were drifting as a result.

It didn't help that Berry Gordy's attention was completely distracted by his chores as producer of *Lady Sings the Blues*, the motion picture biography of Billie Holiday that starred Diana Ross. Motown might have floundered anyway, since the label's rigid, controlling approach was never flexible enough to accommodate changing modes of expression easily. But without Gordy at the helm, the downslope was steep. Several of Motown's best-known performers had left the label, including Gladys Knight and the Pips and the Four Tops. Neither Marvin Gaye nor Stevie Wonder made a record in 1972. The Miracles had broken up, and Smokey Robinson hadn't yet made up his mind to pursue a solo career.

All this ought to have made the Jackson 5 even more precious to the company. Instead, the lack of leadership left it out in the cold, too. The best strategy Motown could come up with was the solo projects by Michael and, for the first time, Jermaine.

*Jermaine*, as his album was called, was only semisuccessful, producing just one hit, a remake of Shep and the Limelites' "Daddy's Home." It scraped the Top 10 but it doesn't begin to compare with the great doo-wop original and didn't sell much. As Aletti commented, "Jermaine simply doesn't have the range and assurance of Michael—he's just right on upbeat, bright numbers . . . but he's out of his depth, sometimes desperately, on other types of songs."

But with Michael's second solo album, Motown stumbled into treasure. While Berry Gordy was off making his motion picture extravaganza, Motown hauled Michael into the studio to cut the theme song for *Ben*, a movie about a wacko teenager's obsession with his pet rat. The song ought to have been a travesty; on the sound track, that's exactly what it was. But on record, without the dippy picture to get in the way, "Ben" was a minor masterpiece, a pure exploration of Michael's ability to project a remarkably, almost profoundly, sentimental vision. The Corporation's production is its most skillful and inspired since the beginning, and the camp tragedy of the lyric is more than redeemed by the simple, gorgeous tones of Michael's singing. Even at its dumbest ("I used to say / I and me / Now it's us / Now it's we," complete with a chorus that would not seem inappropriate in an elevator), Michael's conviction sells the tune.

"Ben" was released in the spring of 1972 but it didn't really explode until the summer, when the teen audience made the movie a hit. Then it rocketed straight to number one, selling two million copies, as many as "I Want You Back." The song gained an Academy Award nomination (a travesty, since the Academy failed to nominate Curtis Mayfield's superior but indubitably blacker score for *Superfly*). At least momentarily, "Ben" revived the sagging fortunes of both Michael and Motown.

But not for long. Motown's lack of organization in this period is typified by the label's inability to come up with a decent album to capitalize on "Ben." Again, production was divided among The Corporation, Davis, and Marcellino and Larson. The latter's ham-handed touch gives *Ben*, the album, the schlockiness of Elvis Presley's mid-sixties sound tracks.

Michael's ability to put over the weepy sentimentality of "Ben" seems to have misled all the producers. The arrangements rely heavily on white-bread choruses—closer to the Carpenters than the Temptations—as though Michael had exhibited an affinity for singing any old pap. *Ben*'s only interesting performance is a cover of Thom Bell's "People Make the World

Go Round." Marcellino and Larson even manage to botch a remake of "My Girl" by casting it as a contemporary show tune.

In fact, what Michael had proved—as he had earlier with "I'll Be There" and a cover of another Bell song, "La La Means I Love You"—was his gift for singing weeper soul ballads. In this mode, little or nothing has ever been too overwrought for him. But the R&B base must be established. Set against strings without zing, he is helpless. Given a backbeat or some hint of ravaged soul, he is superb. It's as simple as that.

But Motown either didn't perceive this aspect of his skill or (more likely) misunderstood it as a willingness to sing any old trash. (Again, the comparison with Presley is inevitable.) Consequently, though the album hit the Top 10 briefly, the label failed to follow up "Ben" with anything of substance. Michael's later Motown solo albums—*Music and Me* from 1974 and *Forever, Michael* from 1975—are flawed in exactly the same way, despite a nice cover of Jackie Wilson's "Doggin' Around" on the former. For the rest of his tenure at Motown, Michael was left to wander in benign neglect as a solo artist.

So 1974 was the nadir of the J5's career. Motown issued two Jackson 5 albums, one each by Michael and Jermaine, and singles from each. None cracked the Top 20; few came close. Little of the material deserved a better fate. *Skywriter*, the year's spring album, is hapless, the material uniformly mediocre and the arrangements self-destructive, burying Michael among his brothers and a welter of overplush instrumentation. The production is split into seven configurations on only ten tracks. The Corporation had disintegrated. Perren would soon leave Motown to begin a distinguished independent production career, while Richards and Mizell were working separately within Motown. Marcellino and Larson remained bathetic. Hal Davis never overcame the lackluster material. In a few places, the producers halfheartedly attempted to incorporate some of the stylistic devices of Philly soul, as practiced by Gamble and Huff, or a touch of the sound created by such black writer/performers as Mayfield, Wonder, and Gaye. But since the Jackson 5 had no hand in creating its songs—allegedly because they were amateurs, though they could hardly have done worse than these particular pros—the latter approach was futile, and the group was still too stamped with juvenilia to put over the sophisticated, highly adult Philadelphia-style material.

*Get It Together,* released six months later, at least allows Hal Davis to hold the helm from start to finish. The material is another stew, but the album is notable for a couple of reasons. One is Michael's closest-ever approximation of his mentor, Diana Ross, on a remake of the Supremes' "Reflections." The other is that Davis finally began to figure a way to make the Jackson brothers sound like a modern group again. For the most part, this simply meant aping the pop-funk approach that Norman Whitfield and Barrett Strong had created for the Temptations. (Whitfield and Strong wrote a couple of the albums' songs.) It was on *Get It Together*'s final track, though, that Davis concocted the best J5 hit single since "The Love You Save." "Dancing Machine" was more than just a good record. It tapped the Jackson 5 into the freshest, hippest trend to hit black pop in several years: disco.

Soul and rhythm and blues had always been in large part dance music. But dancing didn't become a full-fledged subculture until the release of such records as "Armed and Extremely Dangerous" and "The Player" by First Choice, Isaac Hayes's "Theme from *Shaft*," "Soul Makossa" by the African Manu Dibango, and Love Unlimited's "Under the Influence of Love." These tracks tended to be longer than the average pop hit, with extended rhythm and percussion breaks that drove the beat through all manner of changes. They were designed expressly for the use of patrons at urban all-night dance clubs. Most of the crowd was black, though the cult soon overlapped into white working-class areas, and there was from the beginning a heavy sprinkling of gay involvement. Fueled by adrenalized horniness, the frustrations of the nine-to-five, and all the bitten-back rage experienced by suppressed sexual and racial minorities, the disco revelers came late and stayed later. At most clubs, the real action didn't begin until about midnight, didn't heat up until several hours later, didn't end until the sun had already cracked the sky.

Wrapped in luxurious fantasy, sped up on drugs and sex, disco culture was a blacker and more blue-collar analogue of white rock's related splurge of hippie hedonism. And like the hippie subculture, disco quickly acquired a proud (though less inhibiting) self-consciousness. Disco songs were often about dancing or just the delights of being at a disco, the characters one might encounter there, loves lost and won within its walls.

"Dancing Machine" was a perfect expression of the disco subculture. Although at three minutes, twenty-two seconds it was brief next to the real extravaganzas, it fit the prototype of later dance records very neatly. As Nelson George wrote, "Supervised by veteran producer Hal Davis and coarranged by the Commodores' producer James Carmichael, it mixed jet-propelled bass and drum tracks, fine ensemble vocals by the Jacksons and a high-octane Michael lead ('watch her get down, watch her get down') that made for joyous dancing."

Until well into the seventies, discos were subterranean even in big cities. It took that long for record companies to begin crafting records specifically for discos—and of course, by 1977, the disco movement had broken loose and become one of the most important musical phenomena of the decade, thanks to *Saturday Night Fever* and the like. But in the early seventies, disco DJs still had to work hard to locate singles and LP tracks that fit the needs of their patrons. So it isn't surprising that it took Motown six months after *Get It Together*'s October 1973 release to release "Dancing Machine" as a single.

But when it did, the song took off on the charts. It was not only a perfect disco record, it was one of the best tracks either band or label had made in years. "Dancing Machine" spent twenty-two weeks in the Hot 100, peaking at number two. It was the Jackson 5's biggest record since "Never Can Say Goodbye," three years before.

This time, the follow-up album was worthy of the hit. Producer Hal Davis and arranger James Carmichael took the "Dancing Machine" track from *Get It Together* and assembled one of the first disco concept albums around it. The chart ranking of *Dancing Machine* (it reached only number sixteen) doesn't reflect its large impact and influence. Carmichael's arrangements were so hot, dug grooves so deep, that they even rescued the half of the album given over to Marcellino and Larson tracks. The follow-up single, Marcellino and Larson's thumpingly tedious "Whatever You Got I Want," flopped, but *Dancing Machine* achieved more coherence, more sense of the J5 as a collaborative effort than any other Motown album the group made. As Pablo Guzman wrote, "Through disco, the Jacksons found a way to grow with their audience without puncturing teen fantasy." He might have added that they had found a way of reflecting their own growth. The Jackson 5 were still teenagers, but they weren't a teenybopper group any longer.

The Jackson family spent the years of their decline growing— mostly just growing up. In 1972, both Tito and Jackie were married and, before long, were parents—not the ideal situation for teen idols, but then Jackie and Tito's status as teen idols had always been shakiest.

Jermaine turned eighteen in 1972, and that spring, gradua- ted from the Walton School. As a real teen idol, he was expected to keep his romantic options open, but a special situation had developed: a romance with Berry Gordy, Jr.'s daughter Hazel. Gordy and his wife had split up around the time of the move to Los Angeles, and Hazel had chosen to continue to live with her father. With one of dad's employees as her suitor, the makings of melodrama were at hand: a classic theatrical cliché, in which the up-by-bootstaps entrepreneur for- bids his daughter to date—much less wed!—the help.

This was real life, not an Elvis movie, so it didn't work out that way. Instead, in late summer 1973, Motown issued a release containing Berry Gordy's proud announcement of his daughter's engagement to Jermaine Jackson. The wedding date was set for December 15.

If anybody's family was upset, it would have been the groom's. As the Jackson 5's star faded at Motown, with greater attention paid to other acts, Joe Jackson began to reassert his control of his boys. By 1974, he was managing the group without any official involvement by Motown, and even earlier he was mak- ing his objections to the haphazard recording process known. Especially, Joe wanted the brothers to have the opportunity to play at least some of the instruments on their records and to write some of their own songs.

The former was mostly a prestige point (none of the Jacksons is a particularly talented player, except maybe Randy, then too young to make his skills known), but the latter point had important economic ramifications. Songwriters are paid a roy- alty on every record sold (two cents per copy sold in those days, split 50/50 with the song publisher). The B-side of a million-seller that never got any radio play at all would be worth up to $20,000. A hit was worth much more, for two reasons: Unlike recording artists, songwriters are compensated—through ASCAP and BMI—for having their work played on the radio, and a hit song will often engender "cover versions," recordings of the song by other performers, each of whom has to pay royalties to the songwriter. This was what made Stein & Van Stock and Jobete, the principal Motown publishing companies, among the most lucrative of all the Motown subsidiaries.

It was also the reason that the company governed song selection so severely. (Motown could drive a hard bargain: Even when Stevie Wonder broke loose in 1970 with his own publishing company, Black Bull, Motown wound up with part of the publishing rights.) The advent of the gigantic album market in the seventies made controlling the songs that filled out an album especially significant. Even if no one ever played the J5's version of "Reach Out I'll Be There" on the radio, Motown still realized thousands of dollars from its presence on a multimillion-selling LP. And this was almost pure profit, since the song was already in established copyright, there was no need to work to promote it, and the Jacksons sang almost exactly the same arrangement that the Four Tops had used. It was found money.

Motown's reply to Joe's insistence that his sons should record their own songs was the same it had originally given Stevie Wonder and even Marvin Gaye. The Jacksons were not writers; they were singers. That was how the Motown system worked.

Whether the Jacksons really were confident of their writing skills was beside the point. At least they wanted the chance to try a few songs, to be used as album filler, if nothing else. But there is some evidence that they were writing songs even in their early days at Motown.

"Even on that first tour, I can remember Michael saying he'd written a song with Jermaine," said Robin Katz, their British fan club representative. "But it wasn't like 'It'll be on our next album.' It was like, 'We played three games of basketball, we wrote a song and we petted the animals.' It was just part of the way they lived."

And Freddie Perren told Nelson George, "I never saw any songs he [Michael] wrote, but I always knew he could. There was an instrumental hit out, "Love Is Blue" [in 1968]. He came in one day and asked me about this section of the song he found interesting. I showed it to him on the piano. He couldn't play but he was able to learn his part and would sit there picking it out. There is a certain talent that goes with songwriting and I could see he had it. Motown just didn't encourage it in performers. At Motown the producer was king."

The brothers also had ambitions of producing themselves. "I was like a hawk preying in the night," Michael has said of his behavior at recording sessions. "I'd watch everything. They didn't get away with nothing without me seeing. I really wanted to get into it." Motown's response remained the same: That wasn't how the system worked.

In retrospect, what should have been obvious to the label even at that time was unavoidable. The system didn't work anymore. With the exception of Diana Ross, Motown was not having production-mill hits any longer. Its biggest artists were Wonder and Gaye, who had been given the freedom to control all of their own music. This was the trend within the recording business anyway, especially for white rock performers, but increasingly for black ones, too.

There was another reason that the Jacksons wished to produce themselves. Motown's method of making records was expensive— to the artist. "Quality control" meant that dozens of songs were cut without being released. But all the studio and rehearsal time (tens, maybe hundreds of thousands of dollars) was deducted from the group's royalties. This further reduced the group's income.

There were plenty of other reasons to be unhappy. Motown got a slice of all the Jackson 5 spin-offs; it shared in management and booking agency commissions through subsidiaries. All of the musical decisions were in the label's hands. This may have seemed reasonable at the beginning, when the Motown studio approach was still alive, but by the mid-seventies the arrangement had become a very expensive albatross.

But even if none of the creative disagreements had existed, there was a basic conflict between Motown and the Jacksons, stemming from the group's stingy record royalty rate. The group had been signed to a contract in 1968, when the typical royalty for beginning groups was about three to four percent of the record's selling price. The Jacksons signed for a royalty of 2.7 percent, small even by those standards, especially since there were such large deductions for recording time and producers' fees. Furthermore, even though by the early seventies it was standard practice within the record business to renegotiate such contracts when an artist became a profit-generating star, the Jackson 5 contract had never been renegotiated.

The difference is enormous. The biggest acts in rock were receiving a record royalty of about 12 to 15 percent (of retail selling price—companies that computed royalties on a wholesale basis paid about twice as much), or roughly seventy-five cents to one dollar per album. On top of this, most were writer-performers who received another approximately twenty cents for each record (ten tracks times two cents each). That meant that a million-selling album was worth about a million dollars to the act.

The Jacksons' contract with Motown provided only about a sixteen-cent royalty for an album that listed at $5.98. That meant a platinum record was worth only about $160,000 to the group—before deductions for studio time, producers' fees, management commission, taxes, or anything else. The Jacksons sold at least ten million albums at Motown—even if you forget about deductions and select the minimum realistic superstar royalty (seventy-five cents), that's a difference of almost six million dollars, a sum worth getting mad about.

Joe Jackson considered himself a student of the business, certainly no rube. "Joe would talk about the business a lot," Motown promotion man Weldon A. McDougal III wrote. "He would really be interested in how disc jockeys felt about the Jackson 5. He was concerned about what people in general thought about the Jackson 5. He would talk about his ambitions of having his own record company and being as big as Motown."

Robin Katz confirmed this view. "He'd sit in the corner of a dressing room and not say a word," she said. "People thought he was the janitor or the roadie. He was very quiet. . . . But he always gave the impression he knew exactly what was going on." As events had proved, Joe Jackson was never an especially shrewd businessman. But he imagined himself one, and anyway, it didn't take a Baruch to figure out that the Jacksons were being highly undercompensated by their Motown deal.

Joe was by nature suspicious of outsiders. He believed in blood loyalty above all. "Years later, when we dropped them off, Michael said something like 'You're gonna make up what you write anyway; you writers all make it up," said Robin Katz. "It wasn't said with malice. It was said with this 'I know [attitude].' I think this was their father. He always taught them manners but you don't give anything away. You don't say what you really think."

So Jermaine's marriage to the daughter of his family's business antagonist could not have been very happily greeted at the Jackson home. As events also proved, Joe's essential mistrust of the Gordy clan never subsided. However, he was hardly in a position to do much about it.

This didn't deter Berry Gordy, who planned a wedding fit for a potentate. Held at the Beverly Hills Hotel, the poshest in Hollywood, on December 15, 1973, it reportedly cost a quarter of a million dollars. The menu and decorations—organized around a "Winter Wonderland" theme conceived by Hazel's father—certainly justify the estimate. The pure white camellias on each of the tables in the hotel's Crystal Room cost seven thousand dollars by themselves. In addition, the invitations were printed on silvery metal which was also used for the napkin rings and the engravings on the special mugs, inscribed with Jermaine and Hazel's names and the date. Gordy brought in mountains of artificial snow. One hundred seventy-five white doves in cages surrounded the main ballroom.

The menu featured papaya with San Francisco bay shrimp and Lorenzo dressing; beef Wellington with sauce Périgourdine; artichoke bottoms Florentine; cherry tomatoes Provençale; and frozen peach mousse in coconut shells. Before you even got to sit down, though, there was a buffet table of hors d'oeuvres highlighted by huge dishes of Beluga Malossol caviar.

Hazel wore a white mink-and-satin dress, designed by Luis Estevez and sporting an eighteen-foot train. The wedding march was written especially for the occasion by Smokey Robinson, who sang it as his mentor and best friend escorted Hazel down the aisle.

Hollywood had rarely seen such a lavish and ostentatious affair since the heyday of Pickfair. For Berry Gordy, it was perhaps more than a wedding—more like his coming-out party as an important mogul. The guest list was naturally star-studded. Just as naturally, speculation was soon rife that Jermaine Jackson was being groomed to succeed his father-in-law as Motown's president. (Jermaine later fueled this speculation, by saying—even after signing with another label in the mid-eighties—that he fully expected to someday become president of Motown.)

The Jackson family still kept mostly to itself. "We think it's important that the public feel the Jackson 5 is still accessible, that they're not isolated from the people who helped make them famous," said security chief Bill Bray. "J5 fans feel there's a strong bond between them and the boys and as long as it doesn't endanger the boys' security, we want to preserve that feeling." That was just talk. In reality, what was preserved was the Jackson brothers' feeling that they were more special than ordinary folks. In fact, the family may have been all too normal, meaning not that happy. It's interesting, at least, that, with the exception of Michael, all the brothers were married and out of the house within a year of their high school graduations. (Marlon got hitched in 1975, although two months later Joe was still denying that he knew anything about it.)

Yet it would be a mistake to assume that Joe Jackson was not in full charge of the Jackson brothers' professional careers. Michael, the meal ticket, remained a minor under his charge. And even though the Motown contract gave the company theoretical control over the group's selection of live performances, in 1973 Joe began booking tours his way, including many dates outside the United States: Africa, Japan, the Philippines. Although the Jacksons' American pop chart numbers continued to sag, they remained a major attraction overseas.

In the summer of 1974, Joe Jackson took a further step, defying Motown by booking the boys into the main room of the MGM Grand Hotel in Las Vegas. It's ironic, in light of Motown's image, that the company opposed this move. But maybe that was just another reflection of the company's conviction that the Jackson 5 was still a bubble-gum group. Or perhaps Nelson George is correct when he remarks that "Motown was loosening its hold on its performers' lives as Berry Gordy's business interests were moving beyond the company's record division."

The purpose of the Vegas shows, at any rate, was to change that teen idol image. To that end, the Jacksons were presented as an entertainment family, including a spot for eldest child Maureen, eighteen-year-old LaToya, twelve-year-old Randy, even eight-year-old Janet. Taking a page from their teen-mag archrivals, the Osmonds, the brothers sang medleys from the repertoire of such pop harmony groups of yore as the Mills Brothers and the Four Freshmen.

The show wasn't an immediate success. "We knew Las Vegas would be different from other engagements," said Jackie, "but we weren't prepared for the total silence. We were used to screaming girls and concert audiences hollerin' and stompin' their feet. The Las Vegas crowd seemed to be saying, 'Show me.' For a split second we were frightened, but then that magic that exists between a performer and an audience came into play. They liked us and we liked them."

But it wasn't only Vegas crowds, used to chorus lines and slick patter, who found the Jackson family routine a bit awkward. When they took the Vegas show on the road, even long-time fans had their reservations. What pulled the group through, needless to add, was Michael. Wrote Vince Aletti: "His stylized show-biz posing (the bends and turns, arms outstretched and sweeping the air in front of him; little self-hugs with his head thrown back) is becoming a little disturbing, at moments even grotesque for a boy who's still a very skinny sixteen. But when he isn't being Engelbert Humperdinck, he's supreme and so controlled it's almost frightening. In his motel room, when he tells you he's in eleventh grade, it might seem strange, but it's believable. Seeing him onstage, dancing and striding confidently . . . you just know he had to be lying."

But he wasn't. Michael was still just a show-biz kid, and though he, above all the others, may have been willing or even eager to sing "Suddenly There's a Valley" and "Graduation Day," that wasn't why he was there. He was there because the family—still a huge one, no matter what its income level— needed the money. He might have been doing what he liked to do best; he might have been doing the only thing he knew how to do; maybe there were a dozen other places he would rather have been. At any rate, at sixteen, he shouldn't have had to do two shows nightly on his summer vacation, not considering what he'd already earned—for someone. His father determined to see to it that none of the Jacksons spent too much more of their lives in the same bind.

The reason that most record labels were willing to renegotiate the long-term contracts of their stars is simple: No contract lasts forever. (Under the law, seven to ten years is about all that's acceptable.) The Jacksons might have felt mistreated by Motown, but they had the same handy option as any other disgruntled pop star: Wait until the contract expires and then leave. If there's still anything left, the performer has all the advantages when the deal is up (which is one reason that companies like to extend contracts when they agree to pay more money). The act can walk away with name and talent; the company is left with a batch of records that used to be hits, but no new ones. At least, that's how it usually works out.

The Jacksons had a little less leverage than some because their recent records had sold poorly. However, there were aspects of their situation that appealed to any major record label. They were an established presence on the black charts, then still dominated by independent labels. They sold a huge number of records outside the United States, and that was attractive to conglomerates like CBS and the Warner Communications group, who owned their foreign subsidiaries. (Motown was distributed around the world by licensees in various countries and territories, with consequent problems of supply and payment.) Michael Jackson was still a teenager; he gave every evidence—to anyone with shrewd ears—of maturing into a significant adult pop singer. Finally, because the Jacksons had been so underpaid at Motown, their expectations from a new contract would be less than an artist who was just marginally underpaid at his old label.

The Jacksons' Motown contract expired at the end of March 1976. As is typical in the industry, Joe Jackson and his partner, Richard Arons, began scouting other homes for the group about a year before. According to Motown's Ewart Abner, there was an agreement between the company and Jackson and Arons. "They were to go and get an offer and then Motown would have the right to match," said Abner, an industry veteran then serving as the president of the record company. "If we did, they would remain at Motown. . . . I was aware of the rumors that they were talking to other recording companies. It didn't bother me because the understanding with Joe was that whatever kind of offer he got, all we had to do was match it and they would stay home."

Joe Jackson and Arons were looking for more than a money offer, though. They wanted a deal that would allow them to begin writing and producing their own material, one that would cut them loose from the kind of creative controls Motown had exercised. These were not unreasonable demands, and for almost any rock act negotiating a contract in the mid-seventies, when the record business was at its most flexible regarding artistic indulgences, it would have been a minor issue in making the group's new deal. (Proven writer/performer/producers were then signing contracts providing only that they submit master tapes of high technical quality, leaving all questions of artistry outside the company's purview.)

If the Jackson 5 hadn't been signed to Motown, it's unlikely that such terms would have been issues at all. But because they had never written or produced anything, other labels had to be wary. Who knew what the group's material would sound like, whether they were embarrassing rank amateurs or as talented as their father/manager swore that they must be. Joe had claimed as early as 1974 that the boys were writing and that he hoped to make some demos of the material they'd done.

In the record business, the hunt for a new contract is called "shopping a deal." Joe Jackson and Richard Arons kept their hunting to a minimum. There were really only two appropriate labels for their act: Atlantic Records, which had a long history in rhythm and blues and soul music, starting out as an independent and being purchased by the Warner Communications conglomerate in the late sixties, and the CBS Records group, which assigned most of its black acts to its Epic subsidiary. CBS and Warner Communications were the richest, most efficient distributors in the industry. But Atlantic chairman Ahmet Ertegun wasn't especially excited about committing a large sum of money to a group that hadn't had a hit in over a year and had spent two years between hits before that.

Ron Alexenberg, the young president of Epic Records, was a lot more enthusiastic. Epic was started, as most major-label subsidiaries are, to pick up some of the spillover from Columbia's overcrowded roster. (There comes a point when it's a mite embarrassing for a radio station to be playing too many records bearing the same label. So a company, as it expands, creates separate divisions for its various acts: Thus, Motown spawned Tamla, Gordy, and Soul.) Epic also was the principal repository of CBS's black and country talent (partly as a result of having absorbed the old Okeh label in the early sixties). By the mid-seventies, as independent producers began to make long-term distribution deals with major labels, Epic also became the center for that part of the CBS record interests.

In 1975, Epic counted among its most important artists the British guitarist Jeff Beck, the heavy-metallist Ted Nugent, singer/songwriters Dan Fogelberg and Michael Murphey, such black pop singers as Minnie Riperton and the trio LaBelle (coming off a number one hit, "Lady Marmalade"), and country singers Charlie Rich, George Jones, Johnny Paycheck, and Tammy Wynette. Long a weak sister to Columbia, the flagship of CBS, Epic had increased its annual billing under Alexenberg from under ten million to over one hundred million dollars annually. In part, this huge increase was because of the division's association with such "custom labels" as Philadelphia International, run by producers Gamble and Huff; country-oriented Monument Records from Nashville; the Isley Brothers' T Neck label, and Kirshner Records, run by TV and music publishing entrepreneur Don Kirshner. But it also reflected the management style of Alexenberg and his team, headed by A&R chief Steve Popovich.

Alexenberg, a burly native of Chicago's South Side (where he was a young protégé of Motown's Ewart Abner), had been head of promotion for Columbia during the halcyon days of the late sixties and early seventies. Popovich was his running mate in the promotion department, and a natural choice to work with him in spotting and signing new talent. Popovich and Alexenberg had made a practice of reviving acts thought to be has-beens—

LaBelle, Nugent, Beck, Riperton, and Rich were all considered finished before Epic hit singles revived them.

So the fact that the Jacksons were not at the peak of their career wasn't at all bothersome. "I've always felt that if someone had a track record and they're cold at the moment, that's not very important," Popovich said. "They're only one hit song away from reviving their career, where with a new artist you're really looking for two or three hits to begin to establish them."

When Alexenberg told Walter Yetnikoff, the head of the CBS Records group, to whom he reported, that he wanted to sign the Jackson 5, Yetnikoff asked why, since the J5 hadn't had a hit in so long. Alexenberg replied that they'd just sold out Radio City Music Hall and that kids were lined up in front of the Warwick Hotel, up the street from the CBS building, where the group was staying.

What did give Alexenberg and Popovich pause was the Jacksons' insistence upon writing and producing for themselves. Here, there was no track record, no basis for experienced judgment. Joe Jackson insisted that his boys could write and produce. With the aid of old pal Bobby Taylor, they had prepared seven demos in their home studio, so Popovich flew to California to listen. Popovich was tremendously impressed by the short leash on which Joe Jackson held his sons, though he was somewhat taken aback when, during their first meeting in Jackson's office, Joe, as was his habit, fell asleep in the midst of the conversation.

He heard the Taylor-produced tracks out at the Encino house but they didn't especially impress him. "I wasn't knocked out," he said, recalling that he was played versions of the Rascals' "People Got to Be Free" and Boz Scaggs's "We're All Alone," along with a couple of songs Michael had written. But he and Alexenberg still insisted on making the deal. A couple of weeks later, they took Walter Yetnikoff to the suburban Nanuet Theatre to see the group. Yetnikoff wasn't knocked out either, but he told them he'd be willing to go along.

So a contract was prepared. The final papers from CBS are dated May 28, 1975, but negotiations of such agreements generally take place over a matter of months. While the Jacksons weren't outrageously well rewarded for their previous successes, they were given a deal commensurate with their star status: a signing bonus of $750,000, plus $500,000 from a recording fund that provided $350,000 per album for the ten-album (minimum) term of the contract. (CBS also had the right to a third album in each of the contract's five years and the right to issue two "greatest hits" albums culled from previous releases.)

All the advance money was to be recouped from royalties, but these were generous: 28 percent of the wholesale price for records released in the United States, 24 percent abroad. In 1975, records sold for about $6.98 at retail, which put the wholesale price around $3.50. This gave the Jacksons a royalty of roughly ninety-eight cents per album (eighty-four cents on international sales)—a star contract. After each album sold 500,000 copies, the royalty escalated to 30 percent (about $1.05 per disc).

By itself, this was a fine deal. It increased their Motown royalty by 500 percent. But there were some drawbacks, especially regarding creative control. CBS retained the right to appoint their producer. The Jacksons had the right to request a particular producer, but CBS could veto the group's choice. (In either event, the Jacksons would pay the producer from their royalties, as is standard industry practice.) Epic also wanted the right to supervise song selection, though here it bent a bit more, specifying only that CBS and the group had mutual approval of the material recorded. Additionally, the Jacksons were given the right to designate the B-side of all singles (important from a financial viewpoint, since they would be able to choose songs they wrote or published for the free ride behind a potential hit), and the group could also select three songs on each LP without interference (except "in respect of obscenity, defamation and advocacy of illegal activity"). If they didn't use those three songs, their rights would accrue, and when they got enough unused credits, the Jacksons could finally pick all the songs for one album.

The contract provided that five of the albums were to be made by the group as a whole, while the other five were to be made by members of the group individually. Epic had the right to decide whether group or solo material was wanted at any given time. Clearly, Alexenberg and Popovich saw Michael's potential as a solo star and wanted to ensure that they were signing him as well as the group.

In another clause, the Jacksons assured CBS that they owned the name the Jackson 5. But the contractual language seemed to anticipate a change, specifying that they also guaranteed owning "any other name that [the Jacksons] may designate and which we approve."

This was important because the Jackson 5 had signed over so many entitlements to Motown. Even though the group had used the name well before signing with Motown, who actually held the trademark was up in the air. "In the event that we request that you utilize the name 'the Jackson Five,' you shall utilize such name as The name, but in such event the warranties and representations [that the Jacksons were asked to make regarding their group name] shall not apply to any claim by Motown Records Corp. You have advised us that Motown Records may claim ownership of the name 'The Jackson Five',", the contract read.

Motown did more than just lay claim to the Jackson Five name—although they definitely did that. They laid siege to the Jacksons, as a group and as a family. The label had seemed fairly disinterested in the group in recent years, but now it had prestige at stake and maybe something more. After all, these were Berry Gordy's in-laws leaving the roost.

The story that the Jacksons might be leaving Motown broke in the June 30, 1975, *Hollywood Reporter*, with the headline: "Motown Denies Jackson 5 on Way to Epic Discs." The article quoted Motown vice-chairman Mike Roshkind: "There may be substance to the reports that Epic has talked to the group or that *some* of them signed to go over to Epic at the termination of Motown's contract."

Later that same day, the Jacksons confirmed the story at a huge press conference that Alexenberg staged at the Rainbow Grill, at the top of the Radio City complex above Rockefeller Center. "My head was really on the chopping block that day," Alexenberg recalled. "The first question was 'Where's Jermaine?' And I said, 'Well, obviously, he didn't want to be here.' And they of course asked me why. And I said, 'Well, Berry Gordy's his father-in-law and perhaps he told him not to be here.' "

The signature page of the Jackson's contract with Epic left a space for Jermaine Jackson to sign. It remained blank. Joe

Jackson had negotiated the Epic contract without consulting his sons—without ever hinting to Jermaine what he was up to—then had imperiously presented it to the boys for their signature. He saved Jermaine for last, theoretically because Jermaine was away on a fishing trip.

Upon his return to Hollywood, Jermaine was summoned to Encino and taken to his father's bedroom, where the Epic contracts were spread out on the bed. "Sign," Joe told him. Jermaine refused to do so without at least consulting Hazel. He left. It was a long time before he spent any time at his parents' house on easy terms.

"I wasn't choosing between families, I was choosing between record companies," Jermaine later said. But it wasn't that simple, because both the Jackson and Gordy families were recording institutions. At any rate, Joe Jackson wasn't about to let such a split be easy. "It's my blood that flows through his body, not Gordy's," he said. Given such angry sentiments, it's possible that Jermaine remained at Motown just to separate himself from the rest of the family.

"Of course my brothers and father thought I had betrayed them," he said several years later, when everyone had cooled down and the family was again functioning as a unit. "My family was mad at me. My brothers didn't really make any comments about the situation, but my father made a statement. . . . And my mother kept asking me why I did what I did. She wanted to know what was wrong with me, why I had broken the family apart. You can imagine, it was a very tough time for me. I had a lot of things to think about. I had a lot of major decisions to make. . . .

"The stories that came out in the press said my reason for staying with Motown was because I was married to Gordy's daughter. But that wasn't nearly the entire story. For me it had a great deal to do with loyalty. Motown really cared about us and I believe that they treated us fairly and had our best interests at heart. Naturally, I realize that they are in the business to make money but I felt there was more to our relationship with them than just that. Motown put time and money into grooming us. They moved us from Indiana to Hollywood and put us in the best schools, saw that we were very well taken care of, including my sisters and parents. It's hard to find another record company that will do that with a group that is so young and that hadn't proved themselves.

"When I think about it, I believe that way of operating hurt Motown over the years. They take a personal interest in performers, work with them when they are unknowns and mold and help develop their talents. Then they build them up to monsters. Then what happens, as what happened with the Jackson 5, is that other record companies come along and offer these groups more money and better contracts. And these performers leave, forgetting all the time and effort Motown took to mold them into successful talents."

This is pure party line. Motown went so far as to claim that Epic, as part of a huge conglomerate, could never treat the Jacksons with the tender loving care to which they were accustomed. "Not only did they get stage coaching, great production and strong promotion, but they even lived with Gordy for a while," former Motown staffer Tom Noonan told Nelson George. "If they had signed anywhere else someone would have cut a record on them and left them right there in Gary to fend for themselves."

But Motown had been incredibly well compensated for the risks it had taken and the largesse it had doled out: the 2.7 percent royalty took care of that obligation and then some. At any rate, the company's sense of obligation was a one-way street, as such paternalism always is. When the Jacksons wanted to grow, the company had not been so generous. It had blocked their path, just as it had blocked the paths of Marvin Gaye and Stevie Wonder.

Besides, the Motown of 1975 was not the company it had been. As even Jermaine acknowledged, "Motown was feeling the pressure (economic and otherwise) and was in the process of reorganizing [its] staff. Also, our records weren't selling like they had, so my father felt it was time to leave."

Jermaine's position was that Joe "should have been closer to Gordy and should have tried to work things out. But it seemed like his mind was made up. The next thing I knew, they were gone." And for his part, Joe felt that getting any closer to Gordy was not really a possibility. "Every time I went in there, trying to get them to do something, they said, 'Oh the Jackson

5 aren't writers and producers, they're entertainers,' " he told
*Soul* magazine. "I just don't want them to be like some of the
other guys. I want them to be able to utilize all their talent. I
want the people in the world to know that they can do other
things than just getting onstage."

Jon Landau summed up the dilemma, when he defined the
Motown formula. ". . . [L]ike all great popular art," he wrote,
"Motown confined itself in formal ways to liberate itself in
other ways. You can't shatter conventions when none exist. And
conversely, you can't invent a meaningful convention if you
don't feel it. . . .

"The beauty of Motown is that it gives great artists something to work with and against. It gives them saleable good
songs and a beat and a producer and musicians and supervision.
But it doesn't give its vocalists their voices, their talents or
their soul." By 1975, the Motown production line could no
longer keep its half of the bargain.

If the dispute had been just about creative differences, the
fight could have ended there. As Michael said, "Being at a
record company is like being at a school. If you're not happy
with the principal or the school, you go to another. Looking
back, the creativity was there but any kind of direction was
virtually taken away from us. It wasn't like I woke up one
morning and said, 'Hey, here's a great tune that we have to do
on our next album.' It was more like a gradual awakening, a
gradual realization that someone else was controlling our music." Motown still felt that its assembly line, properly modified,
could work. Its executives resented not being given the opportunity to prove it with the Jacksons.

And Motown was good at scrapping in the alley. They sued
CBS and the Jacksons for twenty million dollars, claiming that
the Jacksons' contract had not expired. When a judge ruled in
mid-1976 that after seven years the contract had expired, Motown
still proceeded to allege breach of contract, interference with
prospective advantage, service mark infringement, injurious false-
hood, intentional infliction of emotional distress, and invasion
of privacy. That suit was not settled out of court until 1980,
and it was settled very much in Motown's favor: The Jacksons
paid their old friends $100,000, and signed royalty waivers

and the like that cost the group another half-million bucks. Additionally, Motown kept title to the Jackson Five name.

They couldn't resist rubbing it in. Said Michael Roshkind to the New York *Daily News*, "We can do anything we want with [the Jackson Five name]. After all, we created the group, created the name. There were forty thousand Jacksons running around and we not only made five of them stars, we put them in their own house, paid for their education and worked a full year with them before they cut their first record."

Katherine Jackson should have had the last word. "I just hope Motown has finally learned to let go of my boys. The way Motown was acting, it's like a mother holding on to a child and saying, 'I raised you so you owe me your life.' There has to be a time to let go, in a family or in a business."

In the early days. *(Michael Ochs Archives)*

(*Above*) On *"The Sonny and Cher Comedy Hour,"* 1972. Michael was already as tall as Sonny. *(AP Wide World Photos)*

(*Below*) Gary was never like this. *(Michael Ochs Archives)*

The Jackson 6. Randy's down front. (*Michael Ochs Archives*)

The house in Gary, 2300 Jackson Street, where the eleven-member family lived until 1968. *(Kirk West/Photowest)*

Around the time of *Triumph.* Where's Michael? *(Simon Fowler/Retna)*

Partying with a fellow cast member of *The Wiz* (not Billie Jean). *(AP/Wide World Photos)*

P.Y.T. *(Barry Schultz/Retna)*

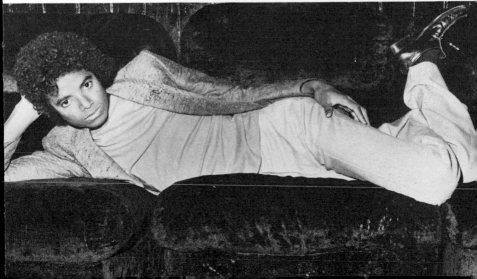

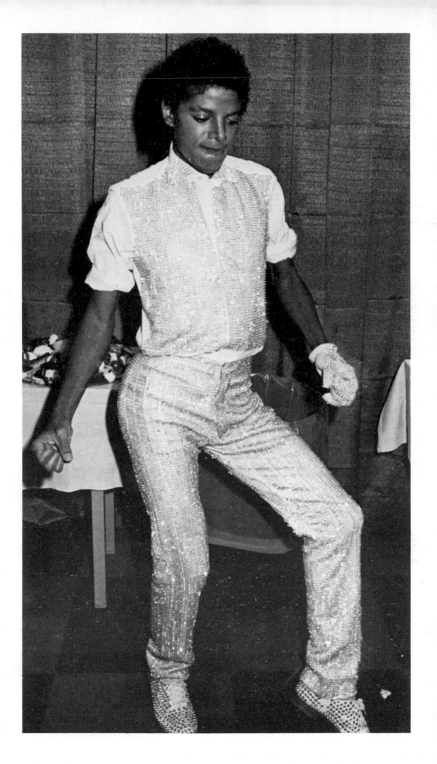

Michael and Quincy reap their reward at the 1984 Grammys.
Ninety days later, the grins faded as the Victory Tour began.
*(AP/Wide World Photos)*

Receiving the Award of Merit from mentor Diana Ross at the
1984 American Music Awards. Barry Manilow looks on envi-
ously at right. *(AP/Wide World Photos)*

(*Left*) Spangled dancer. Note the nose. *(John Bellissimo/Retna)*

A gathering of child stars—Spanky McFarland of The Little
Rascals at left. *(AP/Wide World Photos)*

The Gates of Eden—Encino branch. *(AP/Wide World Photos)*

In the hospital after the public burning. *(Carl Arrington/Liaison-Gamma)*

Leaving the hospital after his public burning.

*(Carl Arrington/Liaison- Gamma)*

"I wanna be where you are.

(AP/Wide World Photos)

"Smelly," Dopey, and Snow White. *(AP/Wide World Photos)*

With his friends at Fantasyland, Disney World, where there are hotel suites named for everyone in this picture. *(Gamma-Liaison)*

At the White House, where he played to an audience surprisingly similar to those on the Victory Tour. *(Judy Sloan/Gamma-Liaison)*

The Victory Tour's announcement turned Michael into the Jacksons' silent partner. *(Robin Kaplan/Retna)*

"Millions now living will never die." *(Judy Sloan/Gamma-Liaison)*

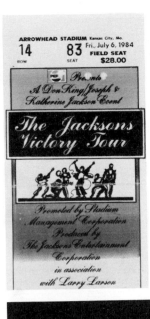

A Victory Tour opening night ticket stub. The price is two dollars low, because it doesn't mention the service charge.

(*Center*) "And behold! The King!"
(*Joe Traver/Gamma-Liaison*)

(*Below*) The starting lineup.
(*Ross Marino*)

In Dallas, the Victory Tour's second stop, the Jacksons were joined by Edward Van Halen, whose "Beat It" solo was the key to *Thriller's* crossover. *(Vinnie Zuffante/ Star File)*

Guitarist Gregg Wright, discovered by Randy and Tito while playing in a bar, grinds out yet another approximation of Edward Van Halen's greatest hit. *(John Bellissimo/Retna)*

In vogue.
*(Edward/Gamma-Liaison)*

# T · E · N

Dear Michael,

At this point, you probably think that I don't like you very much. That's not true, but how can I prove it? Things keep getting in the way: money, politics, sex, religion. But it would be foolish to be blinded by so many big issues and lose sight of the pleasure you've given or the real accomplishments you've made as a recording artist and singer and producer. That's especially true since part of the definition of these letters is that we don't know each other and that maybe we can't, except as images: a writer typing his way into the maw of the monolithic press that you fear; a singer dancing as fast as he can, trying to keep from being pinned down. That's as you like it—you keep your distance and force the rest of us (press and fans alike) to keep ours.

So let me just say right here that in the area where you've allowed anybody to approach—your music—I like you a lot. If somebody wanted to be cynical, they'd say that I should like you, since you're such good copy. But if that were all there was to it, I wouldn't have spent a big part of every day for about a year thinking about you, wondering how things got this way, where they'll wind up, what it all means.

A really tough critic could impugn everything you've done, I guess, if a really tough critic would bother with a pop singer in the first place. But for me, there are a few undeniable moments: "I Want You Back," "I'll Be There," "Dancing Machine," maybe "Ben" from the Jackson 5 days, and then "Heartbreak Hotel," *Off the Wall*, and *Thriller*.

Maybe *Thriller* wasn't a millennial masterpiece, as many critics (including me) tried to convince themselves it was in the late months of 1983 when it seemed that its sales might never slow down. But it's a damn fine record, and its best songs— "Billie Jean," "Human Nature," "Beat It"—are spectacular, as exciting as any pop made in the eighties.

More than anything, I think that the last few months have taught me what a good all-around hand in the record-making game you now are. Diana Ross's "Muscles" and your sister Rebbie's "Centipede" were terrific dance records that sounded fabulous on the radio, which is my way of saying that they fulfill everything they wanted to be. Of course, as ambitions go, that isn't much, and the fact that you sometimes make music just for the pure pleasure of capturing a great groove and slamming it home misleads some people into thinking that that's just about all you aspire to do. But that's wrong—what you aim to do isn't always what you achieve, but from time to time, it's been very clear that Michael Jackson reaches out not only for the sky, but for a standard of expression that's beyond most pop stars.

It would be silly to claim that your music has been as consciously and consistently developed as Stevie Wonder's has been, or that it reflects the essential unity of purpose that characterizes all the records made by Prince, to choose two extremely relevant examples. Such precision wasn't possible through the first decade of your career. Your progression was haphazard, ranging from moments of real inspiration to ones that are profound only in the depth of their banality.

But the reason isn't that something essential was missing from your artistic makeup. In the early days, you were trebly limited by your youth, your status as a member of a group that did not always recognize your leadership, and your subordinate position with producers who didn't always understand your potential or your limitations. Neither Motown nor Gamble and Huff were equipped to teach you how to express yourself—

neither was especially interested in having you do that. For them, you were a tool.

Motown's formula worked for Stevie Wonder and Marvin Gaye in their early days because the label provided them with an environment in which they were consistently challenged by collaborators of the highest caliber. By the time you came along, top-notch songwriters, producers, arrangers, and session players were in short supply. As a result, you got the chance to make excellent records only sporadically. (The shows were always good, even those odd dates in 1974 and 1975 when you took the Vegas show on the road. But you can get away with a lot more raw, unprocessed talent on the stage than in the cold, harsh atmosphere of the recording studio.)

By 1976, when you got together with Gamble and Huff, the limitations of their production team were equally evident. The Philadelphia sound was a formula in a more negative sense than Motown—it was a lot more restrictive, a lot less of a foundation on which a personal style could be built. (The biggest reason, I always thought, was Thom Bell and Linda Creed's leaving so early. After that, Gamble and Huff themselves were the only truly outstanding writers and producers in town.) So the material you worked with on *The Jacksons* and *Goin' Places* was unresponsive to what you might have wanted or needed to express. As a thorough pro, you never rebelled—within the imposed limits, you did as good a job as was possible. When they offered silk, you turned out gorgeous purses; when you were saddled with sow's ears, you still fooled many people, though the illusion didn't last long.

In that sense, the commercial failure of *Goin' Places* in 1977 was a blessing. Because it didn't crack the album chart Top 40 or even go gold, CBS finally cut you loose to make your own music your own way. The immediate result was *Destiny*, entirely written and produced by you and your brothers, which became your first real smash since *Dancing Machine*, reviving your career and establishing your credentials.

But even if *Destiny* was the first album that had much to do with what you were really trying to say, it was still compromised. You and your brothers were presented as equals, which is a long way from an accurate description of the true balance within the group. As a result, *Destiny* offers only a slight improvement—much hipper dance music, a more individual and attractive sound, a sense of slightly broader horizons. The best track, "Shake Your Body (Down to the Ground)," is nothing less than a dance masterpiece, but that's all. Only on "Things I Do for You" and "Bless His Soul," credited to the Jacksons but bearing your unmistakable stamp, do you begin to sing out about the issue that had been driving you all along, about the force that will spur you on in the next five years.

The topic was control, of your self, your money, and your work, of your sex life and your public image, of all things under the sun. Not necessarily power, but just the ability to stand on your own two feet, to reap rewards for what you did, not what somebody else made you do. Alongside that need for control is another feeling: the sheer terror of what it means to lose control, a desperate fear of the consequences of emotional (particularly sexual) self-abandon. This comes out pretty bluntly in those songs from *Destiny*: "No one could help me but myself / And I gave everything I had," you sing in "Things I Do for You," while complaining about those who took but offered nothing in return. And in "Bless His Soul," you outline the problem such urgent needs create when left unfulfilled: "The life you're leading is dangerous / It's so dangerous, dangerous." Far more than a mere assertion of your right to control your own life, that's a statement of fury at your inability to cut loose from the obstacles stacked—deliberately and purposelessly—in your way.

*Off the Wall* has only three songs written by you, but even in some of the material you didn't write, these themes emerge. The record is mostly about the disco nightlife, a more advanced version of *Dancing Machine*. But the best songs are about the quest for control ("Don't Stop 'Til You Get Enough") and what happens when you give it up ("She's Out of My Life"). They're about control subordinated to desire ("It's the Falling in Love") and sublimated in your complex understanding of work and play ("Working Day and Night").

Curiously, the metaphor you use for this search for control is most often dancing, a medium most often understood as a method of attaining sheer release. In "Working Day and Night" the dance floor actually becomes an arena in which partners joust to see whose dream will dominate. At the other extreme, the willingness to surrender, to give it up, is portrayed as a decision that leads to tragedy or disaster: This concept of catastrophe is probably what moved you to tears while recording "She's Out of My Life." (Given what you say about your sex life, how else could you have taken it so personally?)

In general, your expression of these ideas has been melodramatic and sentimental. But with "Heartbreak Hotel," your only solo composition on the Jacksons' 1980 album, *Triumph*, and most of the self-written songs on *Thriller*, you deal with these themes quite differently. "Heartbreak Hotel" still presents the consequences of giving it up as doom and disaster, but the writing is more convincing, even in its pulp-thriller format. Trapped for ten years against your will in a palace of seduction where the only remotely sympathetic figure has been held for fifteen already, you're more than scared, you're petrified: "Hope is dead," you declare. "Live and sin," you sing, as though you'd committed some ultimate offense against the biblical injunction to "go and sin no more."

In some senses, this is an infantile vision. It is deeply misogynistic: the hotel is run by predatory women; you wind up there as punishment for not following through on your commitment to your girlfriend; the women just won't believe the truth, that you've wronged no one in trying to be yourself. And it is a vision based on a paranoia about sexuality—acting out your sexual desire is what condemned you. So you invert not only the Bible but secular poetry as well, declaring that it is better not to have loved at all than to be damned for trying. Self-sufficiency becomes not only an answer, but a necessity for survival.

"Billie Jean," the greatest song on *Thriller*, is "Heartbreak Hotel" in real life, and a lot scarier because of it. If it's true, as it seems to be, that there really was a Billie Jean–style paternity case in your life, it seems to have confirmed all the suspicions behind songs like "Heartbreak Hotel" and "Things I Do for You." "Beat It" and "Wanna Be Startin' Somethin' " ("Someone's always . . . / Talkin', squealin', lyin' ") present you with situations that you obviously can't control: being outrun by gossip, overtaken by bullies.

This theme emerges all over the place in your work from this period. The video of "Billie Jean" is built around surveillance, the attempt of outside agents to know you (and thereby, run you). The "Thriller" and "Beat It" videos similarly play off images in which somebody—you, Ola Ray, the street gangs—is losing control to outside forces, none of which ever quite reveal themselves for what they are. Except you, the white knight at the end of both videos. Of course, "Thriller" undercuts this, but then, "Thriller" is also a song you didn't write, a vision you've denied (willingly or not), an altogether ambiguous statement. One thing's for sure, though. The fear in your voice as you warn Ola Ray that you're about to be transformed into a werewolf stems from some essentially authentic well of emotional knowledge—it's convincing but it's barely acting. This is the half-hidden downside of your obsession with being "special."

Why am I bothering you with this? Probably because I think that so far you haven't dealt consciously with these subjects. The pattern that links these songs is there, all right, but it's a found pattern, not one that's been deliberately planted. As a half-hidden hobgoblin, your obsession and fright can just as easily curdle your ambitions as help you realize them. Out in the open, as an approach to your future work, they might prove useful.

But there's another reason. I think that your fixation on patterns of dominance and assertion explains a lot of what has happened to you in the past couple of years, all the more so if it's developed unconsciously. After all, the drive to control—acquiring control, manipulating it, avoiding it—is a major issue in all of rock music, from Elvis Presley to John Lennon to Marvin Gaye. It's not so surprising that it should crop up with you.

But your approach to the theme is unavoidably tied to your passivity: to your attraction to "escapism," your links to the Jehovah's Witnesses, your relationship with your father, your love of infantile literature, your determination to live your life, so far as it remains possible, as a child. The contradiction is self-evident. In order for a grown-up to live like a kid, he must have an unusual degree of authority over his own life. But in order to acquire that authority, some very adult decisions have to be made. You can leave them to others, but eventually you'll lose the things that let you have so much latitude in your everyday behavior: money, for a start, but also the luxury of having your life run smoothly enough to worry about it no more than a prepubescent youngster would. So you have to continually reimmerse yourself in mundane life in order to be able to afford the periods of withdrawal that deny the importance of that kind of living.

This was never clearer than in the summer of 1984. You sleepwalked your way through the tour, and your contributions to the *Victory* album are nothing less than grudging: a lackluster cutting contest with Mick Jagger and the deliberately opaque "Be Not Always." You could say that you really were getting at the essence of the matter here and in the song you cowrote with Randy and the Toto guys, "The Hurt," but that means that the essence of the matter is that hell is other people, meaning you'd just as soon not be involved in any situation you can't . . . control. So you just kind of dusted yourself off and stood up there as a dropout from your own existence. And reaped the whirlwind.

If that's what happened, it's a shame, because there was opportunity for a lot more. But then there you are. In a word: trapped. But by nobody but yourself. I don't know what you're going to do next, but I hope you'll be the boss. It's the only chance you've given yourself.

# E · L · E · V · E · N

Through early 1976, CBS and Motown fought it out in courthouses and through press releases. Motown displayed a real talent for such roughhousing. When its other acts had left (such stars of the label's golden age as Martha Reeves, David Ruffin, Eddie Kendricks, and the Four Tops were long gone), Motown had made little or no public comment. However, its litigation against CBS was news by definition because that corporation's fortunes were important to Wall Street financiers, as well as record industry folk. Dragged out into the open, Motown's remarks were sharp and tough. The idea was that Motown *owned* the Jackson 5.

It backed that idea up, too. Over the next eighteen months, the label issued two more Jackson 5 albums (*Moving Violation* and *Joyful Jukebox Music*), two compilation albums of the group's hits and highlights from Michael's solo albums, and continued to reap high profits from back catalogue sales. (In January 1973, when the Jacksons were finally given their first royalty statement, which covered the period from "I Want You Back" through the end of 1971, the sum they received was only $90,000.) Over the next ten years Motown repackaged the Jacksons catalogue in innumerable configurations (particularly in the year after *Thriller*). Each reissue was more profitable than the last, especially after the 1980 royalty waiver settlement. Motown's aggressive assertion that the Jacksons had been disloyal was a beautifully conceived smokescreen that obscured the real victims of the story.

Understandably, the Jacksons felt bitter about Motown. *"Joyful Jukebox Music* never even made the charts. I don't think Motown promoted it too heavily," said Michael. "We don't feel as limited with Epic. At Motown, our music had to be written by certain people. Producers were another issue. On the *Dancing Machine* album, we used several producers but we just wanted to use one. But they wanted us to do it their way, so we came up with a bunch of different sounds on the same record, which happens when a lot of producers are used. That wasn't the best way to do it."

For the family, the hardest part was the split with Jermaine. That summer, they played Las Vegas again, their final dates with him. They were strained, unhappy gigs. Jermaine went back home and cut his first solo album in a couple of years, *My Name Is Jermaine*, working within the system: the album was made by a hatful of producers, with Berry Gordy credited as "executive producer," which seems mostly to have meant that he was paying attention. It contained a minor hit, "Let's Be Young Tonight," which was to be Jermaine's last appearance on the pop charts until the label let him duet with Stevie Wonder in 1980, which produced the Top 10 "Let's Get Serious."

Meantime, he was estranged from his folks. His mother would ask him why he was doing this to the family; he could only ask why they were doing it to him. Later, Jermaine told the Los Angeles *Times* that he called repeatedly to patch things up with both his brothers and parents without immediate results. The brothers claimed publicly that the split was nothing personal, but Jermaine would not appear onstage with them again until 1981, and then only as an encore guest.

Jermaine's dilemma might, in fact, have been an opportunity. Joe Jackson *ruled* his roost, brooking little meddling by anybody else. Leaving his brothers was difficult for Jermaine, but staying with them might have been no easier. And anyway, as he later said, "Berry and I had a father-child relationship from day one. I was one of his students. He taught me quite a bit and did a great job of it."

Jermaine's Motown solo career was rocky, but he demonstrated acuity as a talent scout. He signed Stephanie Mills, who played Dorothy in the Broadway play, *The Wiz.* Jermaine ran into the group Switch in an elevator at the Los Angeles Motown offices, helped them find a place to stay, rehearsed them, got them a live showcase, and ensured that they were signed by Gordy. Later, he discovered a family gospel group, the DeBarges, in western Michigan and helped them negotiate their way out of a small label contract so they could make a pact with Motown. (His sister Janet later married a DeBarge.) Together with Hazel, who became his manager, Jermaine had a real flair for the business side of the music industry. Even when he left Motown to sign with Aristo, in 1983, he still vowed he'd be the company's president one day.

Meantime, the Jacksons plugged on with young Randy in his place, continuing to tour while waiting for the final separation from Motown. (Their contract with the label didn't expire until next spring.) For the summer of 1976, they were signed to do a CBS TV variety show, *The Jacksons.* It ran only a few episodes, first as a summer fill-in, then as a regularly scheduled production, before being canceled due to low ratings. (Alexenberg remembered the TV series showing so poorly in the ratings that CBS, Inc., president Arthur Taylor later had second thoughts about the record deal.)

In some ways, signing with Epic was out of the frying pan into the fire. The Jacksons' hope that they could work with Bobby Taylor as their outside producer was quickly crushed. Epic was convinced that the proper approach was to record the group with Kenneth Gamble and Leon Huff, the masterminds of disco's Philly sound.

If this had really meant Gamble and Huff themselves, it might have been a great idea. But Gamble and Huff weren't at the peak of their form in 1976. Creatively, they'd topped out the year before, with Harold Melvin and the Blue Notes' "Bad Luck," a magnificent swan song to an era that saw black pop expand and recreate itself. In 1975, the production partners were under federal indictment for payola, and although the charges against Huff were dismissed in early 1976, Gamble's difficulties dragged on. (He was eventually fined $2500.) Whether coincidentally or not, Gamble and Huff's sound began to dry up about the same time. Not that they didn't have hits, but they were smaller ones, and the inventiveness the team brought to the studio seemed to diminish.

Anyway, *The Jacksons,* the group's first Epic album, wasn't even entirely produced by Gamble and Huff. They assigned important chunks of the work to Dexter Wansel and the team of Gene McFadden and John Whitehead, both good songwriters who had never come close to equaling their bosses as producers. Although Gamble and Huff came up with "Enjoy Yourself," a good Philly-style dance hit, for the Jacksons (as they had been rechristened), one Top 10 hit wasn't sufficient. The album peaked at number thirty-six on the *Billboard* chart, just as *Moving Violation* had.

In public, the Jacksons were enthusiastic about the pairing with Gamble and Huff. "It's a lot of fun working with Kenny Gamble and Leon Huff; they're great producers and good writers," said Michael. "They know what they're doing. They've proven themselves to be great. Look at all the hits they've had in the past. They go way back. . . . It seems like they're just mass producing acts, but I don't think they are. When they wrote the tunes for our album, they went to the mountains in a trailer and stayed for about a week. It was a special project for them."

Never has Michael—or anyone else—sounded more like he was trying to talk himself into something. Nor should he have believed in the power of Gamble and Huff to get the Jacksons out of their uncommercial rut, for just as they had landed at Motown at the exact moment when that company's production line was disintegrating, so had they come to Philadelphia International at exactly the wrong time.

Even at their best, what Gamble and Huff did wasn't what Michael and his brothers were about anyhow. As Nelson George wrote, "It was, musically, an uneasy relationship. Gamble and Huff's best work had always been with older, gospel-based vocalists, such as Teddy Pendergrass of the Blue Notes and Eddie Levert of the O'Jays. Michael's voice was deepening at age seventeen, but it still had that young and spirited pop quality that was his trademark."

In the end, what's most interesting about *The Jacksons* is the pair of songs the brothers wrote and produced themselves. Neither is great, but both offer hints of what was to come. Michael and Tito wrote "Style of Life," a Latin-inflected dance groove that tried to keep pace with the Philly feel of the Gamble and Huff tracks but never quite gelled into anything more. On the other hand, "Blues Away," written and produced by Michael, has a light touch and a breathy vocal that suggest the direction in which his style would develop.

Despite such mixed results, CBS had nowhere to send the Jacksons for their second Epic album except back to Philadelphia. Prior to acquiring Gamble and Huff's distribution rights, CBS, despite being the largest record company in the U.S., had virtually no presence in the black record market. Its resources in that field remained essentially limited to Philadelphia International and a few self-contained performers, such as the Isleys, Sly, and Maurice White's Earth, Wind & Fire. So the Jacksons went back to the Mainline.

This time Gamble and Huff did make an effort to accommodate the Jacksons: Tito played guitar, Randy congas. But, in general, Michael was correct when he later complained, "That sound wasn't right for us. We sounded too much like the other Gamble and Huff artists."

Gamble and Huff and they were no more able to come to terms with the Jacksons'—and in particular, Michael's—talents than their Motown producers had been. This is reflected in the songs themselves, a hodgepodge of standard ballads and dance tunes on which the group, especially Michael, acquit themselves competently but to no special effect, mostly because there simply isn't anything special about the material. An exception might be made for the light ballad, "Even Though You're Gone," but even there, Michael isn't pushed to take chances as he later did on his own. At nineteen, he was still audibly trying to forge a style—and, equally audibly, every chance he took was made without much sympathy or support from his mentors.

The problem was compounded by Kenneth Gamble's psychic convictions. He frequently used Philadelphia International albums as a medium for espousing his vague, soporific plans for world peace and cosmic harmony. *Goin' Places* contained one song, "Man of War," which espoused metaphysical pacificism, and on the sleeve, Gamble continued the thoughts of the lyric, referring to a "Divine Vanguard," which would wage a "war against ignorance, hatred, racism, unrighteousness." Certainly what Gamble was saying was well-meaning, but his presentation left more than a lot to be desired: "When communications reach the point of no reasoning, because one party cannot agree with another, violence has been the solution to communication breakdown."

Gamble and Huff had no answers, nor could they provide the key to unlock the Jacksons' very real creative impasse. In fact, it became even more evident on *Goin' Places* that the Jacksons were ready to write, if not produce, for themselves. The album's one really excellent track, "Different Kind of Lady," was one of the two the brothers wrote. Their other contribution to the record, "Do What You Wanna," is imitation Gamble and Huff, but "Different Kind of Lady" was also a different kind of record, just the kind of lightly sung but heartily grooving dance track that Michael would later perfect with "Rock with You" and "Wanna Be Startin' Somethin'." Michael's singing is grittier than it later became, but the song is more than just a piece of dance floor fodder. It was a big club hit, and although never issued as a single, it has the kind of pop surface—call-and-response vocals, gimmicky wah-wah voice interjections, some real dynamic development—that could have made it a pop smash.

If the Jacksons had only been rank beginners, such a polished production would have been astounding. But, of course, the Jacksons really had been woodshedding. They were ready to write their own material—and produce it, too. "We were writing songs at Motown, but we were never allowed to put them on our albums," Michael had said several times, and based on "Different Kind of Lady," it must be true. Just as it must also be true, given the sophisticated production of that track, that he had really watched both his Motown and Philadelphia producers "like a sponge with eyes."

"Different Kind of Lady" was the breakthrough the Jacksons needed. "People went bananas for that song," Michael said. "And Gamble and Huff went back and wrote another song, in competition with ours. *They* went back to the drawing board. They stayed in that room a *long* time. In fact, they left the producing up to us. And we said, 'Wow, look at this.' 'Cause Gamble and Huff were like the best songwriters." Kenny Gamble told the brothers, "You are good enough to do your own stuff."

And the brothers told CBS. Michael, accompanied by Richard Arons and Joe Jackson, arranged a meeting with Walter Yetnikoff, at which they pleaded their case for self-production. Yetnikoff, with little reason to doubt their talent (and no place else to turn now that the Gamble and Huff liaison hadn't panned out), gave the okay. The Jacksons' next album would for the first time contain only songs written and produced by themselves.

But Michael wasn't able to rush back into the recording studio. He was already preparing for his first movie role, in *The Wiz*, a remake of *The Wizard of Oz*, based on the Broadway hit. This version had an all-black cast. The producer was Motown.

The rights to *The Wiz* had originally been purchased by Twentieth Century-Fox, but Motown purchased them and arranged for Universal Pictures to distribute after Diana Ross had a dream in which she saw herself as Dorothy. Ross was now a bankable star (one of very few black ones), and Motown, with twenty-nine-year-old producer Rob Cohen (who had worked with the company on *Bingo Long and His Traveling All-Stars,* Motown's film about the twilight of Negro league baseball), was quickly able to get the project financed. In addition to Ross playing Dorothy as a twenty-four-year-old schoolteacher (Ross was thirty-four) and Michael as the Scarecrow, Mabel King (Eviline, the Wicked Witch) and Ted Ross (the Cowardly Lion) were signed from the Broadway cast. Nipsey Russell as the Tin Man, Lena Horne as the Good Witch, and Richard Pryor as the Wiz rounded out the cast. Sidney Lumet was hired as director, Quincy Jones to supervise the music. Preproduction began in New York in July 1977. Filming took place from October through December 1977 at Astoria Studios in Queens, the birthplace of American commercial cinema but unused since the major studios completed their move to Hollywood in the twenties.

Rehearsals began in July at the St. George Hotel in Brooklyn, the actors reading the script with Lumet in a small room while choreographer Louis Johnson ran one hundred twenty dancers and forty models through their paces in the main ballroom. For the first couple of weeks all went well. Then, on a Fourth of July outing to Coney Island, Michael had an attack of pneumothorax. "The doctor said it was bubbles on the lungs and the bubbles burst and you can't breathe," he said. "Mostly slim people have it. He said there was a little bit of pleurisy there, too. It reminded me that Buddy Ebsen was supposed to be the Tin Man in the original *Wizard of Oz* and he broke down sick before the thing."

It naturally reminded others that Michael was a high-strung, inexperienced kid who might have been feeling the pressure. Although he claimed "anybody can act," Michael must have been feeling terribly uncertain as he embarked on his Hollywood dream. Quincy Jones said that they began to grow close around this time, when Michael was having trouble with one of his line readings—mispronouncing "Socrates." "When they took a break, I took him to the corner and said, 'Michael, it's 'Sock-ra-tease,' " Jones said. "We kind of looked at each other and we felt a real strong bond. It was a little thing in a way, but . . . our relationship began to grow from that point." Yet, except for Diana Ross, Michael seems to have been basically unprotected on the set. He claimed to have learned much from Lumet, but the evidence didn't reach the screen. Michael had some raw ability, but it remained unprocessed for the moment.

By the time shooting began, the nineteen-year-old Michael was his usual ebullient self. "Film is my dream," he said. "I love music and film and want to integrate them like it's never been done before." It was an ambition he'd realize—but not yet.

*The Wiz* was a catastrophe. Almost everything about it went wrong. Ross was probably inherently incapable of playing ten years under her age, but she was hopelessly lost given makeup that meant to make her look dowdy but wound up giving her a pallor more commonly associated with severe illness. To top it off, she wore a short haircut that overemphasized her age. The script was another loser: Broadway musicals rarely transfer well to the screen, but this one was filled with implausibilities. (Dorothy is supposed to be a twenty-four-year-old schoolteacher who has "never been south of 125th Street." So where'd she go to college?) Richard Pryor is wasted as the Wiz. Jones had scored thirty films, but asked to come up with some competent dance music for this one, he flopped—the music tries to play strings off against harmonica, and the result is a battle both sides lose. The best song, "Ease on Down the Road," was better sung and arranged on the original cast album, and the new material, contributed by Charlie Small (who also wrote the theater music), isn't much either, even though Michael's "You Can't Win, Pt. 1" from the sound track LP hit the low rungs of the Hot 100. Lumet was coming off a string of hits—*Network, Three Days of the Condor, Serpico, Dog Day Afternoon*—but he had never done a musical before and demonstrated zero sympathy for the style. Lumet was always a rather wooden director; *The Wiz* was cut from teak.

And the film sank both with reviewers (with whom Lumet had never been a favorite) and at the box office: It cost twenty-four million dollars, at that time one of the most expensive movies ever made and by far the most expensive black-oriented film. Its box-office revenues were about twelve million dollars. (Films generally need to earn two to three times their negative costs in order to break even.) Ross, who had gotten good notices in *Lady Sings the Blues* and decent ones even in the dire *Mahogany*, was ripped this time. As for Michael, critics sometimes noticed his potential, but it was impossible to say that he lit up the screen.

Yet his preternatural enthusiasm left Michael glowing. He had only praise for all involved and once again displayed his singular ability to turn any negative into a positive in the space of a paragraph: "I spent four hours a day for five months getting made up and it was well worth every minute. Man, that was painful. I'd finish a day's shooting in all that stuff and then I'd leave the set with my skin all blotched and marked and my eyes red and sore. There'd be fans outside and they'd point at me and say, 'Hey, that guy's on drugs—look what it's doing to him! I'd explain that I never touch drugs, but I don't think they believed me. Sometimes I would go home in costume and makeup and the people would say, 'Trick or treat!' It was beautiful!''

Michael's power of self-persuasion came close to self-hypnosis. He actually managed to convince himself that *The Wiz* exceeded the merits of the original *Wizard of Oz*. (And *The Wiz* couldn't have sold Stevie Wonder on that proposition.) "It was a heavy script, real heavy. A lot of people look at it as just a children's story but it isn't. It's dealing with faith and belief and courage, and when you deal with those subjects, you're dealing with things that make kings of the world." Michael actually said that he not only enjoyed making *The Wiz*, but that it was "really wonderful to know that something you've done, something you've been a real part of, will be around for just years and years." You'd have thought he was speaking of "I Want You Back." But then, Michael was inculcated with the standard show-business hierarchy of importance, in which pop music success comes a long way down a list topped by making it at the movies—any old movie will do.

Or maybe *The Wiz* was just further confirmation of his view of how his world ought to work. "What's wonderful about a film," he said, "is that you can become another person. I love to forget. And lots of times you totally forget."

The Jacksons hadn't been together since the previous May, when they played a Royal Command Performance for Queen Elizabeth II's Silver Jubilee at King's Hall, Glasgow, Scotland. The Jacksons remained a huge overseas attraction, and England was one of their biggest markets. (Ironically, it was during the Jubilee that the Sex Pistols reached the peak of their revolutionary counter-marketing assault on British pop by releasing "God Save the Queen," which savaged the whole idea of British royal tradition and respect for authority. Naturally, the two groups were oblivious to one another.)

Now it was time for the brothers to regroup, in order to begin recording their first self-written, self-produced album. Epic wasn't yet entirely confident of their abilities, so it assigned two of its staff A&R men, Bobby Colomby (formerly drummer with Blood, Sweat & Tears) and Mike Atkinson, to serve as "executive producers": company overseers. By all accounts, Colomby and Atkinson didn't meddle. They were around to make sure, that's all.

The Jacksons themselves may have had some reservations about what was going to happen. It was during the months just before the release of *Destiny* that Joe Jackson and Richard Arons terminated their relationship and Joe signed the group to a management contract with Weisner/DeMann Entertainment. Jackson later claimed that he felt he needed white representation to get along effectively with CBS management. But there must have been something more to it, since Arons was also white.

Ron Weisner and Freddy DeMann were experienced in the entertainment business, the former as a personal manager, the latter as a record executive and promotion man. In a short time, they'd built a reputation as shrewd deal-makers. Even though pop music artists are signed to long-term recording contracts, each album release is a separate deal in a sense, requiring that the releasing label pay attention to the new music's special strengths and drawbacks. Joe was apparently convinced that Weisner and DeMann were the best men available to crack the whip at CBS.

Musically, the Jacksons knew they were ready. "We had saved a lot of material that we couldn't do on the [Gamble and Huff] albums," said Marlon. "We kept saying, well, we'll use that on the next album. Finally, when it got to the point where we could do all our own material we found that we had more than enough. . . . When they said, 'Go write your own material,' it was like a weight was lifted. We were turned loose and we really wanted to show how good we could become."

Nor was the Jacksons' self-confidence misplaced, in the opinion of Greg Phillinganes, a young but experienced keyboardist brought in by Colomby to serve as the group's rhythm arranger. "I went out to the house in Encino to work with the guys," he told Nelson George. "I was fairly surprised at how much music they had in them. They were real enthusiastic and excited because this was the first time in their entire careers that they controlled the music. All of them could write but I thought Michael and Randy were probably the strongest writers in the family."

This was certainly confirmed by the *Destiny* album's immediate standout, a Randy and Michael song, "Shake Your Body (Down to the Ground)," which took what the brothers had learned at Motown and in Philly, combined it with the hottest dance ideas currently on the radio, and distilled it all into eight minutes of bone-rattling, joyous music—a disco classic, a Top 10 hit (after the first release, "Blame It on the Boogie," flopped), and just what the Jacksons needed to take their album sales back past the million mark.

*Destiny* was more than a one-hit wonder. It was the first time in their career that the Jacksons had sustained an entire album from start to finish. Perhaps this really was due to stockpiling material; it's a frequent phenomenon among new groups that what's been stored up over several years and finally cut loose for the first time in a studio results in a much more satisfying product than the group ever achieves working on a shorter schedule. (It's also true that the Jacksons had the full advantage of Michael's involvement for perhaps the last time—he had not yet initiated his Epic solo career, so the group still had first call on his best work.)

With very minor exceptions, everything on *Destiny* works. If the title track is somewhat plodding, at least its arrangement is fascinating: It starts off as soft rock and eventually becomes as heavy as the brothers knew how to get (sorta middleweight). Michael does a beautiful ballad turn on "Push Me Away." "Bless His Soul" is one of the most complex harmony arrangements the group ever recorded, and they pull it off seamlessly. And while the dance tracks, with the exception of "Shake Your Body," are somewhat dated now, they're serviceable in context.

When it reached the shelves in mid-December 1978, *Destiny* rejuvenated the Jacksons' career in every sense. Their 1979 world tour, which occupied the first several weeks of the new year, was more widely anticipated than anything they'd done since the teen idol days. And once "Shake Your Body" hit the airwaves in mid-February, they were clearly back to stay. Epic's Alexenberg arranged a lavish Beverly Hills party to celebrate their tenth year of hits. It was held in a posh Beverly Hills bank, outfitted for the occasion with a dance floor and mega-watt sound system. That night, as the Jacksons descended by escalator to the main floor, "I Want You Back" blasting the room while the guests cheered, Joe Jackson must have felt that for once his plans were working perfectly.

On January 22, they went off on their world tour, with an itinerary that took them first to Bremen, West Germany, then on through Nairobi, Kenya, Madrid, London, and Paris before bringing them back to the States for a route through the major American urban areas. The brothers were working together superbly, Randy proving a more than adequate replacement for Jermaine. They had shown the record industry and the world what they could do together. "When we were mixing the album, a lot of people thought each one of us would have a knob on the board, but we outslicked all of them," said Marlon.

Behind the scenes, things were less smooth. In November, Michael had gone into the studio to make his first solo album in four years. The idea wasn't to split the group, but the trajectory of a successful solo career would eventually pull things that way. It wasn't so evident right then, but the Jacksons still had no substitute for Michael. Without him, they would never be able to make their era of good feelings last.

Evidently, Michael had thought of doing a solo album for some time. His reasons are obvious enough: If the Jacksons didn't do well with *Destiny*, the group would have little future. Anyway, Michael was not especially interested in spending the rest of his life sharing equal credit with brothers, who weren't his equals in imagination, talent, and ambition much less in taking orders from his dictatorial father/manager. Michael had already had solo success at Motown; the CBS contract implied that they wanted him to do more. *The Wiz* was his first step toward creative independence from his family (while he lived in New York during the shooting, only sister LaToya was with him). A solo album was the logical progression by any measure.

Despite *Destiny*, he wanted and needed an outside producer. "One day I called Quincy to ask if he could suggest some great people who might want to do my album," Michael told Stephen Demorest. "It was the first time that I fully wrote and produced my songs and I was looking for somebody who could give me that freedom, plus somebody who's unlimited musically. Quincy calls me Smelly and he said, 'Well, Smelly, why don't you let me do it?' I said, 'That's a great idea.'

"It sounded so phony—like I was trying to hint to that, but I wasn't. I didn't even think of it. But Quincy does jazz, he does movie scores, rock 'n' roll, funk, pop—he's all colors, and that's the kind of people I like to work with. I went over to his house just about every other day and we put it together."

Quincy Jones had indeed done everything, from producing Lesley Gore to arranging big bands. Born in Chicago in 1934, he grew up in Seattle, where he began playing trumpet. When he was thirteen, his next-door neighbor was a transplanted sixteen-year-old blind piano player from Florida—Ray Charles.

Together, they joined the big band led by local butcher shop manager Bumps Blackwell. Blackwell would go on to produce, write songs for, and manage Sam Cooke, Little Richard, and dozens of other rock & roll, rhythm and blues and gospel stars. At that time, he was a magnet for jazz musicians playing in the area. They'd stay at his home, and when they fell asleep, Blackwell's teenage trumpet player would copy their orchestrations.

In 1948, Lionel Hampton brought his band—which Jones has called the first rock & roll band—to Seattle. Quincy came to see him with a suite he'd composed. It impressed Hampton enough for the vibraphonist to take the kid on the road for a few weeks, until his wife sent Jones packing back to Seattle, with instructions to finish high school.

When he did, Jones won a scholarship to Boston's Berklee School of Music, from which he graduated in 1952. Jones then rejoined Hampton's band for a couple of years. In 1956, he was appointed musical director of Dizzy Gillespie's orchestra, with which he toured Europe, Asia, and the Middle East for the U.S. State Department. Entranced by Paris, he moved there, working with producer Eddie Barclay, observing other expatriate American musicians (notably Joe Turner) and studying with Nadia Boulanger, the compatriot of Ravel and Debussy, "a living textbook of European tradition."

In 1960, Jones returned to the States, where he got a job as director of A&R for Mercury Records in Chicago. The next year, Mercury made him the first black vice-president of a major American record label. He worked everywhere with everybody: producing Frank Sinatra and Count Basie's joint session in Las Vegas, making Lesley Gore's hit, "It's My Party," in New York.

Over the next decade, Jones built a career as an independent record producer and arranger. He also became one of the most prolific composers of film scores in Hollywood, working on more than thirty pictures. Although he lacked cachet among jazz purists, Jones was well regarded in pop circles and he worked with an wide range of names: Sinatra, Basie, Charles, Aretha Franklin, Sarah Vaughan, Louis Armstrong, Ella Fitzgerald, Duke Ellington, Jacques Brel, and Edith Piaf among them. He once estimated that since age thirty he had spent an

average of fifty hours a month in the recording studio. He did
the music for the entire *Roots* television series in eleven days
"without sleep." The resulting stress caused Jones to have a
stroke in 1974 when he was barely forty. But within two years,
he was back working full time.

In the seventies, Jones made a series of his own instrumental
albums. (He had begun dabbling with such recordings while at
Mercury.) They were disparaged by critics, but sold very well.

Jones had his own musical philosophy. "Producing an album
is simply a matter of finding a mood that inspires you and
plunging into it," he said. That outlook, and his ability to
produce hits for late seventies acts such as the Brothers Johnson,
made him an excellent choice to get along with Michael Jackson.

There were doubters. Jones was a rather traditional, stuffy
figure, the epitome of the bourgeois gourmand and aesthete.
Michael was the space-cadet child star. "Everybody wasn't sure
we were going to make that work," Jones told Gerri Hirshey.
"Unfortunately, we had a lot of people on our backs that were
saying it was a ridiculous combination, it wasn't a good creative
combination. Because people are strange; people have precon-
ceived ideas. I've spent most of my life trying to stay out of
slots—they've always got to get you in some kind of slot: 'He's
a film composer,' he's a jazz, he's this or that. The comments
we heard were it's going to sound like the Brothers Johnson; it's
going to be too jazzy; it's going to be ridiculous. Inside his
[record] company, there wasn't a lot of faith. I didn't feel any at
all. And I could feel this resistance and I love that because it
gives me great motivation. I told Michael that at the time. I
said don't worry about it, man, people love to do that, you
know. And it will be the same people that when it works will
be giving you the smiles."

Michael himself had doubts, not about the collaboration but
about his ability to establish a name independent of the group's.
"He wasn't at all sure that he could make a name for himself on
his own," said Jones. "And me, too. I had my doubts. But he
had a real intensity and I couldn't stop myself from accepting
[the assignment]. People take him for a simpleton with a head
full of silly songs but he's a complex young man, curious about
everything, who wants to go further and further. He behaves

like an adolescent and at the same time like a wise old philosopher. I feel kind of responsible for him."

Jones told Hirshey that he had been impressed with Michael's talent ever since he saw him sing "Ben" on the Oscar telecast in 1973. "You just knew he was a notch above, he was going to be around a long time." But the experience that linked them was making *The Wiz*. Michael, the self-professed "sponge with eyes," must have been thrilled to find that the composer of the film's score was sympathetic enough to quietly help him with his lines. And Jones was deeply impressed by what he was seeing. "Watching him in the context of being an actor, I saw a lot of things about him as a singer that rang a lot of bells. I saw a depth that was never apparent, and a commitment. I saw that Michael was growing up."

Their relationship became so friendly that some saw Jones as a surrogate father. Michael was a frequent visitor at Jones's home, and became close with Quincy's wife, Peggy Lipton (she had starred in *Mod Squad*, the antihip sixties TV series), and their children. Jones took to calling Michael "Smelly" because Michael was squeamish about the term "funky."

That doesn't mean that they were a perfectly balanced set. In the wake of later success, Jones has taken what some see as too much credit and the very jazz buffs who slammed Jones for being too pop years before now claim that it is only Quincy's genius that created Michael's massive hits. Jones and Jackson themselves seem pretty competitive about which of them deserves more credit for *Off the Wall* and *Thriller*.

Keyboardist Phillinganes, who worked on both albums, put their partnership into perspective. "Their ideas just blend into each other," he said. "You see, Michael is not like a lot of other singers who come around just to add a vocal. Michael is involved in the whole album. 'Q' [as his cronies call Jones] is basically an overseer who runs the show without really running the show."

In other words, Jones's contribution to Michael Jackson's solo career has been as much psychological as musical. Jones has never produced any other pop records with the quality of *Off the Wall* and *Thriller*, and his one attempt to repeat the formula he'd developed with Michael, working with Donna Summer in 1982, was an unqualified failure. In the studio, Jones serves as an interpreter of Jackson's ideas to the musicians, as a skilled technician who can solve the innumerable creative problems such an intuitive performer faces, as a general intermediary who has much more rapport with the world at large than Michael chooses to have. The result is an approach to record making that so far has managed to convey Michael Jackson's musical persona in unmistakable terms—no mean feat, considering that two of the great production staffs in black pop, Motown's and Philadelphia International, failed to do it. In general terms, Quincy Jones has succeeded where others failed because he understands that "when Michael commits to an idea, he goes all the way with it. . . . It's a long way from idea to execution. Everybody wants to go to heaven and nobody wants to die."

Michael could always sing like an angel. The basic problem in making each of his records has been finding appropriate material. Then, if the arrangements are at all compatible with his style, he turns in superb performances. Musically, Jones's greatest contribution has been piecing together that acceptable body of songs. With *Off the Wall*, this was a special problem because Michael had so little experience as a songwriter.

In fact, coming into the sessions, he had written only one song, "Don't Stop 'Til You Get Enough." In the course of the production, he put together a second, "Working Day and Night" (which he later told Demorest was "very autobiographical in a lot of ways, though I did stretch the point. . . ."). Jones put him together with Louis Johnson, of the Brothers Johnson, for a third, "Get on the Floor." All were about the disco nightlife.

Jackson's problem in writing songs is specifically verbal, not musical. Michael told journalist Vernon Gibbs that "writing lyrics takes me a long time, but writing melodies I love. I make them up all the time." Since he's generally inarticulate, that's not surprising. The problem, then, was to find songs good enough to make a listenable album while still helping the album add up as a whole.

The obvious place to turn was to friends and associates, in the process perhaps attracting some celebrities who would strengthen the budding image of Michael Jackson as an adult pop star. For the solo album didn't just need to establish a persona for Jackson, it needed to subtly shift him away from the teen idol mold. In this respect, even though the songs weren't the best things on the album, Stevie Wonder and former Supreme Susaye Green's "I Can't Help It" and Paul McCartney's "Girlfriend" were among the most important tracks on *Off the Wall.*

The most important songwriter with whom Jackson worked, however, was the relatively unheralded Rod Temperton. Temperton, an Englishman, who lived in Germany, was a leader of the disco group Heatwave, best known for its 1977 hit, "Boogie Nights." He left the group in 1978, to begin a career as an independent songwriter/producer, though he continued to work with Heatwave in the studio.

Temperton was in New York making *Heatwave Three* when Jones rang him to ask for songs for both Jackson and Rufus, featuring Chaka Khan, with whom Quincy was also working. "I said it was impossible [since] I was doing the Heatwave project," Temperton said. "Finally, he wrangled out of me that I would do one song for each artist."

For *Off the Wall,* he wound up contributing three, including the title track; the breakthrough hit "Rock with You," and the last song on the album, "Burn This Disco Out." Only "Rock with You" surpasses disco conventions, but because they were so similar to the songs written by Michael himself all of them helped the album establish Jackson's new image. And it was "Rock with You" that began to drive a wedge into the resegregated American radio scene, opening the album to an audience that was broader than that of any other black artist of the time.

Once they'd assembled the songs, putting the album together was a relatively simple, if painstaking, process. Describing Jackson's working process, Jones has said, "Michael starts with basic tracks, then adds overdubs, then fixing—you've got to put it together like an Erector set and try to help Michael realize, or embellish, what he has." He estimated that the entire process consumed about three months.

*Off the Wall* took considerably longer to complete, because the tour intervened. Fragile Michael must have been stretched pretty thin during this time; he wound up canceling seven dates on the Jacksons tour due to throat trouble, a problem often aggravated by stress and overwork. As a result, the first single, "Don't Stop 'Til You Get Enough," wasn't released until late July 1979. But CBS might have been reluctant to release a single much earlier anyway because "Shake Your Body (Down to the Ground)" didn't leave the pop charts until late June.

When it finally appeared, *Off the Wall* exploded, going straight to number one. This time, there were singles galore. In November, after the album had been out for two months, "Rock with You" was released, and it also marched up to number one, staying there for four weeks, the sign of a really massive sales and airplay hit.

Disco had splintered the pop music world more decisively than any style since rock & roll itself. The result was a reinstitution of the same racial barriers that had existed before Elvis Presley, Little Richard, Chuck Berry, Fats Domino, and their cohorts tore down the walls twenty-five years before. Once more, there was white radio for white artists, black radio for blacks. "Rock with You" breached the wall—not much but a little. It wasn't alone (Donna Summer's Rolling Stones–style "Hot Stuff" preceded it by a few months), but the FM stations that had maintained lily-white playlists at least had to reckon with not playing "Rock with You," an obvious across-the-board smash.

"It was bad when we did *Off the Wall* because there were stations that wouldn't play 'Rock with You' after it was number one; they wouldn't put it on the radio station *until* it was number one," Jones told Hirshey. "And those were stations that we needed to get it to number one." Yet, once it got broad airplay, *Off the Wall* chewed up the charts in the midst of a major national recession that had caused the greatest slump in overall record sales in post-Depression history.

"It's like any place else," Jones continued. "England didn't notice the West Indians and the Pakistanis too much until times got really bad. That rub didn't get rough until the economy got bad and then they said, 'Hey, you might be taking my job away.' All of a sudden, we don't need West Indians and Pakistanis anymore. And it's the same thing in the situation [for blacks] here. When the record business is shrinking and the economy is bad and everything else, there are probably a lot of whites that feel that if anybody should *not* [prosper], it should be the black people. It's a funny balance of sociology because a lot of program directors tell me it's not the station so much, it's that the people will call up and say 'We don't want to hear that black music."

By playing into this bias (as the white radio stations had done by staging antidisco rallies and orienting their playlists to demographic segregation in the first place), the programmers fulfilled their own prophecies. When the time came, the same programmers described those who made racist phone calls as cranks.

In this malign maw of dubious intentions and warped rationalizations, the success of "Rock with You" spurred album sales even more than a number one hit ordinarily does. The Epic Records promotion department stayed on the case and "Rock with You" was followed by two more Top 10 hits, "She's Out of My Life" and "Off the Wall" itself. The album became only the second by a single artist in history to produce four Top 10 hits. (The other was Fleetwood Mac's *Rumours,* though a couple of sound tracks had done it, too.) Before it was over, *Off the Wall* sold more than eight million copies, making it one of the half-dozen best-sellers in record industry history.

Despite this, *Off the Wall* never topped the album chart. It made number three, but during its active life, it was outranked by the Eagles' *The Long Run,* Donna Summer's *On the Radio— Greatest Hits,* Pink Floyd's *The Wall,* and Bob Seger's *Against the Wind.* Partly, this was just a statistical anomaly—the *Billboard* charts report what's selling best that week, not cumulative purchases. But every one of those other albums was by a white artist, except Summer's, which made number one on the heels of "No More Tears [Enough is Enough]," a duet with the highly Caucasian Barbra Streisand.

Segregation in radio and records works both ways. Jackson's next single was the gorgeous ballad "She's Out of My Life," perhaps the most fully realized track on *Off the Wall.* The performance was the kind of tour de force Michael had come up with on "Ben" but hadn't had the chance to do since. He sweeps through the song in beautiful voice, trembling and wavering through its melodrama. (Jones and Jackson have both admitted that Michael actually broke down crying when he got to the lines "And it cuts like a knife . . . she's out of my life." Shades of Johnnie Ray.)

Yet because "She's Out of My Life" lacked a dance beat or

even a hint of gospel-based soul singing, black stations mostly wouldn't touch it. As a result, the song stalled at number forty-three on *Billboard*'s black chart, the same week it went Top 10 on the pop Hot 100. Such are the ironies of musical apartheid.

*Off the Wall* isn't a masterpiece. It produced the first number one single of the eighties, but its music could have been made any time in the past three or four years. Nelson George correctly summed it up as a classic example of L.A. studio groove, "its rhythmic but well-rounded texture corresponding to the way cars in that city roll along the freeway or skaters twirl along the palm-lined boardwalks on the beach. *Off the Wall*'s aura is sweet, sunny and bright—and characteristic of so much middle-of-the-road black Seventies pop, offers philosophical bromides about rockin' the night away in place of any real personal vision."

In the end, *Off the Wall*'s emotions were heated, at times overwrought, but there seemed to be nothing concrete spurring them. The fault lay in Jackson and Jones's shared concept of pop music as basically mood music. The result was to update Michael Jackson's public image without redeeming it from its essential triviality. He now had a new persona, but it remained as trivial and juvenile as the old one.

At the 1980 Grammy Awards, Michael fully expected to win for either Album of the Year or Record of the Year, but when the statuettes were handed out, he was given only an award in the token Best R&B Vocal Performance, Male, category. The big awards that closed the nationally televised broadcast went to the Doobie Brothers' "What a Fool Believes" and Billy Joel's *52nd Street*. Michael felt snubbed by his peers. "It bothered me," he later told *Billboard*. "I cried a lot. My family thought I was going crazy because I was weeping so much about it. Quincy said not to worry about it. He said the important thing is knowing that people like the album. That should be my reward."

Yet given Michael's confusion of quality with quantity, how else could he have reacted? After all, *Off the Wall* had far outsold its competitors. *52nd Street*, another CBS album, sold about five million copies worldwide; *Off the Wall* sold that many in the United States alone. Each of the four singles from Michael's album sold more than a million copies. What more did they want?

# T · W · E · L · V · E

Dear Michael,

This afternoon, taking a break from trying to decipher you, I accompanied a friend to a gallery with an exhibit of paintings by Marsden Hartley, whose entire audience—even now, forty-odd years after his death—probably barely equals the number of people who've heard your Steeltown singles. The best pictures, most of them from his later years, had a somber aspect—some were quite religious and all were suffused with a sense of mortality, an acceptance of death that made Hartley's life seem complete.

Would these pictures have met with your approval? I can't say. Your favorite painter is supposed to be Maxfield Parrish, king of *kitsch*, all bright, easy surfaces, as far removed from Hartley's understatement and completely personal vision as is imaginable. Come to think of it, those characteristics of Hartley's work don't have much to do with your style, either. But they manage to create a world, one that you enter with some effort but with a big payoff: understanding a lot more about your own humanity.

Afterwards, we went to a bookshop on Madison Avenue that had given over its front window to a display of a new book about Red Grooms. Grooms was what they call a "major figure" in the pop art movement, and his cartoonish style has frequently been applied to personages from Hollywood and rock &

roll: Jean Harlow, Fats Domino, Chuck Berry. Grooms did the
window display himself, and it created another kind of world,
full of visual puns, comically chaotic samplings of an artist's
studio, a self-mocking cardboard figure of himself. My favorite
was a bookshelf full of crazy volumes which included the tril-
ogy, "Eggs," "Toast" and "Bacon," as an odd homage to
painter Francis Bacon and Grooms's answer to the perennial fan
magazine question: "What do you like to eat for breakfast?" I
think Grooms would like to be interviewed by *Sixteen*—or
maybe *Rolling Stone,* anyway.

What makes Grooms stand out in modern art is his sense of
humor. We walked away from that bookstore feeling that Red
Grooms was one of the last funny guys in the art world—maybe
even the whole world. He's somebody who knows how to do his
job and have a good time to boot. He's also a "serious artist"
who is willing to risk his mystique by doing things like
commercial window displays—a task supposedly reserved for
apprentices and hacks. (Reminds me of your Pepsi commercials.)

Ultimately, of course, Grooms plays with fire. He's toying with
the idea that to be an artist is not only a highly serious thing but
also a kick. He's saying the world and our place in it is somehow
inherently absurd—more than that, ridiculous. Grooms says all of
this without a hint of complaint, but I'm pretty sure he's laughing just to keep from crying, as the blues singers used to say.

It bugs me that I don't really have much idea of how you'd have
responded to Grooms, either. Weeks ago, I accepted that nobody
was going to make much progress figuring you out until you got
a lot closer to figuring yourself out. You can't solve a puzzle
that hasn't found its own solution. But that doesn't make
running into the brick wall of your opacity any more pleasant.

You may say that you know more than an outsider like me
(or anybody else in the everyday world) thinks that you do, that
you just aren't getting it across in your public activities. But I
don't believe it. If you were less confused about things, it
would show. People would be less confused about you—maybe
not about their feelings about you, but at least less mixed up
about who they think you are. Instead, what's most obvious is
the things that are missing. One reason Red Grooms made me
think of you was that his sense of humor is exactly what you

lack. (I know there are jokes in the "Thriller" video—where else?)

Of course, you and Grooms are facing opposite problems. Grooms makes his living off the cachet that high art possesses. While it's impossible to imagine him (unlike Marsden Hartley) doing his work without an audience to show it to, high art isn't supposed to become too popular—if it becomes too widely known, it is labelled cliche. People don't pay big prices for cliches (at least, in theory they don't). So unlike you, Grooms has to find another formula for dealing with his status as a commodity—Biggest is Best won't work. Yet he still needs an audience to laugh at his jokes and get swept up in his fantasies. That's exactly the contradictory situation that Grooms finds so damn funny. I don't mean he thinks it's ironic; that's too arch. He finds this dilemma outright laughable.

Your problem is that you started out as a teen idol and had to fight to be taken seriously. But obtaining that serious attention means being called on your pretensions—also not so good for the bank balance. So you get upset all over again and proclaim that you're just an entertainer, people shouldn't take it so seriously. That's pretty funny to me, but you don't seem to appreciate the joke—in fact, you're pretty damn grim about the whole process of music making, which you define as escapism, fun, a way of having a good time. I guess what I'm really wondering is: *are* you having a good time?

If you are, it's all but impossible to tell. Hidden behind your sunglasses, you almost never smile in public. On stage, you bear down as hard as anyone I've ever seen—if your show is unsatisfying, it's never because you're not trying. Up there, it's easy to believe that "Working Day and Night" is how you feel about life. It's a job. It was the same when the TV news showed you at Madame Tussaud's Wax Museum, weeks after the Victory tour ended. Looking over the likeness of yourself, you gave a quick, dutiful grin for the cameras then immediately went back to pursed lips.

Is this what your obsession with control is ultimately all about? "Fun" (whatever that is—it's an abstraction whose precise meaning isn't very well understood) means letting go, finding a release: giving it up. You can't, not because you don't want to but maybe because you don't know how. All your vocalizing, whoops and gurgles and expostulations don't cut you loose. They rein you in. In your best songs, the tension tightens and tightens, but it's never released. The skin of your songs (their surface) insists that you must and will explode but down in the meat and marrow of them, you're doing your best to deny it. What comes across isn't fun but aching desperation with overtones of fear. If I do this thing, you seem to say, I'll regret missing out on this other one. And if I don't do it, then I'll have missed out on that, too. Every step you take is a self-conscious denial of a stride in the opposite direction. Every offer accepted builds resentment for the better—or even just different—one that might have come along.

When I was a kid and didn't want to go to bed, my parents would say, "What's the matter? Afraid you'll miss something?" Some of your best songs work off that principle: On a record like "Rock with You," what comes through those happy-days lyrics is an unbearable sadness. It's expressed in the way you don't sing "all night," but leave it to the chorus, in the pleading way you phrase the word "rock," as though you weren't asking for sex but for something even more intimate. The ache is nothing big; it's just a tug, a certain drift, but it's what takes such songs out of the ordinary, gives them your signature.

Maybe I'm wrong or just plain crazy. Hardly anyone seems to think of you as a trapped, frightened person. Either you're accepted as a happy-go-lucky dancing boy or else resented for not living up to expectations. I guess that's the source of your lust for "escapism." What you're trying to duck isn't responsibility so much as the moment of choice itself. If you could just cruise along in a childlike dreamworld (no matter how false that dream might be), then you'd somehow be safe from choosing wrong. You would never need to fear passing up the best available offer.

That attitude can only come from a sense that you make every choice alone. If you're wrong, no one will support you. If you're right, it'll just lead to another inscrutable set of alternatives that you'll once more have to wade through all by yourself. There's nothing funny about that, because there's no way to convert decision making into anything enjoyable when that's the only way you know how to choose.

*Off the Wall* came out on September 1, 1979—less than a week after you'd turned twenty-one and were legally liberated from parental authority. You spent that week visiting lawyers, accountants and business managers, looking out for your own interests for the first time. In a way, you were doing what any intelligent, wealthy celebrity does: shopping for the best advice available. But it's hard not to feel that you were also hunting for some support.

I wonder if it wasn't already too late. You had become a star as a child and your guidance was provided by people who saw and imagined less than you did. Your father wanted to get out of Gary, to be comfortable and respected. Motown wanted to make you the flagship of a bubble-gum enterprise. Gamble and Huff hadn't much more interest in what *you* wanted. And you wanted to do so much, it must have been written all over your face. Somehow, though, almost no one could see it.

Well, that's no fun. It sure ain't funny. So, while I still think you could stand to lighten up, I'll just take the opportunity to say, once and for all, that given the cards you were dealt, you played the hand pretty well. Too bad there wasn't another joker in the deck. At the very least, you deserved to enjoy the game.

# T·H·I·R·T·E·E·N

After *Off the Wall*, Michael Jackson finally had most of what he wanted. His solo album firmly established him as an important individual performer. If he wasn't the biggest star in the pop music world, there certainly wasn't anyone bigger. Although he'd lost out in the industry-selected Grammy Awards, he was definitely the people's choice. Wealthy, young, and attractive, he had every reason to be ecstatically happy. But his behavior wasn't that of a happy man.

Michael was a full-grown adult, yet he described himself as protecting his private life "just like a hemophiliac who can't afford to be scratched in any way." He added that his greatest fear was of being misquoted. He seemed to worry excessively about his real self being exposed to the public, as if that would blow the whole thing.

The concept wasn't unreasonable. At twenty-one, he continued to live at home with his parents, younger sisters, and brother. But he also purchased a pair of Los Angeles condominiums as personal retreats. (Their existence didn't become known until a 1982 *Rolling Stone* cover story.) His very existence seemed riddled with contradiction. "I think I'd die on my own," he said. "I'd be so lonely. Even at home, I'm lonely. I sit in my room sometimes and cry. . . . I sometimes walk around the neighborhood at night, just hoping to find someone to talk to. But I just end up coming home." And on the other hand, he also complained that he was "never alone," that he couldn't simply go out walking and sit in a tree without winding up on TV or in the newspapers, that "you'll drive outside and there'll be all these girls standing on the corner and they'll start bursting into screaming and jumping up and down," that finally he couldn't "really go any place at all," because if he showed up at a disco or a nightclub, "it becomes work instead of pleasure. They announce that I'm there over the loudspeakers and they play all my records and I'm signing autographs. So it's not fun." Talk about trapped in a prison of your own devise.

He developed an odd, ritualized life-style, in which he was at once king of all he surveyed and his own most oppressed subject. His parents finally forced him to learn to drive, since living in Los Angeles, you were all but crippled without a car. He did well enough at his lessons, but he had a tendency to daydream, he later confessed to Gerri Hirshey. He hungered for friends, yet admitted that he didn't trust himself around "regular people." "I hate to admit it," he said, "but I feel strange around everyday people. 'Cause my whole life has been onstage. And the impression I get of people is applause, standing ovations and running after you. In a crowd, I'm afraid. Onstage, I feel safe. If I could, I would sleep onstage. I'm serious." He professed to see dancing "as the most wonderful thing of all because people communicated through bodily movement before anything. . . . Dancing is really showing your emotion through bodily movement." Yet he expressed himself thus mostly on Sunday afternoons, when he would lock himself for hours in a room above the Encino garage to boogie until he was dripping and exhausted, drained of emotion without ever communicating what he felt to anyone except the mirrors and mannequins that served as the perfect, passive receivers of his gift. And for all his love of the stage, when he was asked onstage at a Quincy Jones concert at the Rose Bowl, he was terrified. "I was ducking and hiding and hoping he wouldn't see me hiding behind people when he called me on."

Maybe it was nothing more than a game he was playing. Once he got up on the stage with Jones, he said, "I just went crazy. I started climbing up a scaffold, the speakers, the light gear. The audience started getting into it and I started dancing and that's what happens."

His weirdness, if weirdness it was, was self-ordained. He had many women friends, mostly young starlets (Stephanie Mills, Tatum O'Neal, Brooke Shields), yet sex seemed to represent little more than another potential trap. He professed to believe in the God of the Jehovah's Witnesses. He said dancing was God. He took no drugs, but maybe he was on the headiest trip of all: the power and confusion of his own self-image. Yet he denied to Stephen Demorest that he even had an ego. "I mean, everybody has an ego but it's not in thinking I'm great and I'm better than this or that person because of what I do. I feel totally sorry for people who have that feeling." Well, maybe that was a consistent statement: It was self-evident that, from his songs on out, he spent a lot of time feeling totally sorry for himself.

He convinced no one except the most gullible fans of anything. At the height of Michael's fame, four years later, Boy George, the cross-dressing vocalist of Culture Club, pinned him down astutely. "I don't believe he's as shy as he's made out to be," George said. "I believe that's a big myth. . . . He's much more confident than most people give him credit for. I say Michael Jackson lives Michael Jackson because it's all he's got. He channels every bit of his energy into becoming Michael Jackson."

To become the Michael he imagined, rather than the one who slumped panting before the mirror after the Sunday dance marathons, he retooled his body. He became a vegetarian, and then, so determined to change the shape of his body and avoid the family tendency to thickset midsections that he all but stopped eating. "First he found out that eating meat wasn't good for you," Katherine Jackson told Gerri Hirshey. "And now he doesn't like the idea of killing things to eat them. He always says that if he didn't have to eat to stay alive, he wouldn't. My son just has no interest in food."

As Michael slimmed down, he made more radical alterations. He had cosmetic surgery to give himself a thinner, less Negro nose. (He continued to make statements about his pride in black culture, however.) He adopted a strange dress code, focusing on uniforms and insignia (anything from a cop to a doorman), but he made his secretary and family do his shopping, partly because he hated the mob scenes when he shopped himself, partly because he couldn't be bothered with selecting clothes.

He remodeled his public image, too. Discarding his identity
as a child star was risky for a lot of reasons—not least because
adults had duties kids didn't. So Michael talked almost incessantly about his love for children and the need to be childlike.
He hung around with twelve-year-olds like Emmanuel Lewis,
"Webster" of television fame. But as much as he loved children,
he was never interested in procreation—or, for that matter,
sexual recreation either. At least not in public. He acquired an
odd image as a boy-man, but not in the teenage sense. If he was
horny, he kept it well concealed. Yet his other emotions were
worn on the narrow edge of his sleeve, ready to be knocked
loose at a moment's notice. He cried easily, and the rest of the
time, he and his advisers often led you to believe that he was
holding back tears: "He's got a lot of people trying to get to
him and bother him and he has to smile when he wants to cry.
It can be rough sometimes. But that's show biz," said papa Joe,
no pushover.

But even among show folk, Michael seemed a little strange.
Jane Fonda recalled some of the crew of *On Golden Pond*, when
they met Michael once again after working with him three years
earlier on *The Wiz*. "They described Michael as a performer
who, when there was no music and the lights weren't on and
they were sitting around and reading and kind of rehearsing, he
almost faded away, he almost wasn't there. And then the
moment the music would start, the lights would go on and the
costume would come on, this creature would come to life and
just overpower everything. It was the most amazing transformation any of them had ever seen."

Yet Michael maintained that all that he did was spontaneous,
not just spur of the moment but beyond his control. "I never
knew what I was doing in the early days, I just did it," he told
Stephen Demorest. "I never knew how I sang. I didn't really
control it, it just formed itself. . . . My dancing just comes
about spontaneously. Some things I've done for years until
people have marked them as my style, but it's all spontaneous
reactions. People have named certain dances after me, like the
spin I do, but I can't even remember how I started the spin—it
just came about. There's nothing where I get in a room and try
to think hard." But he didn't want to be known as an innocent,
letting it out that his first act on reaching twenty-one was to

hire his own business advisers and that he could recite his
foreign royalty figures down to the last decimal point. (Of
course, he also claimed that talking about material wealth was
"tacky.")

"There is a mystique about Michael that is also a feeling,"
said disc jockey Frankie Crocker, himself mystifying nicely.
"The public doesn't know exactly anything about Michael." Or
as Jay Cocks of *Time* wrote, "A good friend is right when he
suggests that, ultimately, 'Michael's appeal is universal less
because of his music than because of who he is.' Jackson has
been in show business for most of his childhood and all of his
adult life—and there are those who argue persuasively that he
has had no adult life—and, with a few other tricks, he has
mastered the techniques of fusing his life with what is thought
to be his image."

Precisely. Each nuance of admission and denial had been
plotted—or maybe just kept after he stumbled upon it—to
create a picture that kept the world away from his weak point:
his cloudy self-image. Michael Jackson was reclusive for several
reasons: He was shy, overexposure could ruin him, and too
much scrutiny would demolish his carefully sculpted public
front. The truth was that Michael Jackson knew a hell of a lot
about how to prosper in show business but almost nothing
about the real world of adult emotion and activity. "He spends
a lot of time—too much time—by himself," a sympathetic
Diana Ross told Hirshey. "Michael has a lot of people around
him, but he's very afraid."

When he became a legal adult, then, Michael's rebellion was
not to leave home or shack up with a lover; it was to go out and
get into show business for himself, by hiring his own advisers:
business manager Marshall Gelfond and attorney John Branca.
Both were well-known Hollywood figures, Gelfond a veteran,
Branca young but the hot hand among West Coast music-
business attorneys.

"He came to the first meeting with his accountant, just after
the release of *Off the Wall*," said Branca. "He was twenty-one
and wanted to establish independent representation. He seemed
very shy, but also very observant. In the meeting, he was trying
to read and gather every piece of information he could. Behind

his sunglasses, he studied the entire conversation, which was conducted primarily by the accountant.

"Michael had definite objectives. He wanted all his business affairs reviewed, including his publishing and recording deals. And with the success of *Off the Wall*, he wanted a new [renegotiated] contract.

"I soon learned that Michael is the kind of person who always makes his own decisions and he makes them well. The genius in his artistry speaks for itself. His business acumen isn't necessarily as obvious because it is conducted behind closed doors. . . ."

It's easy to dismiss that last paragraph as sheer Hollywood hype. That's *not* all it is; the language is more inaccurate than the idea. Michael was a show-biz savant, someone who probably could not figure out how to get his own shirts to the cleaner's but knew much of what was important in a complicated business negotiation with a major corporation. (Branca renegotiated his contract, prior to the release of *Thriller*, so that it became one of the highest-paying at any major record label, earning slightly more than two dollars a record.)

One suspects another reason for making his business move that summer. Michael was still contracted, along with his brothers, to Weisner/DeMann and Joe Jackson as personal managers. He surely needed counsel of his own, but seeking it outside the family, as it were, once and for all set him apart from the other brothers and his parents. It was also a subtle slap in the face for his father, whose ego was on the line.

"The bottom line here is control," said a family friend, some months after the rift between Michael and his father became public. "Joseph sees himself as the family patriarch and he feels he should have final say and approval over all business matters relating to the Jacksons. Michael is his own man and has proven beyond a doubt that given total control he can produce a superior product."

If Michael already had notions of cutting himself entirely free of his family, it was not yet to be. In fact, he spent all of 1980 and 1981 working with his brothers and father on projects related to the Jacksons, producing two albums and two tours. It was symptomatic of the basic conflict between his solo career and the group's that his brothers had done nothing—no records, no tour or TV shows—in the period between the release of *Off the Wall* and the start of sessions for *Triumph,* the fourth Epic Jacksons album. (Jermaine, of course, had his Motown solo career.)

In order for the Jacksons to have a future, Michael had to put his solo aspirations aside. This meant that whatever songs he wrote, whatever time he had for planning and touring would be drained away into the fiction that the Jacksons were a group, rather than just a vehicle. In making decisions, Michael possessed the same relationship to the group as the other boys: one brother, one vote. Michael could have balked or quit but when it's family doing the bargaining, people are a lot more malleable, even against their best instincts.

Not that Michael was being dragged away from music. His mind was still on movies. After completing *Off the Wall,* and doing a round of interviews immediately after its release, he took some time off. Aside from recording *Triumph,* the only event of note on his 1980 schedule was a month spent in New Hampshire, where his friend Jane Fonda was filming *On Golden Pond,* costarring her father, Henry, and Katharine Hepburn. It was probably the closest Michael ever came to the middle-class institution of summer camp. He spent his visit peppering (not to say pestering) the veteran actors with endless questions about movies, acting, the theater, and related dramatic matters. He became fast friends with both the elder Fonda and Hepburn, a real accomplishment because they were among the most reserved of the old Hollywood movie stars. (Michael was one of the first to call on the family when Henry Fonda died a few months after winning his only Academy Award for his performance in *On Golden Pond.*)

But offers for roles in the movies and plays that continued to come Michael's way weren't acceptable. Michael wasn't especially interested in Broadway; he saw doing a stage play as a challenge but resented the idea that one's best performances could go to waste, lost forever without being preserved in any form. And the movie roles were wrong, either because they stereotyped him as a black entertainer (as with the offer to play Bojangles Robinson) or because they violated his sense of propriety in other ways (as with the offer to play the gay dancer in *A Chorus Line.*)

Under those circumstances, *Triumph* might have been a welcome return to harness, but that's anything but immediately evident from Michael's performances, which are relatively muted, making little use of the "vocabulary of grunts, squeals, hiccups, moans and asides" (to swipe critic Robert Christgau's description) he'd perfected on *Off the Wall*. Neither were Michael's songs—he wrote or cowrote six of eight tracks on *Triumph*—on the same level as those on the solo album, with the single exception of "Heartbreak Hotel," the only song he wrote all by himself.

That's not to say that *Triumph* isn't an excellent record. But it's basically a genre piece, stamped from the mold of early eighties black pop. It makes wise use of the Latin-tinged horn riffs and sophisticated string charts learned from Gamble and Huff, but the production lacks the sheen Quincy Jones provided. A major share of the difference between *Triumph* and *Off the Wall* is due to the rhythm sections: bassist and drummer Louis Johnson and John Robinson on *Off the Wall* and Nathan Watts and Ollie Brown on *Triumph*. The latter are competent where the former played as if committed to jet propulsion.

Another significant difference is the kind of songs that the Jacksons recorded. "The songs I do with the group are different from what I do as a solo artist," Michael had said, as a way of explaining his need to make a solo album in the first place. "On my own album I can do some things I can't do on the Jacksons albums. I can do the ballads I want." This was indeed Michael's forte, but the only ballad on *Triumph* is one of the two songs Michael didn't help write, Randy and Jackie's pedestrian "Walk Right Now." (Significantly, both that track or "Can You Feel It" flopped as singles in mid-1981.)

*Off the Wall* was exceptional because it managed to create a fundamental unity from disparate sources, building an overall musical statement that incorporated even its slightest tracks. On *Triumph*, something was lacking: Jones was part of it, but so was Michael's comparative reluctance to project himself forcefully. It's as if he is holding back, trying not to show his brothers up. As a result, *Triumph*, a pretty good record, just doesn't add up. Its best tracks, the hits "Lovely One" (a bright, jumping dance tune right out of the Gamble and Huff mold) and "Heartbreak Hotel" (the most mature pop track the group ever recorded), are so good they would have fitted well into *Off the Wall* or even *Thriller*. ("Heartbreak Hotel" is almost an outline of the musical and lyrical themes of the latter.) But on *Triumph*, they operate on their own, and they just aren't enough.

Michael did try to turn the album into a "statement," with a note on the back sleeve explaining the peacock sleeve that appeared on the covers of both *Triumph* and *Destiny*. "Through the ages," he wrote, "the peacock has been honored and praised for its attractive, illustrious beauty. In all the bird family, the peacock is the only species that integrates all colors into one, and displays this radiance of fire only when in love. We, like the peacock, try to integrate all races into one, through the love and power of music."

Obviously, such superstitious anthropomorphism—note the assumption that a horny peacock acts like a romantic human— was no substitute for the musical and lyrical unity that *Triumph* needed. But at least Michael was trying.

Although *Triumph* was released a couple of weeks before Christmas 1980, the Jacksons didn't begin the tour in support of it until July 6, 1981, in Memphis, Tennessee. One major reason was presumably Randy Jackson's March 30, 1980, automobile accident, in which he wrapped his Mercedes-Benz around a Los Angeles utility pole. Doctors at first feared Randy would never walk again, but he rehabilitated himself well enough to open each show in medieval armor, leading his brothers to the center of the space-age set designed by Michael.

The 1981 tour was the biggest of the group's career, covering thirty-six cities and grossing more than five and a half million dollars. (The figure would have been higher but Michael insisted upon donating all proceeds from their two Atlanta dates, which amounted to about a quarter of a million bucks, to the city's poor. This was during the midst of the headline-making crisis over the murders of black children there.) The show also incorporated video footage from the album, depicting the Jacksons as enormous unearthly godlings who revived a featureless mass of humans with a golden light radiating from their hands. The imagery harkened back to Michael's album-note claims for the

potential power of their music—and also to the religious symbolism of the Jehovah's Witnesses. (On the other hand, Michael
also incorporated Broadway magician Doug Henning's most
un-Witnesslike sleight of hand into the program.)

Musically, of course, the show was still built around Michael,
although a very different Michael than the pudgy little boy of "I
Want You Back." Now he was a lithe, long-limbed figure who
had mastered the mock-elegant gestures of Diana Ross and the
dervish dance devilry of James Brown, the falsetto glissandos of
Marvin Gaye, and the sheer, sweet crooning of Al Green.
Together with a band booted along by drummer James "Sugarfoot"
Moffet, he created a show so slick it could easily have played
any Vegas main room. It was filled with explosions and rocket-
ing light displays, a solid evening's flash. Its best moments,
nonetheless, were the simplest of all: Michael in a hot-white
spotlight singing ballads like "She's Out of My Life" or twirling
through the fast ones, a marvel of speedy kicks and spins.

Epic eventually eked out a live album, *The Jacksons Live!*,
from this tour. It features an odd, off-mike excerpt from an *Ed
Sullivan Show* film clip, projected above the stage. You can't see
the film on the LP, but it's the sound track that tells the tale:
Michael singing "I Want You Back" at twelve, followed, after
some rote patter, by him singing the same number eleven years
later. His range is lower, but that's far from the only difference.
Michael's phrasing is tighter; he restricts the notes, cramps
them together, and pushes them harder. It's the difference
between a kid who really is just doing what comes naturally and
a singer who has arrived at a mature style capable of accommo-
dating almost anything.

Michael doesn't seem especially engrossed in the old songs
until he gets to "I'll Be There," which concludes with unexpected vocal glossolalia. Then in a twinkling, as he shouts "I
wanna rock!" the song becomes "Rock with You." It's not a
transition; the point is forced. But the grand gesture does drive
home the continuity between Michael's career as a child and his
career as an adult.

Continuity there may have been—*complete* continuity simply
wasn't possible. Michael's needs and ambitions had now outstripped his brothers'. *Newsweek's* Jim Miller described the opening video sequence of that 1981 tour (a sequence supervised and

planned mostly by Michael): "Set to the music of 'Can You Feel It' . . . the tape consists of images inspired by *Close Encounters of the Third Kind* and Busby Berkeley's gilded Depression-era musicals. At one point we see the Jacksons drift to earth, each encased in his own bubble. In another sequence, the Jacksons are portrayed as super-human giants, lift a rainbow, light the heavens and sprinkle stardust on the cities of the earth, causing small children of all colors to glow with gratitude, bathed in rainbow hues, reaching out to touch and hold one another. These images, which betray a naive megalomania, have an undeniable poignancy. Here is a black giant who sacrificed his childhood to become a pop idol, a demigod detached from his fellow men, now sealed in a transparent bubble—a lonely prophet of salvation through the miracle of his own childlike, playful, life-giving music." In its world-encompassing grasp and its very vagueness, this vision—which is certainly Michael's and barely comprehended let alone shared by his brothers—forcibly reminds one of Stevie Wonder, Motown's first great child star, himself given to vagaries on a cosmic scale.

Not surprisingly, Michael said Stevie Wonder is the person who most influenced his music. "I've learned so much from him: sitting in on his sessions and talking to him and listening—he's just phenomenal. . . . You can't explain what Stevie does. The way he creates lyrics and melodies so effortlessly. He hears your voice and even if you're trying to disguise it, he knows you. I'll come in the door and he'll start singing my name and just instantly create a song. It's incredible."

But Wonder's self-expression wasn't born so easily as Michael wanted to believe. Stevie had to wage a long fight, alongside Marvin Gaye among others, to force Motown to let him do his music his way. Anyway, Wonder was a more strong-willed artist than Michael, and one with a wider range of skills, which he had begun developing much earlier in his career. Stevie cowrote many of his best early hits—including "Uptight," the best of all. He was a virtuosic multi-instrumentalist, a prolific collaborator, and, most of all, a battler against all that limited him, from his own lack of sight to Motown's absence of long-range imagination.

Michael was no fighter, and the battle he faced was a lot more difficult. It's one thing to stand up to your record company. It's another to go to the mat against your own family. And he'd seen how Jermaine was cut off—reduced to one sad, uneasy guest appearance on the 1981 tour.

The *Triumph* tour ended in Los Angeles, where Michael did a rare interview with Robert Hilburn of the *Times*. "I love being on stage but I don't like the other things that go with touring," he said. "I didn't even want to do this tour. It was going to be cancelled except that we wanted to do the benefit for the children in Atlanta.

"I think it's important to grow and I've been doing this for so long I sometimes feel like I should be seventy by now. We've been around the world twice, performed before kings and ambassadors. It's time to move on. I still want to make records, but I also want to do films. That's how I want to spend my time the next few years."

What a strange statement from someone who once said, "something is really missing when I'm not on stage. It may sound crazy, but I'm a stage addict. When I'm not on stage for a long time I have fits and I get crazy. I start crying and I act . . . I guess you might say 'weird' and 'freaked out.'

"On stage is the only time I really open up. I say to myself, 'This is it. This is home. This is where I'm supposed to be, where God meant me to be' . . . I eat it up. Performing is better than anything else I can think of!"

Faced with such contradictions, the press and public drew the logical conclusion: The Jacksons must be breaking up. Epic's release of the live album suggested as much—live albums are a typical end-of-the-line move among record companies. The fact that *Jacksons Live!* didn't sell well (it failed to even go gold) further reinforced this suspicion.

Michael denied a split. "My brothers and I get along fine. There's no ego problem with us; each of us knows what the other can do and we think everybody has a role in our act. Right now, we feel the Jacksons are still in evolution. It's just not the right time to make any drastic change. I'll do more films and my own albums but right now the group comes first. . . . Anyway, I don't do very many things until a certain force tells me to do them. The force tells me when and then I make my move."

\*      \*      \*

For the Jackson family, 1982 was tumultuous. Joseph and Katherine were not getting along. By the end of the year, she had filed for divorce. Joe moved out of the Encino house, leaving only Michael, Katherine, Janet, and LaToya living in the huge old place. Michael soon after began to completely remodel it after the fashion of the Tudor homes he had admired on his visits to England. Nelson George notes that the house remained "the center of the Jackson clan [but] Michael's taste and money decided its new shape, representing an unspoken acknowledgement of his special place in the world and his family." Talk about taking over for your father.

Meantime, Michael made preparations to make another solo album. This could not have been especially thrilling news to his brothers. In periods when Michael was working on his own music, they had no income other than whatever back royalties came in and whatever investments they had made. Yet what could they do about it?

Michael may have been prodded by his family, but there were plenty of other provocations to spur him along. Even Quincy Jones felt the pressure created by the mammoth sales success of *Off the Wall*. "During the first record that I produced for Michael," he said, "I saw him looking worried one day and I said: 'Michael it's nothing, don't fret, just keep your mind on making the record!' And we made it, a huge hit in America." But how did you expand from there? In recording industry history, less than a dozen albums had surpassed the sales of *Off the Wall*, and several of them were anthologies. None had been made by a black artist. (*Saturday Night Fever*, the sound track to John Travolta's disco movie, featured black sounds and many black performers, but its main hits were cut by the Australian/English Bee Gees.)

"We didn't have that precedent to follow with *Off the Wall*," Jones told Hirshey, "because nobody ever thought of him having a record that big. . . . Now everybody's an expert at what we're doing. The first time we didn't have anything to live up to. Everybody knew who Michael was but we didn't have that 'Man is it going to be like the last one?' "

It was like the last one in the most uncomfortable way. Michael still wasn't writing very many songs—and one of the best that he did write, "Muscles," he gave to Diana Ross, also producing it. Michael made it his old friend's biggest hit in a couple of years. Between solo albums he also did a few other songs for other artists: Betty Wright's reggae-flavored "She's Older Now," two songs for sister Janet's solo debut ("Young Love" and "Say You Do," the former a hit, the latter a recapitulation of "Don't Stop 'Til You Get Enough"). For himself, however, he'd written only two songs that would eventually find their way onto his second solo album: "Wanna Be Startin' Somethin'," which kicked it off, and "The Girl Is Mine," which he asked Paul McCartney to sing as a duet with him. (To return the favor, Michael did two duets with McCartney, "Say Say Say," another hit, and "The Man.")

It was up to Jones to find more material, but even though he surveyed more than three hundred songs, the going was tough. Although this time he had the full attention of Rod Temperton from the start, and Temperton wound up with three songs on the album, it could hardly be argued that his contributions were as substantial as those on *Off the Wall* (even though Temperton once again provided the title track).

Furthermore, Jones said, there was a "serious deadline" on the record: Epic was desperate to get it out in time for Christmas, which meant a release date no later than early November. "Donna Summer's album took longer than it should have," Jones told *Downbeat*, "so when we got to Michael, we only had three months to do *Thriller*. That's pretty scary after a record that did eight million. On top of this, Steve Spielberg asked us to do *The E.T. Storybook* so we had three months to do *both*. It almost killed us, but we made it. I had two studios going. We just rocked around the clock until we finished." As it was, Jones had to briefly interrupt the summer session to catch Paul McCartney while Paul was in L.A.

Jones and engineer Bruce Swedien developed a complex recording process involving two twenty-four-track tape machines, rather than the usual one. On top of that, they'd assemble the tracks from up to four or five reels of tape—often over a hundred separate tracks. Swedien simplified the process somewhat by working primarily with work tapes and employing a third twenty-four-track during mixing. The process gave glossy sonic results, but it was expensive and extremely time-consuming.

Such details sometimes give the impression that the Jackson albums are more assembled than performed, and that's not fair. Although they are built up from basic rhythm beds, Michael's vocals, around which everything else must whirl, are often done in whole takes. Swedien told Nelson George that there wasn't even one punch-in (a line dropped in during rerecording) on the complex "Billie Jean," the album's most successful song.

Nor was there much question about who was boss. Jones was there to make sure that Michael Jackson expressed his vision, not the other way around. "Michael always knew how he wanted ["Billie Jean"] to sound," said drummer Ndugu Chancler. "I came in and cut a live drum track over the overdub so that at times during the recording there is just one and then the two together." Bassist Louis Johnson concurred, saying that Michael spent considerable time with him to select just the right bass to use on the track. And these things happened at the tail end of a session already overdue.

The first time they thought they were finished, they were wrong. "We cut nine songs, at first," Jones said, "and had it finished and then threw four out to get four more that were *really* strong. That's a nice psychological thing to do, because you're competing with yourself." But they were also battling the clock and some of the heaviest commercial expectations anyone had ever stared down.

In the end, however, it was a good thing that they did go back for more material, because two of those new songs were written by Michael himself and they proved to be the real making of *Thriller*: "Beat It" and "Billie Jean." Interviewed by French journalists Pierre Edelman and Jean Pierre Lentin, Jones explained further. "We had everything in the can for *Thriller* and we were about to leave the studio," he said. "I played the tapes a few more times and I didn't get that feeling. I told Michael that he had to write some stronger material. Everyone thought I was crazy. Over the next few days, he wrote 'Beat It' and 'Billie Jean.'" And according to someone who's heard them, Michael delivered the songs as demos that were completely arranged. Thus, he and Quincy just had to concentrate on getting the sounds right, not start out by looking for what they should be.

And even when "Billie Jean and "Beat It" were recorded and

mixed, they had to go back a third time. "We finished *E.T.* and Michael's record was down to mix and master. We were really tired by then, but you have to keep the enthusiasm up. So we mixed the record and were ready to have it mastered," Jones said.

"We finished about eight A.M. and Michael came by my house and slept on my couch. We had to be back at the studio by noon, and Bruce was going to bring the test pressing, so we could listen to it before it went out. This is *the record,* you know?" Jones said, meaning that the test pressing is the last stage in the process that leads to production, the final opportunity to catch errors and make changes.

"Everybody was nervous to hear what was going to happen. Well, we had been in such a hurry that we had put twenty-five and twenty-seven minutes on a side, and you know that's a no-no, because it takes the sound away [reduces the record's dynamic range]. We'd like eighteen minutes on a side, max.

"That record sounded like shit, man. We knew it wouldn't hold. It was *terrible.* Michael cried. So we decided to hell with the deadline, 'cause they were really on our backs. So we took time off and came back, took one tune a day and brought this baby home. And that's what we did. If that record had gone out, it would have never been *over,* it would have been a *disaster.* I'll never forget that day. It was horrible."

Finally, it really was finished: *Thriller,* the album of the century, was on its way into almost thirty-five million homes around the world. The first single hit the charts on November 6. The album leaped into *Billboard*'s listings in the last issue of 1982, dated December 25. Even a Jehovah's Witness would have to appreciate the metaphors. After all, Michael Jackson was about to convert the world.

# F · O · U · R · T · E · E · N

Dear Michael,

Listening to *Off the Wall* and *Thriller*, it's impossible to feel anything but optimistic about you and your music. The best of the songs there aren't just better than what you've done before—they're the products of a new sensibility, one that actually shows incipient signs of maturity. Hearing "Billie Jean," which is for me the very best thing you've done, makes me think that your future in music is exactly as unlimited as you've claimed.

But when the music stops, I remember. For you, the sales records that *Thriller* set were the essence of unlimited. In that sense, *Thriller* was the future as you conceived it. Now that it's over, there's no guarantee that you're really interested in music anymore because you've reached the only goal you ever set. In order to continue growing as an artist, you'd need to make changes that would be commercially inconvenient and maybe even a little dangerous to your stardom.

"Beat It" and "Billie Jean"—the parts of *Thriller* that matter the most—were instants of freedom in which you broke into a clear open space with unlimited horizons. The mania after the record came out built a wall between you and that space so high, wide, and mighty that there's no hope of ever seeing over or around it. (Since your approach is more that of an elephant than a termite, I don't suppose there's any chance you'll burrow

underneath.) On the other side of that wall, though, the hori-
zon still stretches—you haven't reached it, no matter what you
think. I'm not sure it's a place you can reach; it's only something you move toward (or in this case, away from).

It's tempting to think that the answer to getting you going
again lies in less success—if only *Thriller* had sold, say, a
million copies, some fractional amount of what *Off the Wall*
had, you'd still be struggling to advance. But the idea isn't to
get to be an artist in a garret (or a slum). In a sense, we all start
out that way; it's no big feat to stay unknown or, for that
matter, to retreat back to anonymity when the weight of your
creations becomes too hefty. This is a crazy world, but it's not
so crazy that, once you've succeeded in reaching and moving
millions of people, the proper response is to throw away all the
power and opportunity it gives you just because it's unwieldy.
The idea is to learn how to handle success or to treat it like a
wave and surf along its crest. If you can—if *anyone* can.

In a recent issue of *Playboy*, James Baldwin wrote an article
about "freaks." Mostly, it's about feeling freakish, about a
lifetime spent as a black, gay writer who has been treated as a
freak everywhere he went. Toward the end, he addressed a
paragraph to you. "The Michael Jackson cacophony is fascinating in that it is not about Jackson at all," Baldwin wrote. "I
hope he has the good sense to know it and the good fortune to
snatch his life out of the jaws of a carnivorous success. He will
not swiftly be forgiven for having turned so many tables, for he
damn sure grabbed the brass ring, and the man who broke the
bank at Monte Carlo has nothing on Michael. All that noise is
about America, as the dishonest custodian of black life and
wealth; and blacks, especially males, in America, and the burning buried American guilt; and sex and sexual roles and sexual
panic; money, success and despair. . . ."

Baldwin is talking about a concept of androgyny that tran-
scends mere sexual categorization. For him, it's an attempt to
fit in, despite rules that say that a person who lacks certain
equipment, or bears certain burdens, does not fit. A person who
is black, poor, gay, or who in any other way fails to fulfill the
strict demographic definition of the ideal consumer of corporate
products is now constantly bombarded with messages that say
he has no place in America. One key to your fame is that you fit

the model of the outcast well enough to make other "freaks" identify and want to help you along.

Outcasts are always desperate to get back into the game. Like them, you play by the rules of Big Is Best because you think you've got a shot at winning that game, or at least that you have a relatively equal chance of showing up well in it. In other games (Art Snob, for instance), the deck is stacked against you. This isn't something you feel is true; it's something that *is* true for you or anyone else without wealth, money, and the right connections. Art Snobs easily dismiss winning at Big Is Best because they've got another playing field all to themselves. (The rules require them to ignore the fact that it was purchased by their own—or their ancestors—winnings at Big Is Best, of course.) What you haven't grasped yet, Michael, is your potential to win at an ever bigger game, a game that might wipe out the need to play either one. I don't know what you call that game. Maybe it's name is Art Revolt.

*Thriller* spent thirty-seven weeks at number one on the charts because it was more than a piece of musical entertainment. It was a vehicle. For you, it was a means of escape. For CBS, it was a vehicle for maximum profit. For Art Snobs, it was a vehicle with which to whip the public for its lack of taste and imagination. (The first rule of Art Snobbery is that what's popular loses). For the outcasts, it was a vehicle that made them feel more like they'd been playing in the big game. (For others, it was just a nice toy, but they're not playing any of these games—they're playing dead.)

To all of these groups, *Thriller* mattered way out of proportion to its quality as a piece of music; the best popular music ever made wouldn't necessarily be outfitted to fulfill so many roles. But *Thriller* had the tools so it crossed over: into the mass market and the white rock world, taking you all sorts of places where no one like you had been seen before (at least, not recently enough to be remembered).

While I accept the idea that you programmed *Thriller* to do exactly this job, it seems unlikely to me that you envisioned what the consequences would be. The forces that came surging into your face as a result of *Thriller* fulfilling your ambitions were the one element you couldn't calculate. If you'd bothered to sit down and figure them out, there's a very good chance you'd have scrapped the project.

In the past decade, the dream of all black pop artists has been crossover. This isn't anything new. Black entertainers, like all other black Americans, have been fighting to get out of various ghettos and into wider circulation for decades, if not centuries. What was new was the term: crossover. It implied that there was a boundary that needed to be breached. It also hinted that maybe there was no easy way back once you'd made the move to the other side.

I've never been able to figure out why that word came to symbolize so much. The idea is basic to the record business: You try to take a record and cross it over from the black market, radio, and charts to the pop ones. But (though I'm sure nobody realizes it) "crossover" has gospel roots as surely as rock & roll does. It evokes the whole idea of getting over the River Jordan into the Promised Land. (Gospel singer Sallie Martin even has a song called "Crossing Over.")

In the seventies, that's what the pop charts were for black artists: a Promised Land of opportunity. Again, that's nothing new. What was new were the fifties and sixties, when black performers had something like an equal chance of being heard, when Chuck Berry, Little Richard, Fats Domino, Marvin Gaye, the Supremes, Diana Ross, Dionne Warwick, Sly Stone, and Jimi Hendrix could rip it up right next to the Beatles, Stones, Bob Dylan, and everybody else. People wonder why pop music lost its sense of possibility and enchantment in the seventies. What other goddamn reason do they need? Segregation is precisely what choked off the spirit that lifted sixties music. Once black performers had to ask, beg, twist, and contort to get their fair share of attention, *everything* was distorted and corrupted—including the white rock world.

Well, you can go back and back in American history without encountering a period as open as the sixties were. But to find out the results of a crossover mentality, you don't need to go back much further than the beginnings of black show business— back, again, to the minstrel shows of the nineteenth century.

Most minstrels were white, but there were also black ones, who also wore burnt cork as a way of distancing themselves from the caricatures they had to portray. Both black and white minstrels shared a common vision. It's epitomized in the songs of Stephen Foster, who was to minstrelsy what you are to contemporary pop. "He intensified the emotional impact of many of his love songs by directing them toward dying or dead lovers, which also ensured that the love was free of sexuality," wrote Robert C. Toll in *Blacking Up,* his history of the minstrel era. (That's the same book that describes the primordial moonwalk.) "Foster's songs offered . . . welcome symbols of escape . . . distance in time (childhood, old age, the 'good old days'), distance in space (the South), distance from reality (dreams) and distance from life (death)."

Change a few details and there's *Thriller,* like a white whale off the bow: love free of sexuality, distanced from reality through symbols of escape, childhood, and dreams. There's more to *Thriller* than this, of course, but there's more to Foster's songs, too. Still, Toll accurately describes what makes both your songs and Stephen Foster's work. It's how they got over, to paraphrase Mahalia Jackson.

Toll also says that the vicious parodies of black people in minstrel shows were a means of reinforcing what white people wanted to believe about blacks, whom they divided into two categories: a Northern black who was "lazy, pretentious, frivolous, improvident, irresponsible and immature," and a clownish, docile Southern Negro "who loved to entertain whites." These stereotypes became fixtures in American culture and retain their power today although they're no longer associated with specific regimes. Ugly as it is to say it, your appeal is intimately linked with fulfillment of these stereotypes. (Not yours alone, but yours above all.)

It would be reckless and probably inaccurate to claim that *Thriller* sold mainly to whites. But it obviously sold to enormous numbers of white people, most of whom had almost no experience of the context that bred it: pop music in the segregated black musical environment of the late seventies and early eighties. Most of these white listeners never questioned the assumptions of musical apartheid, any more than they thought about or challenged any of the other racist presumptions of American life—that is, of their own lives.

Why did they find *Thriller* so attractive? I'd say because both you and your album let them see what they expected, a "lazy,

pretentious, frivolous, improvident, irresponsible and immature" black "who loved to entertain whites." Now, Michael, I
know you aren't improvident—you have lots of money. Maybe
you aren't lazy when the chips are down, but intellectually,
you're a sloth. You go ahead and deny meeting the other
standards. There's no way I can.

To me, your real victory with *Thriller* came when you united
an audience of almost unprecedented diversity and forced blacks
and whites, rich and poor, young and old, boys and girls, and
all the rest, to recognize each other for an instant. But maybe
that was just wishful thinking. Maybe *Thriller* just let everyone
go on about their business, reinforcing their opinion of themselves as open and liberal good guys because they'd bought some
black dude's record while walking right by a dozen daily in-
stances of racism that should have touched their lives.

In this sense, if *Thriller* made a difference in history, it was a
negative one. Its contribution was to make the people who
bought it think that everything was all right, when it was
anything but. That may have been the most masterful of all the
illusions you spread, and I'd guess that it's the real reason that
Ronald Reagan wanted you to come to the White House.
Wherever Michael Jackson went in 1983 and 1984, things were
all right. That was the message sent and received, at least until
your tour began. Then the problems you'd been covering up
emerged in a new form and sat atop your shoulders like hobgob-
lins, eating away the spell of "community" that had been
created around you until it was revealed as nothing more than
the shrewdly crafted skeleton of a profit-generating machine. By
playing suburban stadiums for a thirty-dollar ticket price, you
turned your back on the people who most needed you, the ones
to whom you were something more than just another blackface
cartoon character. That made a fraud not only of your battle to
integrate MTV, which can only be seen in retrospect as a battle
for nothing other than increased profitability, and it made a
mockery of your giving away all your money to charity, especially when the charities chosen were mostly irrelevant to the
problems faced by those you shut out: the poor of all colors.

This is why the war fought over the racist programming
policies of MTV was fought almost entirely within the music
industry. Your audience never participated because it didn't

know how and you never tried to integrate it into your fight. MTV's audience, concentrated in the same white suburbs where the stadiums (and cable systems) are concentrated, could have cared less that they were being cheated of one of the hottest guitar solos that Eddie Van Halen laid down because no one ever proposed to them that they, as well as you, were being cheated.

On radio, where MTV's bias was genetically duplicated, the record company again did the fighting, the stations again did the resisting, while the audience sat on the sidelines because you couldn't call them out. Why couldn't you? Because if you had said something indicating that *everybody* had a stake in what happened here, you would have destroyed the message you really wanted to deliver: that the victory of *Thriller* was due to you and only you.

Look, I'm not trying to diminish the importance of what happened around *Thriller*. If anything, I think what happened is more important than you do, and I'm pissed off because the opportunity to do just one little thing—show people the lie on which racism is based—was squandered, thrown away, pissed upon.

Chances are, even if you'd wanted to do it, you could not have crossed an army over into the Promised Land with you. But you could have gotten them to wade in the water, to choose another gospel metaphor.

Well, you were trapped. Your family demanded your presence, and you went along with it. What else could you do? Since you weren't touring for the money and since it was obvious that the Victory tour could do nothing to enhance your prestige, why in the world *did* you go along with it?

Record business shoptalk says that even though you didn't need the money, your family did. But I think your brothers and parents needed more than that. Like everyone else, they wanted to be a part of *Thriller*, but unlike the rest of us, they couldn't even pretend to participate by buying the album and playing the grooves off it, sitting back and digging the videos, or buying a Michael Jackson doll. Your family didn't need *Thriller*. They needed you. So, with misgivings galore, you gave yourself to them and were handed up for public execution by the media.

Except they didn't execute you; they just chopped off the
popularity and left you trapped and stranded, fenced in for
good, as used up as last year's video game. In the age of the
spectacle, you had provided yours, and when it was done, the
heroic Michael Jackson was filed to be forgotten. In the process
of staging all these bogus events, the media has learned how to
throw a great funeral, and it gave you yours on the Victory
tour.

Oh, you'll keep an audience. But it won't be those surburban
girls who swore their undying love as you sang "She's Out of
My Life" under the stars. By the time they're seventeen, they'll
swear they never cared. It certainly won't be the parents and
grandparents who brought them to the shows. They were just
being dutiful, like taking the kids to the see "The Nutcracker
Suite" at Christmas. It won't be the young white professionals
who took in your show the way they bought mesquite chips for
the barbecue that same summer. They're already on to the next
fad. (Ask Prince.)

The tragedy is that the audience you'll keep is exactly the
audience that your tour betrayed, the audience that you never
had the time for, the people that you never made your other
fans pay attention to. They aren't mad at you. Why should
they be? You only treated them the same way that everyone
else does: sucked their pockets dry, and walked away. At
least you gave them something to dance to, so they still
love you.

Michael, you might feel that I'm asking you to bear a
special burden because you're black. In part, I'd say that I'm
not just talking about being black. I'm talking about being
disenfranchised. There happen to be a lot more disenfranchised black people in the world than white ones. But, then
again, why the hell shouldn't you bear a special burden for
your blackness? All black people have to carry extra weight
in America, Michael. To some extent, you've escaped that
weight for most of your life. Now it's fallen in on you all
at once. What you are going to do about it, I don't know.
Maybe you'll just cast it off, like a modern Samson. But
until you actively apply yourself to getting rid of racism's existence in your life and every other life that it touches, you're
wrong about being special. You're just like every other media

hustler who ever came down the pike. Your crossover isn't a metaphor of liberation; it's a double cross and nothing more.

Until you carry that weight, your music can't mature (and neither can your acting or anything else to which you apply your massive talent). That doesn't mean you should go out and write "political music," whatever that might be. It means you have to lead by example, by saying no to creeps who want to squander your authority, even if you happen to be related to them. *Thriller* was a mighty step in the right direction, but the Victory tour took longer strides backward. So who can tell what's next? Here, you really are on your own.

I hope you make it, but, like anyone else who witnessed your passage through the long and sordid summer of 1984, I feel entitled to my doubts.

# F ◆ I ◆ F ◆ T ◆ E ◆ E ◆ N

*Thriller* was supposed to be an "out of the box smash," as they say in the record business. Epic desperately wanted Michael's new album for pre-Christmas release not only because a substantial proportion of the entire year's records are bought between Thanksgiving and the end of the year, but also because 1982 was one of the worst years the record industry had faced since the prerock era. In addition to a worldwide recession, the industry was paying the price for its rampant overexpansion and overproduction in the late seventies. In 1979 and 1980, the bottom had all but dropped out, and by 1982, albums ordinarily expected to sell in the millions were considered big hits if they edged their way past five hundred thousand.

*Off the Wall* was one of the few real hits during the recession, in part due to the increasing tendency of consumers to spend the fewer dollars they had available on known quantities, in part because the dance audience had a functional need for such records. Its seven hits were as much a symptom of the increasing concentration of power—musical, political, economic—in fewer hands as a testimony to the quality of the record itself. Epic was counting on *Thriller* to do something similar, though of course the record company couldn't imagine the degree by which it would surpass its predecessor. (Michael had no such doubts. Weeks before its release, he told both his sister Janet and Gerri Hirshey of *Rolling Stone,* with whom he did his only interview that year, that he expected his *Thriller* album to be the biggest album ever made.) The company was upset when the last-minute mixing and mastering difficulties pushed its release back to mid-December. Ordinarily, no records are released in the last couple of weeks before Christmas. But this one was so important that Epic geared up a crash production schedule to get it into the stores at the earliest possible moment after delivery.

MCA Records faced no such production problems with *The E.T. Storybook*, which featured Michael as narrator and singer of one song, "Someone in the Dark," written by show tune songwriters Alan and Marilyn Bergman. But in order to use Michael on the record, MCA had to arrange a release from CBS. Since the album would consist primarily of the narrative material, this was relatively easily done. CBS made only two stipulations: the *Storybook* could not be issued before Christmas and "Someone in the Dark" was not to be released as a single. Obviously, Michael's home label didn't want this outside project to get in the way of its biggest LP of the year.

Michael was enthralled with Steven Spielberg's film *E.T.: The Extra-Terrestrial*. When he found out that Quincy Jones knew its young director, he insisted upon meeting Spielberg as soon as possible. No wonder: The most powerful children's film in a couple of decades, *E.T.* was the embodiment of Michael's belief in childish innocence, a modern-day *Peter Pan* with live action and superior special effects. Spielberg allowed Michael an audience with the E.T. robot and Michael was overjoyed. "He grabbed me, he put his arms around me," Jackson reported. "He was so real that I was talking to him; I kissed him before I left. . . . The next day, I missed him a lot."

Spielberg was fascinated by Michael, so much like the naifs who populate his films. "If E.T. didn't come to Elliott, he would have come to your house," he told Michael. And Spielberg told the press, "Michael is one of the last living innocents who is in complete control of his life. I've never seen *anybody* like Michael. . . . He's in full control. Sometimes he seems to other people to be sort of wavering on the fringes of twilight, but there is great conscious forethought behind everything he does. He's very smart about his career and the choices he makes. I think he is very definitely a man of two personalities." A rather self-contradictory statement and one which posits as opposites things that aren't—surely Spielberg had been around show biz long enough to know that many people who are very smart about their careers are also "wavering on the fringes of twilight." But his comments struck all the notes Michael longed to hear coming from the biggest (and therefore, in his eyes, best) director in Hollywood. So when Spielberg invited Michael to do a narrative album based on the *E.T.* script, Michael leaped at the chance, predicting it would become "the all-time storybook album."

MCA slipped the record into the shops in mid-November, and CBS reacted furiously. The November 27 issue of *Billboard* contained two items relating to the *Storybook,* a review which wondered "How long can the *E.T.* phenomenon go on?" and a page-one story about a CBS lawsuit to block MCA from selling and distributing the record. MCA, a corporation at least as familiar with such litigation as CBS, fought back on an unexpected front. "If CBS has a case against us, then we have a case against Michael Jackson. Michael Jackson's representatives knew all along we planned to release the record before Christmas," its attorney said.

Epic's first request for a temporary restraining order was turned down, but a later hearing in New York State Supreme Court resulted in MCA being prohibited from further sales of the set. The single was withdrawn. The major effect was to raise the collector's price for *The E.T. Storybook* to about three hundred dollars. (The album was a one-disc box set that also included a poster of Michael with his arm around E.T.'s shoulder.) Michael Jackson was never sued by MCA; in fact, Michael would later hire the president of MCA's record division, Irving Azoff, as an adviser. (The album was finally reissued in mid-1985.)

This teapot tempest would hardly be worth recounting if it weren't such a good example of Michael's obsession with large-scale commercial success and pop sentimentality. But it's also instructive because it points out how vociferously entertainment corporations fight to control their best-selling artifacts: *E.T.* in the case of MCA, Michael Jackson himself for CBS. In a way that it shouldn't, the poster of the two great American cultural icons of the mid-eighties has a kind of equality about it.

*      *      *

Epic executives knew they had a blockbuster on their hands the first time they heard *Thriller*. It picked up where *Off the Wall* left off, adding such excellent touches as Van Halen's heavy-metal guitar solo, the riveting rock groove of "Billie Jean," the Grand Guignol plot of "Thriller," and the duet with McCartney to Michael's already dazzling array of musical and vocal traits. Moreover, the music was perfectly styled to capitalize on the market. "You can dance to it, work out to it, make love to it, sing to it. It's hard to sit still to," said Jane Fonda. As Jay Cocks of *Time* (where Fonda's comments first appeared) remarked, "Since Fonda's litany tidily summarizes the full range of contemporary American leisure activity, it is no wonder that Jackson is in the air everywhere."

But *Thriller* didn't reach such heights of popularity just because it was functional. If that were all there was to it, record companies would regularly issue albums that sell ten million copies or more. In fact, they've managed to come up with only about ten, all released since the release of Carole King's 1971 *Tapestry*. (The Beatles and Elvis Presley never made albums that sold that many copies because the overall record market was substantially smaller in the fifties and sixties.)

The answer to *Thriller*'s overwhelming appeal isn't artistry by itself. Although the album is state-of-the-art black pop, as well engineered as one could ask, and contains three or four genuinely remarkable performances, it has several weak songs. It lacks the ambition of such past breakthroughs as *Sgt. Pepper's Lonely Hearts Club Band, Songs in the Key of Life,* or even *Hotel California* and *Purple Rain*. It doesn't possess the emotional/musical unity of *Who's Next, Blonde on Blonde, There's a Riot Goin' On,* or rock's other benchmark albums. Ultimately, it's what Cocks said it was, "a piece of elegant sportswear: slip right into it, shrug it off."

"Every one of [*Thriller*'s songs] could be faulted for elliptical lines, awkward phrases, even the occasional malapropism," wrote *Newsweek*'s Jim Miller. For Miller, what was transcendent and enduring about the record was "Michael's voice [which] haunts these songs, gives them heart." But it's also true that what made *Thriller* attractive to most listeners was exactly its "shrug it off" quality, it's heartlessness. The great pop records—singles as well as albums—won't let you avoid their core. They nag at you, stay in the back of your mind, prey on idle moments, and soon occupy your full attention, whether you want them to or not.

As a whole, *Thriller* doesn't have that much power—but two of its songs do: "Beat It" and "Billie Jean." Cocks compared *Thriller* unfavorably to Grandmaster Melle Mel's "White Lines (Don't Don't Do It)," but that song would have been literally unthinkable without the expanded vocabulary black pop gained from "Beat It": its sizzling snare and crunching guitar, its background voice introjections, the overall savagery of its attack, its breakdown of bass and voice that erupts into Edward Van Halen's magnificent guitar solo, which careens on the verge of chaos. The guitar is a noisy jumble that lives up to the boldest declaration of the lyrics: "No one wants to be defeated."

"Billie Jean" is another thing altogether. "Beat It" is a brilliantly skillful piece of music, but that's about all. It took a video to really explore its potential. "Billie Jean" is the record that sums up all of Michael Jackson's hopes and fears and drives them home like a jackhammer, creating a musical atmosphere and a story that lives up to his terror and desire. Its introduction alone is unforgettable: a huge disco bass drum and a pulsating bass throbbing for several bars alone before strings zing in like a knife to the heart. Michael's vocal quivers and shakes; he's singing so hard he can hardly spit out the long quasi-vernacular lines.

"Billie Jean" is one long ellipsis—the best part of this story of a false accusation of paternity is what Michael can't bring himself to sing. It's the vocal that fills in the blanks, stamping them with an overdose of paranoia that sits right on the edge of redefining "freak out." This is a record where it seems as though the singer could at any second fly off the handle and start doing almost anything: pounding the walls, banging his head on the floor, sobbing, laughing hysterically, or simply spending the rest of his life cringing in a corner of the vocal booth, unable to utter another note or syllable.

"Billie Jean" tries to deny everything, but in the end, the music admits everything. He didn't do it—but he wanted to. The singer can't separate himself from his lust, the trap he's sure will finish him. He battles back ("no one wants to be defeated") and in the end, he's left exhausted, arguing it out with himself, while the music surges around him like a bad conscience: a nagging guitar, menacing strings, muttering background voices, the pounding insistence of the bass and drums.

Out of paranoia, misogyny, and erotic repression—the links to "Heartbreak Hotel" are obvious—Michael Jackson summoned forth an undeniably shattering record. Together with "Beat It," "Billie Jean" created an aura around *Thriller,* obscuring its defects (Temperton's filler, the gimmicky instrumental accoutrements) long enough to make people sweat to get hold of it. And while the album as a whole is probably too flawed to endure, "Beat It" and "Billie Jean" will unquestionably be heard as long as rock music is played.

In terms of *Thriller's* appeal, what mattered was the illusion of balance its great songs let it create. While it's hard to imagine anyone shrugging off the great stuff, those who wanted nothing more than a comfortable fit could find their moments of blank pleasure within other tracks. And those who needed something more tailored always had "Billie Jean" and "Beat It" to help them ignore the excesses of "Thriller" and the banalities of "The Lady in My Life." The musical appeal of *Thriller* isn't quite that schematic, of course ("Human Nature" is a ballad for ballad lovers; "Wanna Be Startin' Somethin' " compels dancing), but its essence is in that outline.

"Beat It" and "Billie Jean" created much more of an aura around Michael Jackson than his simpy duet with McCartney ever did. They gave *Thriller* an inherent appeal to the white rock fans whose attention was held by the AOR (album-oriented radio) stations that didn't play any black artists. (Those AOR stations played plenty of black music, but it was all performed by whites and mostly wasn't the latest style.) Van Halen's guitar solo was one key to capturing these listeners, but the mystique created by "Billie Jean" was equally important. It lent Michael some of the intellectual pretensions normally associated with the AOR pop stars, British and American.

Michael already appealed to several diverse sectors of the record market: blacks, dancers, preteens (he presented the ideal teen idol image even now, because he still relentlessly abnegated his sexuality), middle-of-the-road adults who liked soft, romantic crooning. "Billie Jean" and "Beat It" made it a grand slam—*if* Epic could find a way to break the AOR color line. Epic had every incentive to do it, too, because that AOR audience bought albums in numbers way out of proportion to its actual size.

Epic needed a wedge. In the past, standard methods of breaking a rock act included touring and the press. But Michael didn't have a band (to be precise, he had a band he wasn't interested in performing with) and he didn't do interviews. (If he had done them, his airhead remarks might have stripped him of his mystique anyway.)

There was a new route: video. Because television was one of the most important means of exposure for popular music in many countries, pop artists had for many years been making film clips for broadcast overseas. It was cheaper and more productive than actually touring abroad. The advent of cable television in the United States left plenty of unused channel space, and Warner Communications, the second-largest record marketer in the country, was also a major operator in cable. The company (through a joint venture with American Express) formed an all-music cable channel: MTV. It went on the air in May 1982, with a clip of the Buggles' "Video Killed the Radio Star." Within six months, it proved itself the most effective new medium for exposing hit records since the invention of the disc jockey radio show.

The problem was that MTV was programmed with an AOR radio mentality. It had broadcast the Tina Turner "Ball of Confusion" video and it had one black "veejay," but that was about the limit of its exposure of blacks. In theory, the problem was demographic. Like the rest of cable, MTV's ambition was to play to an affluent young audience and most blacks aren't affluent. (Neither are their neighborhoods wired for cable.) Like radio programmers, the MTV honchos also had a basic preconception about the racial intolerance of their audience, and a profound misconception of music history. "Black and white music have always been separate," MTV's president, Robert Pittman, told *The New York Times Sunday Magazine*.

Epic knew that MTV exposure could sell records in quantity— its sister label, Columbia, found its latest Eddie Money album, a dog at radio, selling large numbers of albums only in those markets where MTV was available. MTV airplay was now considered a significant vehicle for initiating a new act into the marketplace. As Al Teller, who ran the Columbia label, put it: "The idea in the seventies was to get the act on the road, touring from city to city. But even under the best of circumstances, the number of people that would be reached was a fraction of what you can reach through MTV in a shorter period of time." But a *black* act? Michael Jackson? MTV's image shapers would have a fit.

Epic was reluctant to do anything that would jeopardize its good standing at MTV. Fighting that kind of battle for one artist risked ruining the company's entire future relationship with the channel. On the other hand, Epic had some leverage of its own. As part of CBS, it was responsible for a huge load of MTV's programming, programming that it doled out for free. MTV didn't pay for its clips (aside from fees to the song publishers through ASCAP and BMI); they were handed out in the same way that radio stations were given promotional albums.

According to reports in *Billboard* and rumors rampant throughout the record industry in early 1983, when Michael and English commercials director Steve Baron created a sixty-thousand-dollar "Billie Jean" video for MTV airplay in early 1983, the channel refused to play it. The reports also claimed that CBS Records president Walter Yetnikoff, under heavy pressure from Jackson and his managers, went to MTV and threatened to pull every other CBS clip off the air if "Billie Jean" didn't get added to the station's playlist. Although both Pittman and Yetnikoff deny these stories, there must have been some reason MTV finally succumbed. In March, "Billie Jean" was added to MTV's "heavy rotation" playlist.

However it happened, it was Michael Jackson who did MTV a favor, not the other way around. "Billie Jean" was by far the finest clip that MTV had yet aired, submersing the song in an atmosphere of surveillance, escape, and magic. Beautifully photographed, it was also perfectly paced, surprisingly rare among music videos, and narratively coherent, more uncommon among both videos and Michael Jackson creations than it ought to be. The new story line devised kept the video from directly competing with the record, which would probably have been disastrous, while adding a couple of new twists to Michael's image.

Tom Carson of the *Village Voice* described the video best: "On a rainy, empty stylized city street, a private eye tails a figure, whose otherworldly aura is signaled by a human light-show: everything he touches briefly glows an eerie, lovely white. When the detective comes upon Jackson in front of a store every camera in the window goes off, but their pictures only show the private eye reaching for empty air. Finally, we see the reason for the pursuit: Jackson climbs a rickety set of stairs outside a hotel and comes to a room where he looks down on a woman asleep in the bed. He climbs in beside her but when the detective outside tries to photograph them, the sheet glows and gently collapses where Jackson was lying and policemen come to take his bewildered tormentor away. As they leave the street, a set of flagstones on the sidewalk gleams in rapid sequence: Jackson, invisibly taking his leave."

Michael's image was shifted in several important ways by the "Billie Jean" video. It presented him, for the first time, as a creature with personal magic—in no way are his powers ascribed to an outside force, as the roughly similar video created for the 1981 tour implied. He had cast himself as his own E.T., a benign, enigmatically endowed alien with a sense of fun and, by implication, some vague mission that other powers wanted to stop.

Furthermore, Michael had placed himself in the forefront of pop music's video revolution. "Billie Jean" raised the stakes for everybody. Rock stars who had previously not taken very seriously what was, until now, just a promotional device were so impressed by Jackson's work that they were spurred to additional exertions on their own clips. Record companies, watching *Thriller*'s sales spurt as Michael's music reached new audiences (and touched old fans in new ways), opened their purses wider for video production and pushed harder to get on MTV. "Billie Jean" didn't spawn the video revolution, but along with "Beat It," it vastly broadened the medium's sense of possibility.

The chief beneficiary was MTV, which continued to get its clips for free for the next year or so. (It now pays a nominal fee for clip usage, in return for which it receives "exclusive" rights to broadcast specific videos for limited periods.) "Billie Jean" excited a new range of listeners, since Michael was perfect for the biggest consumers of the channel, the teenagers who watched it for hours while doing homework and yakking on the phone, and it increased the quality of the clips the channel showed. MTV also continued severely limiting the number of videos by black artists that it aired, though after Michael got his foot in the door, about 10 percent of the clips the channel aired were by black artists. (Those clips were shown infrequently and often in the dead of night, of course.)

So everyone was really charged up for the second *Thriller* video. Michael, as always, felt that he had to top himself. He chose Bob Giraldi, an American director of TV commercials, to direct this time. And he more than doubled the budget (he paid for the videos himself and controlled all rights) to about $150,000.

Giraldi was a well-known commercials director; he directed the memorable series of Miller Lite beer ads, which featured old sports stars in odd and witty situations. He told Alan Hecht that he'd wanted to do "Billie Jean," but Baron was hired. "I was in Santo Domingo with my family, Antony Payne [his producer] was in New York, Michael was in California and we kept trying to call each other. Did you ever try to call anybody in Santo Domingo? One day my wife picked up the phone and she hears, 'Hello is Bob there?' It was Michael Jackson.

"Anyway, we talked and he told me it was a go. He said the song to him was nothing more than turning the other cheek. Michael Jackson's never been in a gang war; he's probably never been out of that house. I think the world knows he's been watched and protected all his life. He just said, 'Let's do something street.' "

Giraldi told *Cash Box,* another music-industry trade paper, that he'd initially decided to stay out of the music video field because the profit margin was too small. "But when the first one, lo and behold, became Michael Jackson, I realized, 'Well, I'm not gonna give that to anyone else.' "

Giraldi was quite adamant, however, that he was in it for more than the money. "I think violence stinks. The whole beauty of 'Beat It' is how it shows that the macho trip is a joke. . . . Obviously, if anybody ever analyzes [the video] properly, they will see that it's anti-violence, not pro-violence. And Michael dug it. He said to me, 'Okay, this is my anti-violence statement through music; this is your anti-macho vision as a director. Peace through dance.' "

But Giraldi was also eager to do a black video because he liked black music so much. He later worked with Diana Ross and Lionel Richie, and with the former's "Pieces of Ice" found out the hard way how little MTV's programming policies had changed. "In retrospect, MTV probably didn't play 'Pieces of Ice' because the track wasn't very good," he said. "However, you cannot tell me that 'Pieces of Ice' wasn't as good as sixty per cent of the stuff they play. So why wouldn't they play it? Because saying it wasn't good enough is an excuse for MTV to do what rock radio stations do. I call it racist and it may be that they don't agree with crossover and they'll only play Michael Jackson because you have to play Michael, since his stuff is the most popular in the world. . . . Now, I think they get off on it; they capitalize on the press on it. I think they love that controversy; it's what sets them apart."

MTV did play "Beat It," though, and the clip that emerged from the Jackson/Giraldi collaboration was as much a statement against racism as against violence. Heavily influenced by *West Side Story* and Walter Hill's *The Warriors*, the clip begins with two gang members leaving a grimy diner. As the song comes in, other hoods leave from sewers, doorways, and pool halls. Clearly, they're getting ready for a major rumble.

Back in his lonely room, Michael lies on his bed, singing the song. He rises, puts on a red leather jacket with elaborate, winglike shoulder pieces, and gracefully leaps into the hallway. He dances his way through the diner to the pool hall, then to the warehouse where the gangs have gathered. One gang is all white. The other is black. The leaders dance closer and closer together, glaring, facing down for some serious hurting.

Michael bursts into the room just as "Beat It" reaches it climax. He is wearing his spangled glove. With it, he seizes each gang leader by a fist. Raising the white hand and the black one together, he cools the war and sets everyone else to dancing almost as slickly as himself.

"Beat It" is seamlessly choreographed—the gang members glide, even though many of the extras were chosen from real-life street gangs in Los Angeles. But there is no mistaking the power and symbolism of the shot in which Michael, in one simple gesture, unites the races. Although there is a vague implication of superhero powers, they're presented here as less mystical, more down-to-earth, emerging more from common sense and intellectual understanding than cosmic consciousness. Michael himself, furthermore, is shown conquering his fear, realizing that he can't keep his distance from the fight in the street but has to try actively to end it. In the end, you're left feeling that his gesture worked because he was the baddest dancer in town and that, at least in this video's universe, that's what counts.

(In the real world, naturally, it wasn't so simple to bring diverse gang members together on one set. The L.A. police department helped producer Payne round up the gangs, but told him they thought it was a bad idea. Payne and manager Ron Weisner both were concerned that things could get of hand. Eventually, Payne said, "there was a sort of tit for tat, the understanding that everyone was doing their own thing." The shoot took place in East Los Angeles, the toughest part of town, and it was completed without a hitch.)

Showing such a video on a segregated cable channel had an explosive effect. Michael might have seemed exotic in any context, but in this all-white environment, he was practically coming in from another planet. Whether or not the video effectively communicated its message against racism and pointless violence (maybe not, since it was attacked by professional "antiviolence" do-gooders), it did convincingly communicate the message that Michael Jackson was someone special.

That impression had already been firmly implanted in the minds of the forty-seven million people who watched NBC-TV's *Motown 25* special on May 16. (It was taped on April 9.) Subtitled "Yesterday, Today and Forever," the show brought together all the label's old heroes: Marvin Gaye, Diana Ross (both had finally left Motown), the Four Tops (who'd just returned), the Temptations, the Supremes, and the Jackson 5, along with several of its current ones: Smokey Robinson, Lionel Richie, DeBarge. The brevity of the latter list is symptomatic of the company's dwindling fortunes. The production mill had rusted away, and now there were just random hits (sometimes as massive as Lionel Richie's, more often less so) and more misses than ever. But on this one night, Motown was again the kingdom of popular music glory.

*Motown 25*'s unquestioned highlight was the reunion of the

Jackson 5. Michael, wearing a stage tux and derby, raced with his brothers through a medley of their early hits, then snapped into dancing form as "Billie Jean" began. He whipped himself through a rapid-fire set of moves, then skated into the moonwalk, devastating the live audience as much as the viewers at home. *Motown 25* was the most widely seen event in which Michael had ever participated (the ratings compare with the Super Bowl's), and he had not only been the show's main attraction, he'd stolen it from all his old heroes and competitors. (He had an advantage, since "Billie Jean" was the only non-Motown number performed.) The turn earned Michael an Emmy nomination and, more significantly, the fascinated attention of millions of new fans.

Sales of *Thriller* took off for parts previously unknown. At one point, the album was selling in a day what the ordinary number one LP in the country sells in a week. It passed ten million units without breathing hard. And there was lots more to come.

"Billie Jean" was number one for seven weeks. "Beat It" topped the charts for three. Both were still on the charts when Epic issued the third single from the album on May 28. The choice was *Thriller*'s final Michael original, "Wanna Be Startin' Somethin'." It also headed for the Top 10, though not quite as swiftly or as strongly (it peaked at number five). Album sales continued to boom.

Behind the scenes, things weren't running nearly so smoothly. The comanagement agreement with Weisner/DeMann expired in March. Neither they nor Joe Jackson wanted to continue the partnership, though both hoped to remain Michael's representative. "Everything creative was handled through [our] office, even though it was listed as a comanagement group," Weisner later asserted. "Joe represented the group but our company handled marketing, promotion, material and whatever." Joe, naturally, didn't see it that way. He claimed that Weisner/DeMann had only been hired in the first place "because there was a time when I felt I needed white help in dealing with the corporate structure at CBS and thought they'd be able to help. But they never gave me the respect you expect from a business partner."

The issue wasn't only power. There was a huge sum of money involved. A typical management contract calls for the manager to be paid about 15 percent of the artist's total income. If Michael really was getting a royalty of two dollars per album, as attorney Branca claimed, then *Thriller,* which had now sold about ten million copies and looked good for at least another two or three more, was already worth three million dollars in management commissions alone. (Michael probably paid a business manager about five percent and taxes and other fees on top of that.) Both Joe Jackson and Weisner and DeMann wanted to keep their slice.

In late June, the story of their acrimonious split leaked to *Billboard,* which contacted Joe Jackson, who responded furiously. "With regard to Weisner/DeMann Entertainment," the magazine wrote in the June 25 issue which also announced that *Thriller's* sales had passed ten million, "Joe Jackson was quoted as saying, 'They have been put on notice and it will not be renewed. As far as I'm concerned it's over. They don't have a contract and my boys are not re-signing with them. There are a lot of leeches trying to break up the group. A lot of people are whispering in Michael's ear but they know who they are. They're only in it for the money. I was there before it started and I'll be there after it ends.' " It was in this article that Joe made his accusation that Weisner/DeMann was only hired in order to have a white face representing his boys at CBS.

Weisner responded in more measured terms, though that may only have been a matter of keeping his professional cool. "There's no great love between us and it's no secret. I haven't talked to the man in six months. But we have no problem with Michael or the Jacksons. The problem seems to be with their father more than with anybody else. We're the only ones who deal with the record company. Joe doesn't talk to anybody up there. He doesn't have any relationship and from what I gather, he doesn't want to."

His partner, Freddy DeMann, was more blunt. "He hasn't been involved in any of the major issues for the past five years. We don't have a good relationship with him but I don't think he enjoys a good relationship with anyone whose skin is not black." DeMann also claimed that his company was putting together "several deals on Michael's behalf and at his request."

(It's not unusual for managers to work without a contract while another is being renegotiated.) "He has specifically instructed us to pursue record and film opportunities for him and we will be involved in the next Jacksons' album and the Jacksons tour."

Michael was properly horrified, not only that his dirty laundry was being publicly aired (by this time, any trade paper story about him was sure to hit the wire services), but by what he perceived as his father's racist remarks. He issued a written statement to *Billboard*. "I don't know what would make him say something like that. To hear him talk like that turns my stomach. I don't know where he gets that from. I happen to be color-blind. I don't hire color; I hire competence. The individual can be of any race or creed as long as I get the best. I am president of my organization and I have the final word on every decision. Racism is not my motto. One day I strongly expect every color to live as one family."

As usual with Michael's public comments, this press release had several subtexts. On the one hand, it served to reaffirm the commitment to antiracism expressed in the "Beat It" video. Its last sentence also reflected his adherence to Jehovah's Witness beliefs. Most interestingly, it seemed to constitute a final breach in his relationship with his father. (His parents were still separated, which made breaking the knot much simpler.) It also made a very pointed statement that Michael was in charge of his career and that people acting as his agents were doing his bidding, not their own.

A week later, Weisner/DeMann took out a full-page ad in *Billboard*, expressing their thanks to Epic for the years they'd spent with Michael and the Jacksons. Joe Jackson made no further comments about Michael's management choices.

It was left to Tito to defend his dad. "Everything they're saying about him is totally out of proportion," he told Gary Graff of the Detroit *Free Press* in 1984. "He's the fall guy.

"My father was never fired. He had a contract and his contract was up. The thing that the [media] don't know is our previous managers which were in partnership with our dad, their contract was up and they were released as well. But they were released because they were sorta trying to separate the family, because they were going to take—you don't have to guess—a certain member and just go with him.

"Sometimes people let greed get in their way. And like I say, people don't realize that we're family first and musicians second." You had to wonder if Michael still felt that way.

*Thriller* had revived the moribund pop music industry. *Cash Box* called its maker "the savior of the record business." On July 24, the Los Angeles *Times* wrote, "CBS has rebounded in 1983. The first quarter profit increase of one hundred one per cent was the best January-to-March performance in the unit's history. The gain was sparked by such artists as Michael Jackson whose *Thriller* album has produced four hit singles and sold more than eight million copies—best since the industry's glory days of 1978."

The *Times* had underestimated the story by half. "Human Nature," the fifth single from *Thriller*, had been released the week before, and this time nothing could hold the ballad back. It hit the charts running and wended its way to number seven. Sales of *Thriller* kept pace. At the end of September, CBS announced that *Thriller* had sold more than fourteen million copies worldwide, plus another twelve million copies of the singles derived from it. (Over eight million albums and five million singles had been sold in America alone.) The record reached platinum level in Canada, England, Holland, Australia and New Zealand, Japan, Germany, France, Sweden, Belgium, Spain, Switzerland, South Africa, Greece, Denmark, Italy, Israel, and Norway. It was the first album in history to be simultaneously number one on the album and single charts in both the U.S. and U.K. And Christmas was coming around again.

Pundits were going dizzy at their typewriters trying to explain the phenomenon—or explain it away. Philosopher Marshall Berman said in the *New York Times* that Michael was the "Al Jolson of the Eighties. . . . Like Al Jolson, he's bringing black music to a white audience. And like Jolson, he shows that you can come out of the ghetto and if you have the energy, you can do anything. It's the American dream." Said Charlie Kendall, program director of New York's WNEW-FM, exactly the sort of AOR radio station that never played black artists but did program Jackson: "Michael Jackson is mass culture, not pop culture—he appeals to everybody. No one can deny that he's got a tremendous voice and plenty of style and that he can dance like a demon. He appeals to all ages and he appeals to every kind of pop listener. This kind of performer comes once in a generation."

On October 8, "P.Y.T. (Pretty Young Thing)," the song that Jones and Luther Ingram had written for Michael, hit the charts. It didn't do quite as well as the others, only reaching number ten, but album sales held steady and *Thriller* stayed number one. At Halloween, the costume of choice for preteens was a Michael Jackson look: white shirt, tie, one white glove, black loafers, white socks, high-water black slacks with pipe-stem legs. Michaelmania was everywhere.

Michael announced his Christmas present: He was making a special video of the song "Thriller." It would be about fifteen minutes long and he would work with John Landis, who had directed *An American Werewolf in London,* whose special effects Michael had admired. The "Thriller" video would cost more than one million dollars, have a special theatrical premiere in Los Angeles before the end of the year in order to qualify as an Oscar nominee, and be released as a home videocassette.

Although it wasn't yet obvious to the public (since nothing had come along to replace it), *Thriller* was petering out. Its sales were now nearing an incredible twenty million copies, surpassing *Saturday Night Fever* (whatever was third in overall sales was way back). Its five Top 10 singles broke a record for the most such hits from one album; "P.Y.T." would be another notch in the gun. Although Walter Yetnikoff said that he believed that the more than fifteen million copies sold in the U.S. were just the beginning, the fact was that the album had just about saturated the marketplace. (Albums are generally bought once per household; there are around eighty million homes in the United States. Reaching one-quarter of them was miraculous.) But that was just how it seemed to reasonable people. It turned out that Yetnikoff and Jackson were right. *Thriller* lived.

When John Landis was chosen to direct "Thriller" Michael had seen only one of his movies. It's hard to imagine that Michael would have felt so comfortable with Landis if he'd seen *Animal House* or *The Blues Brothers*, in which all the black characters are treated as demeaning cartoons. And if

Jackson was counting on Landis to get him an Oscar, he'd also chosen poorly. Landis was on the verge of an indictment for criminal negligence, as the result of the helicopter crash on the set of his episode of *Twilight Zone: The Movie,* which resulted in the death of actor Vic Morrow and two Vietnamese children. Whatever the sentiments in Hollywood regarding Landis's culpability, the motion picture academy doesn't give awards to people in that kind of trouble.

What Michael really wanted was Rick Baker and EFX, Inc., who did the makeup and special werewolf transformations for both *American Werewolf* and the "Thriller" video. The makeup effects in *American Werewolf* were spectacular, the main characters changing into a ghoul and a werewolf with excruciating detail, gory precision, and hideous sound effects. Michael wanted to be put through the same changes for his "Thriller" video. Since the process was expensive, he had to concoct a more elaborate video scenario, which he did by extending the story line. The result once more expanded the possibilities of music video.

As "Thriller" begins, a car with two high school kids pulls into a wooded lane. It's night; the time is probably the fifties. Of course they're out of gas and will have to walk to a service station. As Michael and the girl (former Playboy Playmate of the Month Ola Ray—Landis wasn't Jackson's only anomalous associate on this project) walk along, he confesses his affection and asks Ola to "be my girl." She accepts; he hands her his ring.

"I have somethin' I wanna tell ya," he says.

"Yes, Michael."

"I'm not like other guys," he says. She doesn't really comprehend until the cloud that has been obscuring the moon moves away. The moon is full. We see Michael begining his gruesome transformation into a werewolf. With the last erg of his humanity, he screeches, "Go away!" Ola runs.

It takes the next thirty seconds for Michael's face to become a werewolf's. His jaws and ears are extended, with painful crunching sound effects and gestures of fascinated agony. Whiskers sprout from his cheeks; his hands become claws. His skin goes from brown to black. Then he begins to chase Ola, finally leering over her, ready to pounce and. . . .

Cut to a movie theater, where Michael and Ola are watching these events in the present. He happily chews popcorn, but she is frightened out of her wits and rushes into the street. Michael reluctantly follows, and begins taunting Ola for her fears. "Thriller" begins.

They dance along a dark, deserted avenue, Michael clowning and dancing zombie moves, until at last they pass a graveyard. As Vincent Price intones his recitative, ghouls, skeletons, and viscid corpses arise from their tombs and begin to stalk the couple, finally encircling them.

Ola and Michael huddle back to back in terror. They're separated for just a moment and when she turns around, he's become the leader of the zombie pack. Michael now leads the ghouls through a series of posed dance steps during the song's long instrumental break, then snaps back into the "real" him to sing the chorus.

Ola breaks and runs into a haunted house, where the ghouls mount an assault. Just as Michael, back in his zombie guise, reaches out to grab her, she awakes. The "real" Michael laughingly tells her that it's time to go home. As they walk away, Ola shivering with relief, Michael turns and looks straight into the camera. Like an evil cat, he grins as his eyes roll back in his head and become yellow and slitted.

Premiered on MTV on December 2, the fourteen-minute "Thriller" clip was an immediate sensation. When the videocassette, fleshed out to an hour with backstage footage, was released a few days later as *The Making of Michael Jackson's "Thriller,"* it became an immediate smash, selling 350,000 copies at $29.95, a gross of over a million dollars.

More stunningly, the video (aired incessantly by MTV and soon after released as well to the networks TV) revived *Thriller* album sales. The record eventually sold another ten million copies, mostly in the United States, and the song was released as a single, becoming the album's seventh Top 10 hit. If the media had been interested in Michael Jackson before, now they were obsessed. Not a day went by without some new analysis of Michaelmania appearing in a prestigious journal. Articles on the nature of adolescent idol worship appeared in quantities not seen since Beatlemania twenty years before.

The same old battles still raged. A high school in New Jersey barred its students from dressing like Michael. Preacher/agitators like Louis Farrakhan and Jerry Falwell condemned him as a sissy. The Soviet Union weighed in with a denunciation, as did journals both liberal (the *New Republic*) and conservative (the *Wall Street Journal*).

Only a few pop singers had ever found such grandiose glory. No one since Elvis Presley had come close to uniting the forcibly diverged strands of American music, topping the black-oriented charts at the same time as the pop lists. No one since the Beatles had become such a (seemingly) sudden and over-whelming popular success. Except for Muhammad Ali, no black American entertainer had ever found such enormous worldwide fame.

The adulation was not unanimous. In the *New Republic*, the columnist TRB wrote sneeringly of Michael's supposed illiter-acy, as though any educational deficiencies he might have possessed were his own damn fault. The preachers hated him for what was taken to be his "androgyny," though Farrakhan ex-pressed their problem more clearly when he called him "sissi-fied." Like Elvis, Michael was in trouble for doing what's not to be done: exposing the power potential of popular culture, en-gaging in race mingling, acting "too sexy."

When he was a phenomenon solely within the world of music, Michael Jackson had enjoyed nearly universal acclaim. There may have been doubters, but there were no naysayers. Bursting past the normal bounds of pop discourse into the mainstream of American events, Michael became not just a hero but a controversy. Even within the world of music, opinion began to splinter. A Michael Jackson backlash was the next item on the agenda. Just as the press had boosted *Thriller*, it now concentrated upon breaking Michael, cutting him down to size.

But not before he reaped his rewards. On January 3 he was nominated for ten American Music Awards; a week later, the Grammys put him up for eight. When the AMAs were pre-sented on January 16, Michael took home all ten awards, plus a special "Music Award of Honor." Quincy Jones was quoted as saying ". . . we made history together."

On February 7, CBS Records threw a huge party for Michael, renting the vaulted lobby of the American Museum of Natural

History in New York City for the occasion. The black-tie affair was reportedly the most sought-after ticket (actually, the invitation was printed on a white cotton glove) in years. Few of the expected celebrities showed up, but outside, hundreds of girls lined up in subzero cold, hoping for just a glimpse of their idol. The place was packed as Walter Yetnikoff, standing beneath a sign reading "Hall of African Mammals," announced to Michael that the *Guinness Book of World Records* had stopped the presses to include *Thriller* as the best-selling record of all time: Twenty-four million copies had now been sold.

The Grammys were a night of triumph and anticlimax. Michael appeared in his bellman's uniform and marched up to the podium to claim seven of the eight Grammys for which he was nominated. ("Every Breath You Take," by the Police, beat "Billie Jean" as song of the year.) He wore sunglasses and said very little, except to dedicate one award to Jackie Wilson, briefly chastise the people who had prevented *The E.T. Storybook* (which won as Best Children's Album) from being properly distributed, and finally, announce that Katharine Hepburn had told him that if he won all the awards he should lift his sunglasses so the screaming kids in the balcony could see him full-face. Which he did, for about two seconds.

Jermaine's release from Motown made a full-scale musical reunion of the Jackson family a possibility once more. Tito and the others were itchy to start, as was Joe. As usual, none had achieved anything since Michael last worked with them—all had other irons in the fire, but nothing came of any of them.

Capturing Michael's attention wasn't going to be so easy this time. In plain fact, he was in danger of succumbing to one of the worst diseases performers who acquire such vast popularity can contract: over-exposure. Showbiz people believe that there's a saturation point beyond which it is very dangerous to push. Stay visible for too long and people get bored. Then, it's a long time before they want more—if they ever do. With *Thriller* in the midst of a thirty-seven week run at number one, it would be months more before that album was off the charts. The last thing Michael needed was the release of another record.

But his brothers and father had more than a new Jacksons

album in mind. They wanted to tour, and they put heavy pressure on Michael to go on the road with them. After all, they had split all the profits from their years as a group five or six ways. Only Michael had ever had an income he didn't have to share. (It's a perennial problem with groups, and one of the biggest reasons that they disintegrate.) They weren't broke but they weren't rich, either. They had to work.

Without Michael, the Jacksons could tour, but not in the stadiums they wanted to play, maybe not even in the arenas they were accustomed to playing. With Michael plus Jermaine, the tour would be a twofold event.

Of course, no one really knows how Michael was persuaded. His sullen attitude presented at every offstage tour-related event argues forcefully that he was cajoled into doing something that went against his best instincts (and perhaps the advice of his business representatives as well). The Jacksons' organization leaked worse than the White House, so perhaps the word on the street was correct. The rumors said that Joe and the other boys promised that if Michael would just do one more album and tour, he'd be off the hook for good. The plan was to run the show democratically— still one brother, one vote—but the theme behind it all was that profit had to be maximized. If this was their last ride on the merry-go-round with the boy who never failed to snatch the golden ring, they wanted to take home every prize they could.

Michael was beat. He'd done enough in the past several years to exhaust anyone. He had declared in 1981 that he'd do no more touring. Yet he was persuaded or, anyway, he gave in. On October 31, New York *Post* columnist Cindy Adams proclaimed that boxing promoter Don King would promote "a Jackson family tour" of forty dates the next spring.

Who was Don King? An ex-felon who had done four years in an Ohio prison for killing a man in a Cleveland street fight, one of the two most important promoters in professional boxing, indicted for twenty-three counts of income tax evasion, a man whom Norman Mailer described by quoting Engels: " 'Quantity changes quality'. . . a hustler of dimensions is a financier." King wore his graying hair straight up, as though he'd just pulled loose from a socket. He was a renowned bullshitter, a master of hype, a guy who understood that if you talked long enough,

loud enough, used big enough words, a lot of questions that
needed to be answered wouldn't even get asked—your filibuster
would wear folks out before they could get to their point, and
you'd be left with an open field for your own hype.

He turned his florid tongue upon the Jacksons and convinced
them to sell him promotional rights to the tour for three
million dollars, a paltry sum considering that Michael could
certainly have received that much on his own, that King had no
experience as a music promoter, that he was, in essence, being
given a license to go out and hustle as much side money as he
could, without ever having to deliver anything except one
check. Being a promoter is a job; King made it an auction.

King and the Jacksons called a press conference for November
30, 1983. Coming just at the time when media madness over
Michael was reaching its highpoint, the place was packed.
Celebrities who got in the door included Dustin Hoffman,
Herschel Walker, Patti LaBelle, Thomas "Hitman" Hearns,
Ossie Davis, and, of course, Andy Warhol. Michael sat tight-
lipped, making no comments except to introduce the other
members of the family, generally without editorializing. So
King held the floor. He showed a film clip of the Jackson 5 on
*The Ed Sullivan Show,* but also a fifteen-minute film about his
own career. He yammered on and on about the tour as "a union
and a reunion," about family, God, and mother love, "enrapture-
ment," the Beatles, destiny, and *Destiny.* Michael, he said, "has
soared the heights to the unknown." He did not use one
adjective where seven could be crammed in. King fielded every
question from the floor, although when he drew a deep breath,
one of the brothers would sometimes squeeze in a sentence.

What was really remarkable about King's performance was
how little information it delivered. He was announcing that
there would be a tour, but beyond that, he had nothing specific: no dates, no places, no prices, no name (Marlon finally
managed to wedge in the news that it would be called the
Victory tour). The real point of the afternoon's presentation
wasn't clear until King finally introduced the main event: a
spokesman for Pepsi-Cola, there to announce that the company
had signed an endorsement agreement with the Jacksons, "which
is probably the biggest multimillion dollar deal of its type that
has ever been put together." (The brothers split five million

dollars six ways after commissions.) In return for its largesse, Pepsi had the right to "sponsor" the Jacksons' tour. In addition, the Jacksons, including Michael, would do two TV commercials for Pepsi, which would be premiered privately at Lincoln Center, New York City's high culture mall, on February 26 and publicly on the Grammy Awards show two nights later.

Like the deal with King, the Pepsi contract seemed a steal to business insiders. Michael Jackson would receive, after the brothers paid their parents and King 15 percent off the top, a little over $700,000. It was not an especially good image move, tending to reinforce his lingering image as a bubble-gum pop idol. And he would be endorsing a product that he didn't use on principle. (Rumors flew that Michael wanted to endorse something more organic—like Quaker Oats.)

The press conference demonstrated that the tour plans were getting out of hand. Michael had shown himself fairly well able to balance the intense focus centered upon him, but his associates in this venture had a lot less self-control. King made a shambles of the Tavern on the Green event, and his involvement made everyone around Michael dubious about the tour ever coming off and wary that if it did it would be a giant black eye for their client.

Around this time, one of the least private secret letters ever written was sent to King from Michael. It made four key points: King could not collect any money on Michael's behalf; King could not communicate with anyone on Michael's behalf without Michael's permission; King could not approach sponsors or promoters on Michael's behalf; any hiring, booking, promoting, and the like that King did required Michael's specific approval. The document was widely reported, in *Rolling Stone* and elsewhere, and though King denied its existence, there seems no reason to doubt that the message allegedly contained in it was delivered.

Its most interesting implication was that King would not, in fact, promote the Victory tour himself, but would somehow subcontract it. According to *People* magazine, MCA Records president Irving Azoff, manager/promoter Jerry Weintraub, and Bill Graham, the famous San Francisco promoter known as "the Hurok of rock," were all rumored to be involved with the tour. Whether any of them were actually involved (Azoff was later hired as a consultant), Graham certainly hoped to be. As the most experienced promoter of tours for superstar rock bands like the Rolling Stones, he felt he had the best credentials to put on a series of shows with the most popular musical entertainer in the world.

Graham's experience would have been an inestimable asset in preventing many of the fiascos and embarrassments that later took place. Certainly, no individual could have headed off the backlash completely, but Graham has a reasonably shrewd public-relations sense, and no one would have been able to attack the tour on the grounds of unprofessionalism, charges that began to surface in the music world as soon as King's name was announced as promoter. (King's experience as a fight promoter was of little value here, since fights are one-night events that don't present the complex logistics of travel, sound, and lighting that are the essence of concert promotion.)

Graham wrote a letter to John Branca, Michael's attorney, on March 14, 1984, which outlined his concerns. Several of the points in it are valuable because they anticipated exactly the problems that the Victory promoters would later face and be unable to defuse. Graham's letter proposed a series of concerts, two shows at each facility, preferably in domed stadiums. The first of these concerts, he argued, should be played in the daytime, for the younger Jacksons fans. The second show would be an evening performance, with additional theatrical effects available after nightfall.

More importantly, Graham proposed, "Community involvement is absolutely essential . . . the only way to approach the security aspect of the . . . tour is to accept the fact that community pride and spirit must play a vital role. . . ." He suggested that cities be chosen "based on the extent to which the authorities would cooperate," not only on economic issues but on security as well. The Jacksons would communicate via television and radio announcements that they wanted everyone to have a good time and to respect one another. Graham's comments here stem from the concern of many professional insiders that a Jacksons tour could be a large-scale security risk. Precedents such as the rumble following Diana Ross's Central Park free concert the previous summer and the deaths of eleven fans at a Who show in Cincinnati in 1980 made everyone uneasy about an amateur promotion that would bring the volatile elements of Michael's diverse constituency into physical contact. (In the end, the Victory promoters solved this problem another way—by setting prices so high that the low income end of Michael's audience hadn't a prayer of seeing him or expressing its resentment of the high end.)

Graham was also eager to see the Jacksons extend their community involvement to a financial commitment to the cities they played. He suggested that half of the tickets could be sold through ordinary mail-order; the other half, he proposed, could be sold to various civic-minded organizations, which could resell them at ten dollars higher than face value, keeping the profits to help run their programs. (Graham mentioned Sickle-Cell Anemia, poverty programs, Big Brothers and Big Sisters, and the United Negro College Fund as the kind of thing he had in mind.) In return, the organizations would provide volunteers to help with security on the day of the show.

Graham added a lengthy P.S. to his letter, discussing the issue of "key field personnel." "On this Olympian level of touring," he wrote, "there's only a handful of qualified professionals who have the attitudes and professional expertise that is essential. . . . First we must understand the magnitude of who the Jacksons are . . . then think about moving them from hotel to the gig to the airport, then to the next city, think of moving a fifty-man crew with eight to ten trucks, building indoor and outdoor stages, over the course of many weeks. What is necessary is a specialized team of production coordinators, logisticians, top-flight security personnel. . . . In the world of rock 'n' roll, there are very few that have had the field experience to take on this immense project."

Graham was right, and according to some published reports, his arguments convinced Michael. But the letter wasn't talking maximum profit, so the other brothers weren't interested. So Graham spent the summer in Europe, promoting a lackluster tour by Carlos Santana and Bob Dylan, while the Jacksons went on planning . . . after their fashion.

Actually, everybody knew by now that another promoter would have to be found. Don King wasn't exactly interested in spending a month negotiating with caterers and trucking contractors, even if he'd known how. So the Jacksons summoned several more experienced promoters to California for a meeting on March 29. They announced afterward that they had selected Frank Russo, of Rhode Island, to run the tour in association with Danny O'Donovan, an experienced international promoter who had previously worked with the group, though never in the U.S. Joe and Katherine Jackson and King retained their percentage of the boys' income. Presumably, Russo and O'Donovan could professionalize the production without Graham's pie-in-the-sky idealism.

Michael must have felt engulfed in chaos. Despite his sweep of the Grammys, most of the omens were bad. On January 24, while filming a Pepsi commercial directed by Bob Giraldi, which featured the Jacksons in performance in the midst of fireworks, a spark hit Michael on the back of his head and ignited his hair. He was rushed to the hospital with third-degree burns and had to undergo scalp surgery in mid-April to repair the damage. Although the commercials—one based on "Billie Jean," the other on the standard "You're a whole new generation" Pepsi jingle—were well received in most quarters, they were regarded in a few as an example of what was beginning to look like simple greed surrounding the whole Jacksons reunion. And although his brothers could contend that they needed the dough, what could Michael reply? At two dollars per album, *Thriller* had now earned him somewhere between fifty and seventy million dollars. But there was little Michael could say because aside from money, there was no reason to tie up with Pepsi. Pinning the endorsement deal on family greed was out of the question—it would only seem as if the most powerful brother was trying to scapegoat the others.

On top of that, Michael was still searching for a new manager. He finally found one, the first week in April, in the person of Frank DiLeo, formerly vice-president of promotion at Epic. Coming up in the same Pittsburgh scene as Steve Popovich, DiLeo was a first-rate promo man—but he had no experience as a personal manager. To some observers, it looked like Michael was taking the job on himself, with DiLeo serving more as a spokesman and point man than a decision maker. That appearance has yet to be dispelled.

Michael must have felt he was standing on quicksand. The heat was on in all areas now. As the summer grew near, everything had to be finished at once. The new Jacksons' album, *Victory*, had to be slapped together by the start of the tour (whenever that would be), and although Michael minimized his involvement, writing and singing only two tracks, participating in writing a third, and mostly not showing up for sessions when the other guys were doing their songs, it was one more detail in a life that already had an overabundance of activity. Meanwhile, all the details of the tour itself had to be firmed up: The stage design, lighting effects (Michael also wanted to use robots, which cost something like a quarter of million dollars to design and execute), sound equipment, and other gear had to be selected, boxed, and fitted into trucks. Musicians had to be hired and rehearsed, which meant a set list had to be constructed.

Meantime, the deal with Russo had fallen through. Russo sued for forty million dollars, the first among many such suits the Victory tour would incur. He was fired on May 16, only two days after Michael had appeared at the White House with President Ronald Reagan to receive an award for donating "Beat It" as the music for the administration's anti-drunk driving campaign, a controversial move in some quarters, given Reagan's policies toward the poor and blacks, the groups perceived as the heart of Michael's musical constituency. Russo's firing was equally controversial inside the music industry. Who *was* running this show? Did they have a clue about what they were doing?

The lack of communication among the family, the indecisiveness, the "we're only in it for the money," philosophy, Michael's grudging participation were the talk of the music industry, and the press picked a lot of it up. The glow emanating from *Thriller* was dissolving in the backwash of ineptitude with which the Jacksons—an entity that might have been but now couldn't be distinguished from Michael himself— conducted their business.

Thinking to solve the problem, Frank DiLeo contacted Chuck Sullivan, an attorney whose family owned the National Football League's New England Patriots. Sullivan and Edward DeBartolo, the Youngstown, Ohio, shopping-mall magnate who owned the San Francisco 49ers, proposed putting up about forty-one million dollars as a guarantee for the rights to promote the tour. The Jacksons snapped at the deal, by far the richest offer ever made to a rock group. But DeBartolo backed off when he saw the terms, which gave the group 85 percent of the ticket price but required but required the promoters to pay the lion's share of expenses. Even at the planned thirty-dollar ticket price (more than twice as much as the Jacksons had ever charged before, exactly double the current standard for rock concerts), DeBartolo didn't see any profit in the deal. But Sullivan decided to try it anyway. He arranged a twelve-and-a-half-million-dollar loan from the Crocker National Bank in California, putting up the family's football stadium in Foxboro, Massachusetts, as collateral.

What gave Sullivan the idea that he could make a profit where others could not? In the end, a combination of his own inexperience and the very disorganization that made it necessary for the Jacksons to work with a nonveteran in the first place. For instance, the press release announcing that Stadium Management Corporation (Sullivan's firm) was to promote the tour boasted that Sullivan had "twenty-one years of experience in concert and sports promotion, experience which has made him one of the few entertainment industry figures to regularly organize events with audiences of up to two hundred thousand."

The story not told in that sentence is that Sullivan had gained his experience in a sports company. His concert promotion experience was limited to booking a few shows in college and while in the army at Fort Benning, Georgia, in the late sixties, and acting as house promoter for concerts at Sullivan Stadium. There's a big difference in running a one-day show at a fixed site and coordinating the logistics of moving a tour from place to place. In this area, Sullivan's only background was as "project officer" for Bob Hope's 1969 Christmas Show in Vietnam. No doubt that one ran smoothly—although Hope was sometimes booed by GIs who correctly perceived him as backing the policies that were getting them and their buddies needlessly slaughtered—but on the Victory tour, Sullivan would not have the resources of the army at his command. He would have to find, hire, and pay for everything from an acceptable, affordable hotel room for the crew to someone to sit down with the local stadium manager and haggle over disposition of the final receipts. He would need to negotiate with (or hire someone to negotiate with) the various employees he hired— and the Sullivan's family labor-relations record was so bad that the New England Patriots were the single most active team in the NFL

Players Association, united behind the 1982 players' strike where many other teams were split precisely because of resentment over salary negotiations.

As it happened, the Jacksons had hired an extremely competent technical crew, one that was well regarded by its peers. If they hadn't, the tour might not have come off at all. But employees were not the only people with whom Sullivan had to negotiate. There were travel agents, hotels, and the stadiums themselves to make arrangements with.

Here, the Jacksons felt they'd bought themselves a bargain. Sullivan was on the NFL committee that planned the Super Bowl. Surely he knew what he was doing in this area. Sullivan also felt that his experience as a stadium owner would work to his advantage as he did these negotiations. He could drive the same hard bargains for these facilities that the NFL did for its event.

But there's a big difference between rock bands and football teams. Hotels want the sports business because it attracts other trade. Many are wary of bands because they're known to damage rooms and corridors, they look unsightly in the lobby, and there aren't a lot of high rollers who follow them around. Although it is not unusual for travel agents to receive complimentary hotel rooms for large traveling parties, Sullivan apparently thought he could get *all* the Jacksons' hotel rooms for free. In Kansas City and Irving, Texas (site of Texas Stadium, near Dallas), he was nearly run out of town when what he was asking hit the papers.

The stadium deal blew up in his face. On June 20, two weeks before the starting date of July 6 (in Kansas City), the Foxboro, Massachusetts, board of selectmen voted to deny the Sullivans the right to stage a concert in their town. Thus, Sullivan was denied a bonus he was counting on, since any fees paid to Sullivan Stadium would accrue to Stadium Management, adding to his profit as the tour promoter.

(The selectmen's vote had murky rationale. In part, it may have stemmed from racial bias, since Foxboro had previously allowed concerts by white artists—David Bowie, the Police, Simon and Garfunkel—to be held there. But some claimed that it was the result of the town's animus toward the Sullivan family, which it felt had not lived up to its end of the bargain made when the stadium was built.)

Sullivan had similar problems at other stadiums. In part, he was trying to hustle both ends against the middle. The Victory tour was originally announced to start in Lexington, Kentucky, at Rupp Arena, whose 21,000 seats made it the largest arena in the country. Those dates were actually announced, but the arena management balked at the plan to sell tickets only by mail order from an address in New York. So did many other building managers. "I think it's utterly ridiculous to expect the masses to send money to a location outside their normal market area," said Cliff Wallace, general manager of the New Orleans Superdome and president of the International Association of Auditorium Managers, in a *Billboard* story headlined "Jacksons Backlash Seen Building." "I don't understand a system that allows the majority not to get a product, particularly when the money is going to be held for up to eight weeks and interest is going to be made by someone else.

"I don't understand the American consumer permitting that to happen more than once. Right now the consumer is responding to it because it's a novelty and because it's potentially the biggest musical event in our history. But when they stop and realize what's happening, I think there's going to be an outcry."

The plan was to sell tickets in blocks of four seats only at a price of twenty-eight dollars each, plus two dollars *per ticket* service and handling charge. That meant an investment of one hundred twenty dollars even for someone who wanted to see the show alone. The money was to be sent to a New York post office box, where it would accumulate until the orders were picked (by computer if there were more requests than available seats). That meant that, if the tour drew the twelve million ticket requests projected, the tour would be drawing interest on more than one billion dollars. Tour publicist Howard Bloom, always good for a laugh, told the Associated Press that this revenue would be used to cover handling and postage costs for mailing refunds, but others had their doubts. It seemed like a way to skim additional profits from an already egregiously high ticket price—a price so high that some called it deliberately exclusionary, designed to keep the urban disenfranchised who had supported the Jacksons long before *Thriller* out of the shows or, at the very least, heedless of their ability to afford the show they most wanted to see.

This added to the stadium and arena managers' fears of an incendiary situation. Not only was there the potential that fans who hadn't been able to get in would appear outside their building, angry at not being able to get in and in a mood to treat the affluent types who had scored tickets with maximum rudeness, but some feared disturbances caused by the failure of the Postal Service to deliver refunds before the shows. Anyone who didn't get a refund might expect that his tickets had been lost in the mail or fear that he was being taken for his money anyway. Others feared the inexperience of the company in New York that was handling the mail orders, a company created by Sullivan for the tour.

That wasn't all. Stadium managers were annoyed at Sullivan's requests for breaks on the local taxes and rental fees usually paid by rock concert promoters. In New Orleans, it was reported that the Jacksons wanted to pay no rent for the Superdome and to get a complete waiver of the 14 percent city and state taxes. In Houston, the mayor's office said, "The Jacksons want the sun and the moon. They want free stadium rental [for the Astrodome]. It gets to the point where you say 'Thanks but no thanks.' " (The tour played neither city.) In Los Angeles, the 90,000-seat Coliseum was lost to the tour because Sullivan failed to offer more than $200,000 as rental on a four-day series of shows that would gross almost two and a half million dollars, without considering potential revenue from tour programs, T-shirts, and the like.

Building managers could not have made these deals even if they wanted to. How could they have ever charged any other rock promoter more to play their building? Sullivan's problem here was not only his inexperience, but the fact that he was operating outside the normal flow of the concert business, unable to perceive the consequences of what he was doing. "There's no question that this tour would have changed the business drastically and overnight if some of the hall managers had acquiesced to the demands," said the manager of the Indianapolis Hoosierdome, another building where negotiations fell through. "After all, there's no reason ever to pay a performer for the privilege of coming to your town."

Sullivan did have reasons to think otherwise. As a stadium owner, he knew that one of the most disturbing problems with such facilities was that they lay idle several hundred days per

year. (Even baseball stadiums aren't used more than about one
hundred days annually. Football stadiums may be used as few as
ten times.) Rock concerts had become the staple profit item of
indoor arenas for just that reason. But his request for a freebie
simply pushed the building management too far. Rather than
giving him a basis from which to negotiate, his extreme demands in some cases ended the bargaining the moment they
were made.

Making a further mess of tour planning was the chaotic chain
of command. King still claimed that Sullivan worked for him.
Each Jackson brother had his own representative, as well as
overall representation for the whole group. Meetings were attended by phalanxes of lawyers and accountants. The "majority
rules" atmosphere meant that even the simplest decision had to
go through the entire web before an answer could be given; it
also meant that if anybody called for a new vote a day or so after
a decision had been made, the previous action could be over-
turned. "I've spent more time on these contract negotiations
than the last agreement with the Detroit Pistons [a multiyear
tenant]," said Pontiac, Michigan, attorney James Smiertka of
the Jacksons' haggling over use of the city's Silverdome. A
Silverdome employee told the *Oakland Press*, "The only way I
want to look at this Michael Jackson tour is through a rearview
mirror." (Nevertheless, the Jackson's did play there.)

Sullivan was also on the hook in other ways. Black promoters, led by Rev. Al Sharpton, wanted in on the action. Despite
King's involvement, they complained that the Jacksons were
turning their backs on the businessmen of their own community. King was still resentful of Sullivan (according to one
source, the two actually wound up in a fist fight one evening).
In Kansas City and the rest of the Midwestern area where the
first dates were promoted, a major fuss was raised over Sullivan's request for free ad space—as a "public service"—in newspapers that ran the ticket coupon. (He actually got some of the
space, though.) The promoters were limited in the venues they
could even consider booking because the stage and sound equipment was so huge. As one result, Madison Square Garden was
the only indoor arena on the tour. As another, several stadiums,
including RFK Memorial Stadium in Washington, D.C., a
"national park," had to have their loading-dock facilities

remodeled—in the case of RFK, at taxpayers' expense. The load-in requirements were so huge and the load-out so complicated that it took three days before and two days after the concerts took place to move the show in and out of the stadiums.

Sullivan could have dealt with all of this, so long as the tickets had sold well enough. There was some room for a profit in the deal if everything went just right. Or so he thought. But he'd been anticipating two things that did not prove to be true. In the first place, he thought that the Jacksons shows would be automatic sellouts; and in the second, he thought that the stadiums would be played at something close to full capacity. But the size of the stage and sound equipment not only created excavation problems, it caused the shows to play to only about three-quarters of the potential seats. "[Sullivan] still could have made it, but none of us realized until Arrowhead [the Kansas City stadium] how big the stage was," Sullivan's public relations director told the Los Angeles *Times*. The Jacksons were unrestrained in their spending on tour preparations, naturally, because they were working on a huge guarantee—their profit was ensured.

Cutting down the stadium capacities had one salutary effect: By playing to such a small percentage of the house, the Jacksons kept entry and exit logistics simple. And since most of the stadiums were located in suburban areas, without any readily available public transportation from the inner cities, it meant that the expected clash of cultures never took place. Of course, in the end, that was a disgrace. "The *street* people we're talking about—and I don't want to keep saying black and Third World, but that part of our society which is not close to middle-aged Caucasian, have had no experience in the game of ticket getting. The majority of people who, over the years, had the experience of getting *Auntie Mame* tickets, got out there and got Jacksons tickets," said Bill Graham. "The black-white ratio at the Jacksons shows wasn't much different than it was at the [Rolling] Stones shows, and it *should* have been." Graham estimated that the crowd at Madison Square Garden, which *was* in an urban area, was 85 to 90 percent white, which jibed with the perceptions of other observers and conformed to the overall makeup of the tour's audience. But then, as Graham also noted, this was made inevitable by the entire concept of the tour—the ticket price alone would have ensured that only the most affluent persons interested in Michael had a chance to get into the shows. You had to wonder if somebody wanted it that way, if somewhere along the line a conscious decision was made that the simplest way to take care of security problems was just to eliminate what James Watt called "the undesirable element" from the mixture. Deliberate or not, that was the result.

But there was another result, one that embarrassed the Jacksons and cost Chuck Sullivan a lot of money. In cities like Buffalo and even Philadelphia, towns where the Reagan recovery had not been felt, there simply weren't enough ticket buyers to fill even the reduced number of seats. Sullivan told the L.A. *Times* that he needed to sell 40,000 seats a night just to break even. In several cities, that figure was not reached. After several weeks, Sullivan had to renegotiate the contract, down to 75 percent for the group. He was also relieved of the most onerous provision of all: paying twenty-one dollars to the Jacksons for each *unsold* seat. But it was too late. While he was able to persuade the Jacksons to extend the tour through December (it was booked and rebooked so many times that nobody could keep rack of which date was making up for a cancellation and which was an addition to the schedule), the stress gave him a mild heart attack in October, and he was not able to report a profit when the tour ended, although he claimed he still had a shot at about $500,000.

The Jacksons' embarrassment also had long-range consequences. The furor over the tour economics and logistics wiped out the goodwill engendered by *Thriller*, creating an atmosphere of suspicion among both press and public. People don't like being hustled, and the feeling of being cheated isn't easily overridden. Certainly, *Victory* didn't help all that much. Its mediocrity was immediately evident, even though its first single, "State of Shock" (Michael's duet with Mick Jagger), was a substantial hit. In the wake of *Thriller*, the record not only seemed, but was, lacklustre, Michael's contributions minor, its others uninspired. *Victory* sold better than any other CBS Jacksons album—about three million copies, compared to about two million for *Triumph*—but it was kept shut out of the number one slot on the charts by the sensation of the 1984 summer, Prince's *Purple Rain*.

Not much was done to even try to recover the harmony and

unity of emotion that had been lost. Michael announced, the day before the first show in Kansas City, that the mail-order ticket scheme would end because it was unfair (it also wasn't selling tickets in the quantities expected) and that he would donate all of his profits from the tour to charity. Still, the tour wended its way through America that summer and into the autumn as an anticlimax. If the Jacksons did a terrific show, well, after all, that was Michael Jackson, what did you expect? And if they did a bad one, that was unforgivable. It was the spit and image of a no-win situation.

# S · I · X · T · E · E · N

Dear Michael,

Of all the sad remarks in that last chapter, the saddest of all was made by that anonymous arena employee at the Silverdome. "The only way I want to look at this Michael Jackson tour is through a rearview mirror." Before the tour, it would have been impossible to imagine anyone but a snob making a remark like that. The miracle wasn't how far you had fallen, but how fast.

For you, I suppose, what makes this person's statement exquisitely painful is the way he identified the object of his loathing: "this Michael Jackson tour" isn't what Victory was supposed to be. It was sold, to you if not the public, as the Jackson Family Reunion Tour, or something like that.

But the opening press conference ended that. The illusion would have ended pretty quickly anyway, since next to no one was interested in seeing your brothers. But the finishing touch came when Marlon said the name. Victory. That name could only belong to you—what had the Jacksons done to deserve a championship celebration?

Your brothers, Don King, your father, and Chuck Sullivan undoubtedly have answers they consider adequate for every decision that was criticized on this tour. But it wasn't their tour to explain and defend. It was yours, and the first impression is that you just weren't talking. But that's not really true. You made your position known before you played the first show.

On July 5, the afternoon before the first gig, a press conference was called at the tour's media headquarters, the Westin Crown Center Hotel. Kansas City was already crawling with reporters, desperate for stories. You gave them a big one, reading a prepared statement:

> We're beginning our tour tomorrow and I wanted to talk to you about something of great concern to me. We've worked a long time to make this show the best it can be. But we know a lot of kids are having trouble getting tickets. The other day I got a letter from a girl in Texas named Ladonnia Jones. She'd been saving her money from odd jobs to buy a ticket, but with the current tour system she'd have to buy four tickets and she couldn't afford that. So I've asked our promoter to work out a new way of distributing tickets—a way that no longer requires a one hundred twenty dollar money order.
>
> There has also been a lot of talk about the promoter holding money for tickets that didn't sell. I've asked our promoter to end the mail order ticket system as soon as possible so that no one will pay money unless they get a ticket.
>
> Finally and most importantly, there's something else I am going to announce today. I want you to know that when I first agreed to tour, I decided to donate all the money I make from our performances to charity. I know you have questions about all this, so I'd like my manager Frank DiLeo to talk with you now about the details of these announcements.

This brief statement was wonderfully subtextual, written between the lines from the choice of pronouns ("we" are beginning the tour and have worked hard; "I" have asked the promoter to change the way tickets are sold and am donating my money to charity) to its not-so-slight linguistic evasions (the Jones letter had appeared in Dallas newspapers the previous weekend; the promoter granted your request because tickets

weren't selling well in Jacksonville and Dallas, the next two
stops). Only in the last paragraph did you speak bluntly,
although you were already ducking any requests for an answer
to the obvious question: How come?

I think you were making a resignation speech. No one,
including me, quite heard it that way at the time, but what else
could your statement mean except that you were renouncing the
only agreed-upon rationale for the tour's existence, and therefore
were essentially washing your hands of the whole mess. Or,
anyway, you were trying to.

Of course, the possibility remained that you would respond
to the creative challenge of getting up on stage, but the evidence is that you did not. You simply walked through the tour
as though that creative opportunity didn't exist, and there's
nothing surprising about that. All one has to know is what you
said about appearing on Broadway, in an interview done around
the time of *The Wiz:* "What's so sad about the whole thing is
that you don't capture that moment. Look at how many great
actors or entertainers have been lost to the world, because they
did a performance one night and that was it. . . . So much is
lost in theatre, so much. That's what I hate about Broadway. I
feel I'm giving a whole lot for nothing. I like to capture things
and hold them there and share them with the whole world."
You can't do that with a concert tour that plays twenty cities,
either, not even if a few nights are filmed.

You didn't do the tour as a walk-through, exactly. What you
tried to do was walk away symbolically. It's kind of the way you
use the white glove as a symbol. I've heard people say all kinds
of things about what they think that stellar affectation might
mean, but none of it makes much sense. It strikes me that what
the glove really says is: With this one hand, I stay pure,
untouched by reality as you know it; with the other hand, I
manipulate your dirty world. That's just how you tried to do
those shows. You were in them, at their center, but you
projected a kind of anti-intensity, none of the full commitment
that comes through on your records.

Or, that's how the show on opening night struck me. Let
me tell you how it was while we waited for you to come on,
since you were probably trapped in the bowels of the stadium
or waiting across the highway at the hotel and didn't get a

chance to feel the full surge of anticipation that built out there.

To start with, Kansas City is a small town, and hosting such a huge event went to its head. But there was none of the anxiety I would have expected, no fear and trembling about security problems. It wasn't until eight that evening that I realized why. We pulled up to the stadium without encountering so much as a minor traffic jam. I cruised through the security, including the hand-held metal detector frisking (that's unconstitutional, you know), in about three minutes and asked the cop at the gate if there had been any problems. "No." He laughed. "No problems. Football crowds—now those are wild people." Inside, it was easy to see what he was talking about. It wasn't just that about 90 percent of the patrons were white. They were affluent, middle-class, blond-hair-and-blue-eyes, golf-and-tennis whites. It was like a country club convention or something.

Once you'd got through the merchandising area (pretty tacky to put the Pepsi logo on a T-shirt that you were selling for thirteen bucks, I thought, but bought three for my kids back home anyhow) and went to your seat, the perspective changed again. The first sight of all the empty seats, seats that would never be filled because they were behind the huge curtain that draped the back and sides of the stage or were blocked off by the walls of sound equipment, actually made my stomach flip. After fifteen years of pop journalism, you get a sense of what empty seats mean in terms of lost revenue. On that basis it's amazing that Chuck Sullivan only had a mild heart attack.

Even though I know that the stage was supposed to extend to the thirty-five-yard line, it set me back to find my fourteenth-row seat put me at midfield. Arrowhead Stadium is one of those modern Astroturfed bowls that only feels right for football, anyway, but sitting in the midst of it with the sun still up and an hour to kill before showtime, I felt sort of silly. Some of the most reasonable people in the rock business had said absolutely outrageous things to me in the past couple of weeks, and I guess getting there early was to make sure that I didn't succumb to the challenge thrown at me by one of them two days before. "Well, I guess we'll see what the press is made of when they review the show and ignore the blood in the parking lot," he taunted. As I gazed around now, all that came to mind was the idea that most of these people wouldn't know how to start a good bar fight if someone came in and dumped a year's supply of Chivas down their backs. Blood? Not unless somebody got a paper cut from holding their ticket stub too tightly.

There was an anxious buzz in the crowd around me. It was hardly about the Jacksons, but it was about the show. Apparently, suburban Kansas City believed that either Mick Jagger, Diana Ross, or Edward Van Halen would turn up to perform with you on opening night. Gently, I tried to explain that superstars were not in the habit of upstaging themselves on important occasions, but no one was buying that. After a while, I began to tingle with the idea myself, until I recalled that with all the reporters around, Mick Jagger would have had to burrow into town like Bugs Bunny to have escaped notice.

A few minutes later, Chris Bliss took the stage. Chris Bliss is a juggler who does his tossing to records played at crashing volume over the concert sound system. "For my last number, I'm going to do a Beatles classic, 'Sgt. Pepper's Lonely Hearts Club Band,' " he said and began throwing things up in the air. As far as I can remember, he caught all of them. My notes were simple: "Who manages this guy?" (No one seemed to know. I figured either Sullivan, King, or your dad.)

The most impressive sights were the huge Coke stands behind me (ironic in light of Pepsi's sponsorship; Coke has an exclusive contract with Arrowhead, it turns out) and the enormous scrims covering the speaker columns at each side of the stage and running across its top. These were tapestries, painted in Maxfield Parrish/*Watchtower* style, of trees growing out of rocky ground. Having seen a few Witness publications already, the symbolism was easy to decipher: True Life in Jehovah growing out of the unproductive soil of This Earth.

Now it was getting late. At 9:13 (by my watch), some smoke leaked from the stage. It came in traces, not billows, but the crowd pumped itself up anyhow. Fourteen minutes later, a little more smoke spewed out from stage right. The crowd roared again. But since no instruments were visible on the stage, it wasn't surprising that nothing came of this.

Meantime, it had become a beautiful night, extremely warm but with just enough breeze to keep the sweat down and with hundreds of stars visible in a blue-black sky. Helicopters buzzed incessantly overhead, hired by news crews from the local TV stations. At 9:35, the crowd started clapping impatiently and for the next few minutes, each time a track on the sound system finished, you could hear hopes rise audibly. A Van Halen crowd would have been chewing the scenery already, but what you got here was nothing more than a frustrated anticipatory rustle.

You hit the stage at 9:45 on the dot. The lights had been all the way down for several minutes. An object—it was too dark to identify it—was moved to center stage. As a little more light came up, it was possible to discern that it was a rock and a tree stump with a sword stuck in the stone.

Monsters entered the stage and shuffled like bastard Muppet camels to surround the sword-in-the-stone. A portentous narration explained that these were the Kreetons, who held humanity captive against the day when a hero would come along who was sufficiently pure of heart to defeat them in battle with the celebrated sword-in-the-stone. (This was bad myth and worse entertainment, but the preschoolers around me seemed to dig it. They probably hadn't heard it eight hundred fifty times before.) Four humans attempted to pull the sword. None succeeded.

A fifth, dressed in wizard gear, approached and strained to lift it. It came loose and lit up, as a blast of sound delivered cries of "Victory!" Smoke and flashpots were going off everywhere, along with explosions of eardrum-popping intensity, so strong that you could feel them physically even fourteen rows back.

"And behold! The King!" exulted the narrator. Randy (for it was he) reigned victorious over the Snuffalupagus Kreetons as mist covered the stage. The *Watchtower* scrims dropped away, revealing the same speaker columns seen at every other outdoor concert in history. Thunder and lightning and smoke poured off the stage, grander and grander and grander. I prepared for a coughing and choking spasm as it drifted my way.

Just in time, a bandstand rose from beneath the stage, and before it, the Jacksons on elevated risers. Down the stairs you came in unison, light spurting from each riser as you goosestepped toward the mikes that had been hurriedly placed. Reaching them, each of you whipped off your sunglasses and wound up in "Wanna Be Startin' Somethin'," a good, tight performance, well paced and predictable to the nth degree.

The rest of the show was just as slick and professional and banal. The press had been given a handout listing the set you'd perform, in amazing detail, right down to the encores. All that was missing was a script for the between-songs patter, but then, anyone who'd heard *Jacksons Live* could have lip-synched it. All the songs featured you, except for a brief Jermaine medley which got pretty tedious about halfway through the second song, "Do You Like Me," and picked right back up again with your duet with Jermaine on "Tell Me I'm Not Dreaming." The concert ended with "Lovely One," but the false ending was written right on the set list. So I knew you'd be back out for the last three songs: "Beat It," "Billie Jean," and finally, "Shake Your Body (Down to the Ground)." It was kind of tacky to save your biggest hits for the encores, but the whole show had a rote edge to it, and saving the guaranteed killers for the encore is a standard show business practice, at least for those not confident that there will otherwise be encores.

To tell you the truth, if you'd waited for the crowd to call you back, you might never have reemerged. These "fans" just about sat on their hands. Maybe they just had hardheaded Missouri common sense and knew that you weren't going to get away without doing the songs that brought them there. (Although there were three fourteen-year-olds sitting in row fifteen who were plenty pissed at not hearing "Thriller." I told them about your pledge in *Awake!*, but they didn't seem to understand.)

I had a few questions myself. Why in the world would anybody who wanted to play music for people set off so many explosions that *hurt* the ears? How come you didn't do any songs from *Victory?* The line on this, when reporters got close enough to ask, was that the album was just out and people didn't want to hear unfamiliar material—they wouldn't know how to react. Yet no *Victory* songs were ever added, even when the show was extended into December. But by then, *Victory* had stiffed—or at least produced no hits not featuring Mick Jagger—and maybe you all just wanted to forget about it.

And then again: where were Mick and Diana and Edward? (At least Van Halen showed up the next weekend in Dallas, the only non-Jackson to take the stage.) Couldn't somebody have taught Gregg Wright how to acceptably fake the guitar solo in "Beat It"? Where does Tito get his clothes—the circus? Why was the show so short, only seventy minutes before the encore? (Usually, when there's no opening act, two hours is the minimum a group plays.) How the hell did you ever imagine you were going to get away with such a superficial show?

I have no answers to any of these queries, except maybe the last one. For the most part, you did get away with it. The hype sustained ticket sales, except in those areas where you'd priced yourselves out of the market. Of course, no good critic gave the show a positive review, although everyone acknowledged that there were highlights (my picks were "Human Nature," "She's Out of My Life," and the torrid "Billie Jean"). But it was too easy to see the show as nothing more than going through the motions to hustle any enthusiasm out of experienced reporters, let alone critics who came looking for musical fireworks to match, or at least parallel, those on your records. They weren't there, Michael, because you weren't trying. In the end, the show was a rehash of the *Triumph* tour, with a few tunes from *Thriller* for spice.

Even the crowd sensed this, which is why the cheers were sporadic, never as loud as the flashpot bombs that were finally the main auditory memory for many. Here, I think, your Motown training betrayed you. When the audience didn't do what it was supposed to do—go bananas, create a fuss—you had no way of coping, of altering and adjusting to meet a situation different from the one for which you'd planned. And because you never reached out and touched anyone—neither in the flesh nor the heart—the crowd grew that much more passive. Your own exhortations and whoops were so regimented that they had no credibility.

Well, I figured, later on they'll make their adjustments, change the set, figure out what goes over best, bear down, and make it work. (Your tune-out still hadn't dawned on me.) Your singing would always be fine, of that I was sure, and the show was no letdown on the numbers where all you had to do was croon. That was something to build upon.

It didn't happen, and as the tour bumbled through the summer, it seemed to move from anticlimax to anticlimax. Cities got worked up because you were in town, but the people

who went to the shows came away frustrated and depressed by
your remoteness, by the business-as-usual attitude of everyone
on stage. I mean, I saw three shows running in Los Angeles at
the tail end of the tour, so I *know* that Tito egged on the crowd
with the exact same words at the exact same spot every night.
But anybody who saw one show would have guessed it. And
when the crowds failed to get up and boogie their butts off, you
should have figured something else out. You would have, too—
if you were really trying.

For me, the whole sorry affair was epitomized by your first
show at Dodger Stadium on December 7. It was raining, one of
those California drizzles that steadily grows into a downpour. Yet
you played on, singing the same songs, mouthing the same
phrases as on every other night. (The changes from Kansas City
were minuscule.) You exhorted the crowd to clap, apparently
not noticing or caring that their hands were already occupied,
tightly grasping umbrellas against the wind and the rain. Customers (for that is all we were by then) whose socks squished
were implored to dance. Not once did any of the Jacksons,
including you, make a single gesture of commiseration. Not
one word of sympathy was offered to the crowd being drenched
while you stood under a roof. There wasn't even enough wind to
blow the wet back into your faces, so finally I started wondering: Were you even aware of the weather?

Well, maybe you didn't need to be, because you weren't
playing to the crowd, you were playing to the closed-circuit TV
cameras. The crowd responded mostly to shots of your grimac-
ing face during the ballads or your skeedaddling feet on the
dance numbers, no matter what the overall scene on the stage.
Of course, most of the crowd was too far away to make out what
was going on up there without some sort of visual aid.

Once again you had rendered your audience irrelevant.
Interacting with your listeners is the essence of a great concert.
You found ways to make interaction less than an irrelevant
afterthought. You made it downright impossible, even on dry
nights.

For me, the epitome of the whole hoax that you were really
involved in anything but yourself during these shows came
during each night's rendition of "She's Out of My Life." "Can
I come down there?" you would ask. The crowd roared—

maybe the biggest response you got on any of the nights I attended was for that line. Rising, you would step down to a movable staircase, then lay on your back and sing a few lines. Rising, you'd descend another three or four steps, then, at your point of closest contact with your fans, turn your back on them and sing straight into the cameras. If I had seen this once, I would never have believed it. But I saw it three nights running in L.A., and it really spoke to me. It told me that this was the closest Michael Jackson would come to his audience and the closest you wanted to come. Maybe it was the closest you knew how to get, or maybe the whole project was an arrogant, cynical sham. Either way, it was what the show was all about.

Even the dancing was mechanical, uninspired. After the first quarter hour, one had to realize that your repertoire of moves was exhausted, and that what made your dancing so breathtaking in short spurts wasn't its inventiveness but speed and dexterity—a physical talent, almost a quirk, not anything approaching artistry.

The ballads were glorious, every night. The more maudlin and treacly, the better. Soppy as they could be, they were enchanting just for the pure conviction with which you put them over. Of the fast songs, not one sounded better than the records and even "Billie Jean" had lost some of its spark by the end.

Even as a balladeer, Michael, you undid yourself. At the end of "I'll Be There," you appended some gospel ruminations. You'd been doing this for years, but apparently seeing a videotape of Mahalia Jackson spurred you to extend it during the latter part of the Victory tour. Here, all your great gift as a singing mimic came roaring back, and it wasn't hard to see why the chitlin' circuit was so impressed by your mimetic talent when you were a kid. You don't have Mahalia's range, but anyone who has ever heard her sing would have recognized your complete immersion in her accents, intonations, breathing, introjections, every groan and nuance mastered and expressed with redoubtable self-assurance.

The first time through, this was endlessly pleasing to me, even mind-boggling. But as I watched you go through the same phrases and effects in the same order on the second night and then third, all hope was lost. Not only had you turned Mahalia's great improvisatory gift into a gimmick, you were making it a travesty. And the reason why was simple. Michael, you have all the resources any man could ask, but you're completely unable to give of yourself.

That's not just what the Victory tour was about. It's how your career to date adds up: Great talent gone to waste because of a root failure to understand the difference between the artistic and the mechanical.

Was there any room for optimism left? Well, I liked what you said as the final night's show came to an end. Stepping to the microphone as family, crew members, and little kids (nephews and nieces, maybe) danced around you, you spoke carefully, not at all casually.

"This is our last and final tour," you said. There was a firmness in your voice that had not been heard before. "I mean, this is our farewell tour. You've all been wonderful—it's been a long twenty years and we love you all."

That's pretty good, I thought, three variations on "I quit" in three sentences. Maybe this time, no one will misunderstand.

# E · P · I · L · O · G · U · E

The Victory tour crashed into the headlines with more fanfare than any pop music event since the Beatles hit the States. It skulked off, fading away in embarrassment and something akin to shame. The stories about Kansas City made the front pages; the ones about Los Angeles were buried back in the amusement section, filler for a slow news Monday. The two hundred out-of-town journalists who had besieged the Jacksons' opening night were reduced by the end to a visible complement of two. The tickets that were supposed to be so hard to get at the beginning were as easy to find as BMWs in Westwood in the final days.

Meantime, Michael Jackson, the puzzle seeking its own answer, was all but discarded, tossed aside like a contraption that had outlasted its fad—not broken just sort of boring. If he did something (U.S.A. for Africa, Madame Tussaud's) the media would cover, but dutifully, without any of the hysterical urgency that had attended the heyday of *Thriller*. If he did nothing, that was all right, too. Maybe it was even preferable. The self-inflating machinery of hype that had pumped him up into the Biggest Star in the World had finally worn itself out . . . at least on this one topic.

Left was a sour smell, a bitter taste in the mouth, the aftershock of cheat and frustration, a nasty, nagging mood. What was most curious about these sensations was their familiarity. Had we known all along that anyone who flew so far beyond our expectations as Michael Jackson would someday simply disappear, clean out of sight, returning only episodically, like a human Halley's Comet?

No, that's not it at all. Michael Jackson has been removed from orbit. That doesn't mean he has lost a shred of his musical talent or an ounce of his showbiz savvy. It does not mean that he has wearied of public attention and gone into retreat. It simply means that the story of Michael Jackson has burned out, that "everybody" is ready to move on to the next thing: Prince's movie, Bitburg, Bruce Springsteen's wedding, a famine in Africa. It really doesn't matter. Soon enough, these things too will run through their cycle of fascination and the headlines will recede deeper and deeper into the back pages, to be replaced by newer pop stars, scandals and outrages against humanity. Of course, in the cycle of these things, there is always the chance that Michael Jackson will reappear. A "comeback" is always an interesting spectacle.

In this environment, no story is truly enduring and all stories are very much the same, since all have bangup beginnings and their conclusions just sort of fade away. Think of Vietnam and Watergate, the central events of American life in the past ten years. When did the war end? When our last troops left or when Saigon fell? Where did Watergate stop? When Nixon was pardoned or the last trial was complete?

The answer is that those stories aren't over, probably because truly completing them would mean remaking the world and ourselves much more drastically than most story-tellers care to imagine. Nevertheless, the stories linger, hovering just around the corner or rattling around in the attic, locked up like nineteenth-century madmen. Either way, they're gone but not forgotten. The biggest of them lurk into ghosts, haunting our dreams, twinging always at our conscience.

In the context of Vietnam and Watergate, the unfinished story of Michael Jackson seems small and superficial. If he were just a pop singer making a bigger score than usual, that might be true. But Michael Jackson is one thing before he is a singer or a success or a star or anything else. He is a black person in America. As a result, he set some older chains to clanking, stirred some ancient ghosts, incited some venerable dreams.

The ghosts of slavery and racism are four hundred years old but their power is fresh and strong. The dreams he incited are equally old—the fantastic hope that we can somehow be brought together long enough to lay those ghosts to rest. Give the dreams their names, too: Emancipation, integration, liberation. Or call them out with the term show business now uses: Crossover.

But never forget: The similarity between the crossover dream and the hope embodied by the idea of integration is deceptive. Their roots are identical, but their aspirations are polar. Integration implies the liberation not just of an entire people but of a whole society, while the practitioners of crossover ask only to receive individual liberties. It's the difference between Jackie Robinson, whose personal emancipation within the world of baseball inspired not only black Americans but the whole country, and Michael Jackson, whose triumphs in the world of popular music were so private that they were ultimately never shared with anyone and as a result, curdled, turned sour and evaporated into a sickly residue of their original potential.

This consequence was so predictable that it now feels inevitable. Like anyone indulging in the crossover dream, Michael Jackson played a dangerous game. He imagined himself capable of receiving an exemption from the visits of the horrible ghosts of American racism. This is an exceedingly dangerous illusion, for in the end, the ghosts always come to call. The drama of race calls us all to play a part and if you shun the call, all you've done is condemn yourself to a role as villain or fool. There is no exemption, not only because of what fame such as Michael Jackson's stirs among the spirits of the past but because of what it awakens among the living.

Of course, there are those who would like to pretend that time has healed all wounds, that the scores are settled and it's time to move on. Michael's dreams of exemption—like all crossover dreams—play right into such hands. So Michael was held up as an example, living proof that the system worked and things weren't so bad after all.

This version of the crossover dream isn't just a fiction, it's an outright lie. So the minute it showed a crack in its surface, it had to be discarded, swept under the rug, superceded by new distractions. As long as Michael Jackson was simply The Thriller, a disembodied performer on vinyl, a flickering image on the TV screen, his image could hold any meaning assigned to it. The moment that he headed out for the real world, taking the stage as a figure of flesh and blood, the crossover dream cracked wide open and where once unity proudly beckoned, now only divisions were apparent. It was time to go.

In a sense, Michael Jackson walked away intact. He retains a huge audience and a bankroll unrivaled by any popular musician in history. He was well-positioned to begin his long-sought career as a moviemaker. But if it is ever possible or permissible to feel pity for a person who has been given so much, it was in those months when the worm turned and he became, not just a figure of occasional ridicule or the target of various hostilities, but washed-up, yesterday's news, subject to the most dread of all superstar critiques: "Who cares?"

Can Michael Jackson escape this fate? Consider that, if his next album sells, let's say, fifteen million copies, he will have failed—not only by the false standards of the music industry but by his own criteria. If it sells a more reasonable five or ten million, God only knows the reaction—Michael's or the world's.

Suppose the opposite. Imagine that, against all odds, Michael Jackson's next project—be it film or music or something else entirely—reflects what he learned in the cauldron of *Thriller* and *Victory*. Dream that it presents him as the master of a new kind of crossover, presenting with new maturity his perspective as the master and victim of fame and notoriety. In the face of this crossover dream, the question would fall away from him—whether he sold five million or fifty—and descend back upon the rest of us, inhabitants of the world of unfinished stories and restless ghosts. If Michael Jackson managed this kind of crossover, one answer would still be left outstanding. Is there anyone left who can hear?